ALL THE BEST LINES

AN INFORMAL HISTORY OF THE MOVIES

GEORGE TIFFIN

HEAD
of ZEUS

First published in 2013 by Head of Zeus Ltd

This paperback edition published in 2014 by Head of Zeus Ltd

1 3 5 7 9 10 8 6 4 2

A catalogue record for this book is available
from the British Library.

ISBN (HB) 9781781853061

Text design by Carrdesignstudio.com
Printed in Malaysia

Head of Zeus Ltd
Clerkenwell House
45–47 Clerkenwell Green
London EC1R 0HT

www.headofzeus.com

For my parents, who taught me
to look as well as to listen.

Frank Capra, whose winning streak as a director of warm-hearted comedies earned him six Oscars.

CONTENTS

ESSAYS AND FEATURES

Introduction

Cinema: spectacle, stars and spotlights. And, somewhere in the distant background, the clatter of a typewriter. This book celebrates the shimmer of the silver screen but really pays tribute to the men and women who dreamed up its stories: the screenwriters.

> Audiences don't know somebody sits down and writes a picture. They think the actors make it up as they go along.
> **Screenwriter Joe Gillis (William Holden)**
> *Sunset Boulevard* (1950)

> A script has to make sense, and life doesn't.
> **Screenwriter Harry Dawes (Humphrey Bogart)**
> *The Barefoot Contessa* (1954)

In the beginning — the early 1890s — moving pictures were such a novelty that crowds would flock just to see footage of a train pulling into a station, a circus performer or a man sneezing. Before long, directors like D. W. Griffith and Sergei Eisenstein had found ways to shape silent scenes into epic narratives with masterpieces like *The Birth of a Nation* (1915) and *Battleship Potemkin* (1925). But as screen stories grew more sophisticated and engaging one crucial aspect was still absent: the voice.

In 1927 technology enabled feature-length presentations to include a synchronized soundtrack and actors were free to speak at last. Many directors resented this shift in power but producers and public alike embraced the change at once. A subtler shift made itself felt, too: scripts were no longer just structural blueprints but carefully constructed documents filled with description and dialogue that needed pace, sparkle and insight.

The film world was not short of literary talent, and many prestigious authors and journalists soon accepted commissions to write for the movies. But the public had grown used to their stars and no producer wanted to splash the face of a screenwriter across a billboard when he could entice his audience with Errol Flynn or Mae West. Even directors' names remained largely absent from posters for the first half of the twentieth century, but the figures behind the scenes could at least take consolation in their pay cheques. Shortly after his arrival in Hollywood Herman J. Mankiewicz cabled playwright Ben Hecht: 'Will you accept $300 per week to work for Paramount? All expenses paid. $300 is peanuts. Millions are to be grabbed out here and your only competition is idiots. Don't let this get around.' Though Mankiewicz and Hecht may be less well known than their novelist contemporaries Hemingway, Fitzgerald and Steinbeck they penned between them enduring classics such as *Citizen Kane*, *It's a Wonderful World*, *The Pride of St Louis*, *Scarface* and *Notorious*.

The power of a screenwriter to bring a story to life — or to kill it — remains controversial to this day. Alfred Hitchcock famously said 'to make a great film you need three things — the script, the script and the script', while an old industry joke told of the ambitious starlet who was so desperate to break into movies that she seduced a screenwriter. Irving Thalberg, one of the most successful impresarios of Hollywood's golden age, was more astute, remarking that 'the most important person in the motion picture process is the writer, and we must do everything in our power to prevent them from ever realizing it'.

When we see Al Pacino as Shylock in *The Merchant of Venice* we understand we are watching a man interpret Shakespeare's words. When we buy tickets to any theatre production we know we are seeing the work of a particular writer: Strindberg's *Miss Julie*, Beckett's *Waiting for Godot*. But the cinema is a different world. Who wrote *On the Waterfront* or *Apocalypse Now*? Even while lines like 'I coulda been a contender' or 'I love the smell of napalm in the morning' are universally known, few could name their author.

In many cases, the question is complicated by the fact that films frequently have multiple contributors — for story, for dialogue, for individual scenes or even in some cases to tailor lines for a specific actor. Attribution — and remuneration — are often contentious, leading to the suspicion that the business of screenwriting is perfunctory and competitive. Sitting before their typewriter, laptop or iPad no true writer feels this; as this book hopes to show, they want only to deliver something powerful and true which will captivate us after we have bought our ticket and taken our seat in the dark.

Writers have always had a difficult relationship with their paymasters and it remains true that producers are rarely depicted on screen in a flattering light:

We're only interested in one thing, Bart. Can you tell a story? Can you make us laugh? Can you make us cry? Can you make us want to break out in joyous song? Is that more than one thing? Okay!
Producer Jack Lipnick (Michael Lerner)
Barton Fink (1991)

I was just thinking what an interesting concept it is to eliminate the writer from the artistic process. If we could just get rid of these actors and directors, maybe we've got something here.
Producer Griffin Mill (Tim Robbins)
The Player (1992)

If these portrayals seem unfair we should remember the genuine remark by Joe Pasternak, one of MGM's staff during the 1950s: 'You call this a script? Give me a couple of $5,000-a-week writers and I'll write it myself.' Many of Pasternak's contracted writers would doubtless have enjoyed watching him try — or, failing that, to accept his cheque since $5,000 back then would be the equivalent of nearly $50,000 today.

While novelists and playwrights enjoy authorial independence and are revered for their unique voices, screenwriters have to satisfy many different masters: producers, directors and actors. To deliver a coherent story in the face of their conflicting demands can be frustrating, if not impossible. Joseph L. Mankiewicz, brother of Herman and author of *All About Eve* and *Cleopatra*, remarked ruefully that 'writers are the highest paid secretaries in the world'. William Goldman, responsible for *All the President's Men*, *Marathon Man* and *The Princess Bride*, is more candid: 'Screenwriting is what feminists call "shit-work"; if it's well done, it's ignored. If it's badly done, people call attention to it.' True of many professions, perhaps, but at least Goldman has two Oscars to show that the best work is often rewarded.

If the names of screenwriters do not readily trip from our tongues, the lines they have written remain with us — zingers, catchphrases, stirring speeches, whispers of endearment. Their words echo everywhere and they prove fitting tribute to their creators long after the credits have rolled.

This book contains five hundred excerpts of varying lengths as well as one-liners, poster quotes, opening scenes and familiar favourites to delight and enlighten. Essays throughout the text shed light on how the scripts were written, and on their journeys from page to celluloid. No matter who dreamed up the story or bought the rights to a bestseller, no matter what it cost or who was cast to play a role, somebody sat down to write it. *All The Best Lines* is about those men and women.

AUTHOR'S NOTE

The films represented are grouped not by genre or title but by theme; a listing will be found on the contents page. Within each theme the running order is chronological; ideally this will allow a lively juxtaposition of style and author. The index will, of course, lead you straight to any particular film the book contains.

Many films benefit from the contributions of uncredited writers. Because this book is not primarily a reference work I have tended to identify only the principal authors, except in cases where anecdotal evidence suggests a more important role.

Where the essays mention budgets and fees I have adjusted figures in line with inflation; modern equivalents are shown in square brackets.

THANKS

Many friends and colleagues sent suggestions for the book. I'm grateful to them all, and hope plenty of them will find their favourites included.

I would also like to thank everyone who helped make the process of writing the book such a pleasure: Anthony Cheetham, Rosie Alison, Plum Webber, Richard Milbank, Katy Price, Emma Duncan, Edward Tiffin, Titan Fiennes Tiffin, Jane Robertson, Rich Carr and Dan Mogford. The team at Head of Zeus and at the Picture Desk have also been vital collaborators.

George Tiffin, April 2013

The stairway to heaven in Powell and Pressburger's *A Matter of Life and Death* (1946) was rooted in earthly reality on a sound stage at Denham Studios in Buckinghamshire.

Dreams

1933 42ND STREET 1933

The show's star has broken her leg and the producer encourages the chorus girl who takes her place.

MARSH

Sawyer, you listen to me, and you listen hard. Two hundred people, two hundred jobs, two hundred thousand dollars, five weeks of grind and blood and sweat depend upon you. It's the lives of all these people who've worked with you. You've got to go on, and you've got to give and give and give. They've got to like you. Got to. Do you understand? You can't fall down. You can't because your future's in it, my future and everything all of us have is staked on you. All right, now I'm through, but you keep your feet on the ground and your head on those shoulders of yours and go out, and Sawyer, you're going out a youngster but you've got to come back a star!

Dir: Lloyd Bacon • Scr: Rian James, James Seymour • Based on a novel by Bradford Ropes • Cast: Warner Baxter (Julian Marsh)

1937 SNOW WHITE AND THE SEVEN DWARFS 1937

MAGIC MIRROR

Prepare to be amazed beyond all expectations. After all, it is what I do.

Dir: David Hand and five others • Scr: Dorothy Ann Blank, Richard Creedon, Merrill De Maris, Otto Englander, Earl Hurd, Dick Rickard, Ted Sears, Webb Smith • Based on a story by Jacob and Wilhelm Grimm • Cast: Moroni Olsen (voice of the Magic Mirror)

This was Walt Disney's first full-length animated feature and still ranks eighth among the highest grossing films of all time. Although the company focuses on mainstream family entertainment, the director Sergei Eisenstein proclaimed Disney's work 'the greatest contribution of the American people to art' and the critic Mark Van Doren called him a 'first-rate artist [who] knows innumerable truths that cannot be taught'.

1939 GONE WITH THE WIND 1939

SCARLETT

As God is my witness they're not going to lick me. I'm going to live through this and when it's all over, I'll never be hungry again. No, nor any of my folk. If I have to lie, steal, cheat or kill. As God is my witness, I'll never be hungry again.

Dir: Victor Fleming • Scr: Sidney Howard • Based on a novel by Margaret Mitchell • Cast: Vivien Leigh (Scarlett O'Hara)

Polhaus finally has his hands on the Maltese Falcon, a priceless figurine the pursuit of which has caused mayhem and murder galore.

DETECTIVE POLHAUS

Heavy. What is it?

SAM SPADE

The stuff that dreams are made of.

Dir: John Huston • Scr: John Huston • Based on a novel by Dashiell Hammett • Cast: Ward Bond (Detective Tom Polhaus), Humphrey Bogart (Sam Spade)

The *Maltese Falcon* was John Huston's directorial debut, but it was the third screen version of Hammett's novel.

The film's final line is a tribute to Prospero's closing speech in Shakespeare's *The Tempest*: 'We are such stuff/As dreams are made on.'

NOIR FILM

'People like me like dark pictures — dark and mysterious. Most were B-movies made on the cheap, others were classy models with A-talent. But they all had one thing in common — they lived on the edge, told stories about life on the streets, shady characters, crooked cops, twisted love and bad luck. The French invented a name for these pictures: *film noir*. Black film, that's what they called them — about a darker side of human nature. About the world as it really was.'

Richard Widmark (*Kiss of Death* (1947), *Night and the City* (1950), *Pickup on South Street* (*1953*))

Few genres are unique to the movies; novels, plays and musicals had charted the realms of drama, melodrama, tragedy and farce long before celluloid was invented and for a while mainstream cinema seemed content to base itself on these established styles. No medium, however, had ever been able to reach such huge audiences.

By the 1940s cinema-goers in America were buying sixty million tickets a week. Barely able to meet this demand, studios were quite happy to turn out B-movies, projects created to fill theatres and keep their roster of contracted talent busy without requiring the budgets of their bigger pictures. Not surprisingly, these films were less closely supervised and could be made with a greater degree of freedom, which writers and directors were eager to seize, drawing on an unlikely combination of factors to create — almost accidentally — what we now recognize as *film noir*.

Weary after the Depression and now in the midst of a global war, audiences had grown impatient with wholesome, censor-approved material. The rise of the pulp novel, with racier protagonists and sexier women, showed that the public was ready for stronger stuff and film-makers were quick to recognize the appeal of hard-boiled writers like Raymond Chandler, James M. Cain and Jim Thompson.

If mainstream studios were still reluctant to put big budgets behind such risqué material, directors like Jacques Tourneur and Robert Wise made the most of these new opportunities. The influx of European talent had spread the influence of German expressionist cinema which suited cheap production perfectly; low lighting budgets created stark chiaroscuro moods mirroring shady storylines, while the fragmented visuals conveniently hid flaws in flimsy sets and affordable locations.

John Huston, Otto Preminger and Orson Welles refined the genre with bigger budget pictures such as *The Maltese Falcon* (1941), *Laura* (1944) and *The Lady from Shanghai* (1947); today, *noir* remains the most influential and imitated of all film styles and lives on in such diverse classics as *Blade Runner* (1982), *Heat* (1995), *L.A. Confidential* (1997) and *Sin City* (2005). The earliest *noir* quotes still seem as powerfully contemporary today:

    JILL: What's the good of living without hope?
    ED: It can be done.
    I Wake Up Screaming (1941)

Well, well. You're the first woman I've ever met who said yes when she meant yes.
Suspicion (1941)

She was a charming middle-aged lady with a face like a bucket of mud. I gave her a drink. She was a gal who'd take a drink if she had to knock you down to get the bottle.
Murder My Sweet (1944)

A woman doesn't care how a guy makes a living, just how he makes love.
Murder My Sweet (1944)

Personally, Veda's convinced me that alligators have the right idea. They eat their young.
Mildred Pierce (1945)

She was worth a stare, she was trouble.
The Big Sleep (1946)

I can be framed easier than 'Whistler's Mother'.
The Dark Corner (1946)

How I detest the dawn. The grass always looks like it's been left out all night.
The Dark Corner (1946)

Those gates only open three times. When you come in, when you've served your time, or when you're dead.
Brute Force (1947)

LEROY: Is he dead?
CAPTAIN FINLAY: He's been dead for a long time - he just didn't know it.
Crossfire (1947)

ADRIENNE: Do you fall in love with all of your clients?
MARLOWE: Only the ones in skirts.
Lady in the Lake (1947)

KATHIE: Oh Jeff, you ought to have killed me for what I did a minute ago.
JEFF: There's still time.
Out of the Past (1947)

He couldn't find a prayer in the Bible.
Out of the Past (1947)

It was the bottom of the barrel, and I was scraping it.
Out of the Past (1947)

I want you to do something. I want you to get yourself out of
the bed, and get over to the window and scream as loud as you
can. Otherwise you only have another three minutes to live.
Sorry, Wrong Number (1948)

Experience has taught me never to trust a policeman.
Just when you think one's all right, he turns legit.
The Asphalt Jungle (1950)

COP: Can I help you?
BIGELOW: I want to report a murder.
COP: Where was this murder committed?
BIGELOW: San Francisco, last night.
COP: Who was murdered?
BIGELOW: I was.
D.O.A. (1950)

I saw the two of you, the way you were looking at each other
tonight, like a couple of wild animals. Almost scared me.
Gun Crazy [aka *Deadly is the Female*] (1950)

You'll always be a two-bit cannon. And when they pick you up
in the gutter dead, you're hand'll be in a drunk's pocket.
Pickup on South Street (1953)

Every extra buck has a meaning all its own.
Pickup on South Street (1953)

MIKE: You're never around when I need you.
VELDA: You never need me when I'm around.
Kiss Me Deadly (1955)

I'd hate to take a bite out of you. You're a cookie full
of arsenic.
Sweet Smell of Success (1957)

1945   THE LOST WEEKEND   1945

A struggling writer confesses he only feels alive when drinking.

DON

It shrinks my liver, doesn't it, Nat? It pickles my kidneys,
yeah. But what it does to the mind? It tosses the sandbags

overboard so the balloon can soar. Suddenly I'm above the ordinary. I'm competent. I'm walking a tightrope over Niagara Falls. I'm one of the great ones. I'm Michelangelo, moulding the beard of Moses. I'm Van Gogh painting pure sunlight. I'm Horowitz, playing the Emperor Concerto. I'm John Barrymore before movies got him by the throat. I'm Jesse James and his two brothers, all three of them. I'm W. Shakespeare. And out there it's not Third Avenue any longer. It's the Nile. The Nile, Nat, and down it moves the barge of Cleopatra.

Dir: Billy Wilder • Scr: Billy Wilder, Charles Brackett • Based on a novel by Charles R. Jackson • Cast: Ray Milland (Don Birnam)

1950 HARVEY   1950

VETA LOUISE

Myrtle Mae, you have a lot to learn and I hope you never learn it.

Dir: Henry Koster • Scr: Mary Chase, Oscar Brodney • Based on a play by Mary Chase • Cast: Josephine Hull (Veta Louise Simmons)

1953 GENTLEMEN PREFER BLONDES   1953

ESMOND SR

Have you got the nerve to tell me you don't want to marry my son for his money?

LORELEI

It's true.

ESMOND SR

Then what do you want to marry him for?

LORELEI

I want to marry him for *your* money.

Dir: Howard Hawks • Scr: Charles Lederer • Based on a musical by Joseph Fields and a novel and play by Anita Loos • Cast: Marilyn Monroe (Lorelei Lee), Taylor Holmes (Mr Esmond Sr)

Although Monroe had not yet become a major star, she was already behaving like one, demanding time-consuming retakes even after director Howard Hawks was satisfied. When the studio asked Hawks how to speed up the production, he replied: 'Replace Marilyn, shorten the script and get a new director.'

1954 SABRINA 1954

Sabrina refuses to let her father stand in the way of her love for David, a millionaire.

THOMAS

He's still David Larrabee, and you're still the chauffeur's daughter. And you're still reaching for the moon.

SABRINA

No, father. The moon is reaching for me.

Dir: Billy Wilder • Scr: Billy Wilder, Ernest Lehman, Samuel A. Taylor • Based on a play by Samuel A. Taylor • Cast: Audrey Hepburn (Sabrina Fairchild), John Williams (Thomas Fairchild)

1956 THE SEARCHERS 1956

A settler in 1860s Texas contemplates the devastation on both sides as ranchers battle Comanche braves.

MRS JORGENSEN

Some day this country's gonna be a fine, good place to be. Maybe it needs our bones in the ground before that time can come.

Dir: John Ford • Scr: Frank S. Nugent • Based on a novel by Alan Le May • Cast: Olive Carey (Mrs Jorgensen)

1957 THE SEVENTH SEAL (DET SJUNDE INSEGLET)   1957

In a medieval community ravaged by plague, the knight Antonius Block wonders how God can permit such horror.

ANTONIUS

Faith is a torment. It is like loving someone who is out there in the darkness but never appears, no matter how loudly you call.

Dir: Ingmar Bergman • Scr: Ingmar Bergman, based on his play • Cast: Max von Sydow (Antonius Block)

1958 AUNTIE MAME   1958

The wild and unconventional Mame is determined to raise her nephew with a true zest for life.

AUNTIE MAME

Live! Life is a banquet, and most poor suckers are starving to death!

Dir: Morton DaCosta • Scr: Betty Comden, Adolph Green • Based on a novel by Patrick Dennis and a play by Jerome Lawrence and Robert Edwin Lee • Cast: Rosalind Russell (Mame Dennis)

1958 THE MATCHMAKER   1958

Dolly, a divorcée-turned-matchmaker, addresses the audience as she tries to persuade us that adventures lie ahead.

DOLLY

Life's never quite interesting enough, somehow. You people who come to the movies know that.

Dir: Joseph Anthony • Scr: John Michael Hayes • Based on a play by Thornton Wilder • Cast: Shirley Booth (Dolly 'Gallagher' Levi)

1959 PLAN 9 FROM OUTER SPACE   1959

NARRATOR

Greetings, my friends! We are all interested in the future, for that is where you and I are going to spend the rest of our lives.

Dir: Edward D. Wood Jr • Scr: Edward D. Wood Jr • Cast: Criswell (Narrator)

The production was funded by a Baptist church; it took three years to find a distributor who would take it on, only for it to be voted Worst Film of All Time in *The Golden Turkey Awards* (1980).

An aspiring journalist interviews a writer whose answers are always unexpected.

PATRICIA

What is your greatest ambition in life?

PARVULESCO

To become immortal... and then die.

Dir: Jean-Luc Godard • Scr: François Truffaut, Jean-Luc Godard, Claude Chabrol • Cast: Jean Seberg (Patricia Franchini), Jean-Pierre Melville (Parvulesco)

THE NEW WAVE

Jean-Luc Godard (b. 1930) may be the only director in film history to have won his career break by insulting a producer: Georges de Beauregard was so impressed by Godard's scathing honesty about a recent film that he hired the young press agent to work on a script he was developing. Godard quickly became bored of the project but had read a treatment for another film about a petty criminal by two star directors, François Truffaut and Claude Chabrol. De Beauregard was intrigued, Truffaut and Chabrol liked the idea of Godard directing it, and since the budget was modest they quickly secured funding.

Across the Atlantic, the golden age of Hollywood was waning and studios were relying increasingly on glossy epics and musicals in their fight against the lure of television. In Europe, a new school of simpler, more realistic film storytelling was gaining popularity: *Breathless* was the picture that fully captured this spirit in a way that was to transform cinematic narrative across the world. It also established the career of Jean Seberg, the young American who played Patricia; on seeing her performance, Truffaut declared her 'the best actress in Europe'.

Godard's production style would have shocked his American counterparts. Working from an ever-changing script, he shot in real locations across Paris without official permission with a small crew and portable equipment. In order to accommodate low light levels, cinematographer Raoul Coutard used Ilford HPS negative intended for stills cameras and forced its development in the laboratory, giving the image a grainy look. This, combined with the fact that the camera itself was light enough to be hand-held, contributed enormously to the rough-and-ready immediacy of the action.

Godard would write or rewrite scenes each morning in an exercise book nobody else was allowed to read and would sometimes only give the actors their lines as they were being filmed to increase the feeling of spontaneity. On the first day of filming, 17 August 1959, the crew only shot for two hours. Thereafter, the schedule essentially followed the amount of material the director needed, or had prepared. Truffaut, whose involvement had enabled the funding, only visited the set twice and Chabrol never appeared at all. Producer de Beauregard worried that the production was proceeding erratically, and on one occasion got into a fist-fight with Godard when he discovered him in a café after the director had called in sick.

The film also broke conventions in the way it edited the footage together, and the frequent 'jump cuts', which made no attempt to match related action or angles, added to the sense of energy and realism. So bold were the innovations that critics coined a new term for the school of pioneering directors: *Nouvelle Vague*, or the New Wave. If the writing about this new style was occasionally overwrought — Andrew Sarris claimed the jagged narrative revealed 'the meaninglessness of the time interval between moral decisions' — the legacy of *Breathless* and similar films changed cinema for ever, influencing directors as diverse as Bertolucci, Scorsese, Wenders and Tarantino.

1963 THE LEOPARD (*IL GATTOPARDO*)   1963

During the upheavals of the nineteenth century in Sicily, the aristocratic Corbera family take stock of the turmoil around them.

TANCREDI

If we want things to stay as they are, things will have to change.

Dir: Luchino Visconti • Scr: Suso Cecchi D'Amico, Pasquale Festa Campanile, Enrico Medioli, Massimo Franciosa, Luchino Visconti • Based on a novel by Giuseppe Tomasi di Lampedusa • Cast: Alain Delon (Tancredi Falconeri)

1966 THE WILD ANGELS   1966

A Hell's Angel explains his credo.

BLUES

We want to be free! We want to be free to do what we want to do! We want to be free to ride. And we want to be free to ride our machines without being hassled by the Man. And we want

to get loaded. And we want to have a good time! And that's
what we're gonna do. We're gonna have a good time. We're gonna
have a party!

Dir: Roger Corman • Scr: Charles B. Griffith, Peter Bogdanovich • Cast:
Peter Fonda (Heavenly Blues)

Shot three years before *Easy Rider*, Roger Corman's film about motorcycles, rebellion and
counter-culture also starred Peter Fonda. The real Hell's Angels, some of whom appeared as
extras in the film, temporarily abandoned their anarchic beliefs to sue Corman for $5 million
[$35 million] for portraying their organization in 'a negative light'.

1968   PLANET OF THE APES   1968

GEORGE

I can't help thinking that somewhere in the universe there
has to be something better than man. Has to be.

Dir: Franklin J. Schaffner • Scr: Michael Wilson, Rod Serling • Based on a
novel by Pierre Boulle • Cast: Charlton Heston (George Taylor)

Although the actors playing apes were assigned their species randomly they found that even
during breaks they congregated in groups according to whether they had been cast as gorillas,
chimps or orang-utans. Composer Jerry Goldsmith was reputed to have worn a gorilla mask
while writing and even conducting the score.

1969   BUTCH CASSIDY AND THE SUNDANCE KID   1969

*Outlaw Butch Cassidy describes his ambition to his partner in
crime.*

BUTCH

I got vision, and the rest of the world wears bifocals.

Dir: George Roy Hill • Scr: William Goldman • Cast: Paul Newman (Butch Cassidy)

1969   THE PRIME OF MISS JEAN BRODIE   1969

*A headstrong, visionary teacher intends to mould her pupils as
she sees fit.*

MISS BRODIE

Little girls, I am in the business of putting old heads on young
shoulders, and all my pupils are the crème de la crème. Give me a
girl at an impressionable age and she is mine for life.

Dir: Ronald Neame • Scr: Jay Presson Allen Jay, based on his play • Based
on a novel by Muriel Spark • Cast: Maggie Smith (Jean Brodie)

1975 LOVE AND DEATH   1975

During Napoleon's invasion of Russia, Boris, a cowardly intellectual, chats with his cousin Sonya.

BORIS

Nothingness... non-existence... black emptiness...

SONJA

What did you say?

BORIS

Oh, I was just planning my future.

Dir: Woody Allen • Scr: Woody Allen • Cast: Woody Allen (Boris Grushenko), Diane Keaton (Sonja)

1978 CALIFORNIA SUITE   1978

Hannah argues with her ex-husband about their daughter's future.

HANNAH

You're worse than a hopeless romantic. You're a hopeful one.

Dir: Herbert Ross • Scr: Neil Simon • Cast: Jane Fonda (Hannah Warren)

GREYSTOKE: THE LEGEND OF TARZAN, LORD OF THE APES

Explorers sail to the coast of an uncharted Africa.

D'ARNOT

This is not the world, John. Just the edge of it.

Dir: Hugh Hudson • Scr: Robert Towne (as P. H. Vazak), Michael Austin • Based on a novel by Edgar Rice Burroughs • Cast: Ian Holm (Captain Philippe D'Arnot)

Edgar Rice Burroughs created the jungle-dwelling hero in his novel *Tarzan of the Apes* (1912). Several silent film adaptations quickly followed but the character was most famously played by Olympic swimming champion Johnny Weissmüller in various appearances between 1932 and 1948.

With *Greystoke*, director Hugh Hudson hoped to deliver a more faithful representation of Burroughs' original story; Academy Award-winning writer Robert Towne (*Chinatown, Reds*) was so unhappy with Hudson's vision that he asked for his name to be replaced with that of his sheepdog, P. H. Vazak. The dog was duly nominated for an Oscar.

DEAD POETS SOCIETY

A schoolteacher warns his pupils that life passes all too quickly.

KEATING

Now I would like you to step forward over here and peruse some of the faces from the past. You've walked past them many times. I don't think you've really looked at them. They're not that different from you, are they? Same haircuts. Full of hormones, just like you. Invincible, just like you feel. The world is their oyster. They believe they're destined for great things, just like many of you. Their eyes are full of hope, just like you. Did they wait until it was too late to make from their lives even one iota of what they were capable? Because you see, gentlemen, these boys are now fertilizing daffodils. But if you listen real close, you can hear them whisper their legacy to you. Go on, lean in. Listen. Do you hear it?

He whispers:

Carpe...Hear it?

And again:

Carpe. Carpe Diem. Seize the day, boys. Make your lives extraordinary.

Dir: Peter Weir • Scr: Tom Schulman • Cast: Robin Williams (John Keating)

1989 FIELD OF DREAMS   1989

Ray Kinsella is visited by the ghost of his father.

> JOHN KINSELLA

Is this heaven?

> RAY KINSELLA

It's Iowa.

Dir: Phil Alden Robinson • Scr: Phil Alden Robinson • Based on a novel
by W.P. Kinsella • Cast: Kevin Costner (Ray Kinsella), Dwier Brown
(John Kinsella)

1989 NATIONAL LAMPOON'S CHRISTMAS VACATION   1989

*Clark wants to give his family the best Christmas ever but his
plans are thwarted when his boss cuts his bonus.*

> CLARK

Hey! If any of you are looking for any last-minute gift ideas
for me, I have one. I'd like Frank Shirley, my boss, right here
tonight. I want him brought from his happy holiday slumber
over there on Melody Lane with all the other rich people and
I want him brought right here, with a big ribbon on his head,
and I want to look him straight in the eye and I want to tell
him what a cheap, lying, no-good, rotten, four-flushing, low-
life, snake-licking, dirt-eating, inbred, overstuffed, ignorant,
blood-sucking, dog-kissing, brainless, dickless, hopeless,
heartless, fat-ass, bug-eyed, stiff-legged, spotty-lipped, worm-
headed sack of monkey shit he is! Hallelujah!

Dir: Jeremiah Chechik • Scr: John Hughes • Cast: Chevy Chase (Clark
Griswold)

1992 GAS FOOD LODGING   1992

*Teenager Darius tries to persuade his date that women are the
true adventurers.*

> DARIUS

Well, it's like Adam and Eve. He was fine grooving in
paradise, but Eve wanted something scary. She wanted the
fucking edge. She wanted to jump off cliffs just so she
could see what it was like to fall.

Dir: Allison Anders • Scr: Allison Anders • Based on a novel by Richard
Peck • Cast: Donovan Leitch (Darius)

A prisoner risks punishment by broadcasting an opera aria over the workyard loudspeakers.

                        RED

I have no idea to this day what those two Italian ladies were singing about. Truth is, I don't want to know. Some things are best left unsaid. I'd like to think they were singing about something so beautiful it can't be expressed in words, and makes your heart ache because of it. I tell you, those voices soared higher and farther than anybody in a grey place dares to dream. It was like some beautiful bird flapped into our drab little cage and made those walls dissolve away, and for the briefest of moments every last man in Shawshank felt free.

Dir: Frank Darabont • Scr: Frank Darabont • Based on a novella by Stephen King • Cast: Morgan Freeman (Ellis Boyd 'Red' Redding)

Although the film did not prove a hit in cinemas, it has grown hugely in popularity and is now ranked number one in the Internet Movie Database readers' poll. Since one of the inmates keeps a pet crow, the American Humane Association was present during the shoot to make sure it was properly treated; they approved of the bird's conditions but objected to the scene where the inmate feeds it a maggot on the grounds that it was cruel to the bug. Happily, a maggot that had died from natural causes was discovered and used instead.

A passionate affair causes a photographer to review his life.

ROBERT

The old dreams were good dreams; they didn't work out, but glad I had them.

Dir: Clint Eastwood • Scr: Richard LaGravenese • Based on a novel by Robert James Waller • Cast: Clint Eastwood (Robert Kincaid)

IN THE BEGINNING

After the Twentieth Century-Fox searchlight has swept the sky, the MGM lion has roared and (for those of us old enough to remember) Rank's sculpted bodybuilder has beaten the vast gong an expectant hush settles over the audience as we await the first moments of the film. No wonder screenwriters feel the pressure of capturing our attention in the very opening scene, and actors vie for the juiciest lines for us to recite when the lights come up. Here are some of the most captivating opening salvos:

Rosebud...
Citizen Kane (1941)

This is the universe. Big, isn't it?
A Matter of Life and Death (1946)

I never knew the old Vienna before the war, with its Strauss music, its glamour and easy charm - Constantinople suited me better.
The Third Man (1949)

ANTONIUS: Who are you?
DEATH: I am Death.
The Seventh Seal (1957)

Maycomb was a tired old town, even in 1932 when I first knew it. Somehow, it was hotter then. Men's stiff collars wilted by nine in the morning.
To Kill a Mockingbird (1962)

Ladies and gentlemen, welcome to violence, the word and the act.
Faster, Pussycat! Kill! Kill! (1965)

What can you say about a twenty-five-year-old girl who died?
That she was beautiful and brilliant? That she loved Mozart
and Bach, the Beatles, and me?
Love Story (1969)

I believe in America.
The Godfather (1972)

I am not a bum. I'm a jerk. I once had wealth, power, and the
love of a beautiful woman. Now I only have two things: my
friends and... uh... my thermos.
The Jerk (1979)

Saigon... Shit. I'm still only in Saigon. Every time I think I'm
gonna wake up back in the jungle. When I was home after my
first tour, it was worse. I'd wake up and there'd be nothing. I
hardly said a word to my wife, until I said 'yes' to a divorce.
When I was here, I wanted to be there; when I was there, all
I could think of was getting back into the jungle. I'm here a
week now, waiting for a mission, getting softer. Every minute
I stay in this room, I get weaker, and every minute Charlie
squats in the bush, he gets stronger. Each time I looked
around the walls moved in a little tighter.
Apocalypse Now (1979)

I was twelve going on thirteen first time I saw a dead human
being.
Stand By Me (1986)

Today is a good day to die.
Flatliners (1990)

As far back as I can remember, I always wanted to be a gangster.
Goodfellas (1990)

Oh, fuck! Fuck!
Four Weddings and a Funeral (1994)

Come to Los Angeles! The sun shines bright, the beaches are
wide and inviting, and the orange groves stretch as far as
the eye can see. There are jobs aplenty, and land is cheap.
L.A. Confidential (1997)

We were somewhere around Barstow on the edge of the desert
when the drugs began to take hold.
Fear and Loathing in Las Vegas (1998)

My name is Lester Burnham. This is my neighbourhood; this is my street; this is my life. I am forty-two years old; in less than a year I will be dead. Of course I don't know that yet, and in a way, I am dead already.
American Beauty (1999)

What came first, the music or the misery?
High Fidelity (2000)

The world has changed. I feel it in the water. I feel it in the earth. I smell it in the air.
The Lord of the Rings: The Fellowship of the Ring (2001)

I only ever met one man I wouldn't wanna fight.
Million Dollar Baby (2004)

Are you watching closely?
The Prestige (2006)

There's a hundred thousand streets in this city. You don't need to know the route. You give me a time and a place, I give you a five-minute window. Anything happens in that five minutes and I'm yours. No matter what. Anything happens a minute either side of that and you're on your own. Do you understand?
Drive (2011)

1996 TRAINSPOTTING   1996

A junkie celebrates the thrill of oblivion.

RENTON

Choose life. Choose a job. Choose a career. Choose a family. Choose a fucking big television, choose washing machines, cars, compact disc players and electrical tin openers. Choose good health, low cholesterol, and dental insurance. Choose fixed interest mortgage repayments. Choose a starter home. Choose your friends. Choose leisurewear and matching luggage. Choose a three-piece suite on hire purchase in a range of fucking fabrics. Choose DIY and wondering who the fuck you are on Sunday morning. Choose sitting on that couch watching mind-numbing, spirit-crushing game shows, stuffing fucking junk food into your mouth. Choose rotting away at the end of it all, pissing your last in a miserable home, nothing more than an embarrassment to the selfish, fucked-up brats you spawned to replace yourselves. Choose your future. Choose life...But why would I want to do a thing like that? I chose not to choose

life. I chose somethin' else. And the reasons? There are no
reasons. Who needs reasons when you've got heroin?

Dir: Danny Boyle • Scr: John Hodge • Based on a novel by Irvine
Welsh • Cast: Ewan McGregor (Mark 'Rent Boy' Renton)

The first twenty minutes of the Edinburgh-set film had to be redubbed for American audiences.
Director Danny Boyle had hoped to license the theme music to *Mission: Impossible* for one
sequence until he discovered it would have cost three times the production's budget.

1999   THE TALENTED MR RIPLEY   1999

*A New York lavatory attendant passes himself off as a
well-to-do Princeton student.*

RIPLEY

I always thought it would be better to be a fake somebody
than a real nobody.

Dir: Anthony Minghella • Scr: Anthony Minghella • Based on a novel by
Patricia Highsmith • Cast: Matt Damon (Tom Ripley)

1999   THE MATRIX   1999

*Cyber-warrior Trinity persuades Neo to join forces with the
mysterious Orpheus, who leads the fight against the machines
that have enslaved humanity.*

TRINITY

I know why you're here, Neo. I know what you've been doing.
..why you hardly sleep, why you live alone, and why night
after night you sit by your computer. You're looking for him.
I know because I was once looking for the same thing. And
when he found me, he told me I wasn't really looking for him.
I was looking for an answer. It's the question that drives
us, Neo. It's the question that brought you here. You know the
question, just as I did.

NEO

What is the Matrix?

TRINITY

The answer is out there, Neo, and it's looking for you, and it
will find you if you want it to.

Dir: Andy Wachowski, Lana Wachowski • Scr: Andy Wachowski, Lana
Wachowski • Cast: Keanu Reeves (Neo), Carrie-Anne Moss (Trinity)

A child psychologist tries to help a young boy who is visited by ghosts.

COLE

I see dead people.

MALCOLM

In your dreams?

Cole shakes his head.

MALCOLM

While you're awake?

Cole nods.

MALCOLM

Dead people like, in graves? In coffins?

COLE

Walking around like regular people. They don't see each other. They only see what they want to see. They don't know they're dead.

MALCOLM

How often do you see them?

COLE

All the time. They're everywhere.

Dir: M. Night Shyamalan • Scr: M. Night Shyamalan • Cast: Bruce Willis (Dr Malcolm Crowe), Haley Joel Osment (Cole Sear)

Director M. Night Shyamalan described the project to his backers as a cross between *The Exorcist* and *Ordinary People*. Toni Collette (playing Cole's mother) was so immersed in the real emotions of the family that she failed to realize the film was a horror story.

2000 BILLY ELLIOT 2000

A young boy growing up in a tough mining town fights to protect his dream.

BILLY

I don't want a childhood. I want to be a ballet dancer.

Dir: Stephen Daldry • Scr: Lee Hall • Cast: Jamie Bell (Billy Elliot)

2004 I, ROBOT 2004

Detective Spooner questions Sonny, a robot, reluctant to believe it is capable of independent thought.

SPOONER

Human beings have dreams. Even dogs have dreams, but not you - you're just a machine. An imitation of life. Can a robot write a symphony? Can a robot turn a canvas into a beautiful masterpiece?

SONNY

Can you?

Dir: Alex Proyas • Scr: Jeff Vintar, Akiva Goldsman • Based on short stories by Isaac Asimov • Cast: William Smith (Detective Del Spooner), Alan Tudyk (Sonny)

2006 THE DEPARTED 2006

Frank Costello, a Boston mobster, explains his power over the community.

COSTELLO

I don't want to be a product of my environment. I want my environment to be a product of me.

Dir: Martin Scorsese • Scr: William Monahan • Cast: Jack Nicholson (Frank Costello)

When Martin Scorsese received a Director's Guild of America award for the film, he claimed: 'this is the first movie I have ever done with a plot'. Jack Nicholson relished the opportunity to play Frank Costello, describing his character as 'the pure incarnation of evil'. With Scorsese's approval he improvised much of his performance, including the scene in a porn theatre where he startles Matt Damon by pretending to ejaculate on him with a dildo.

2008 SEX AND THE CITY 2008

Carrie sets the scene for the romantic adventures of her group of friends.

CARRIE

We were perfectly happy until we decided to live happily ever after.

Dir: Michael Patrick King • Scr: Michael Patrick King • Cast: Sarah Jessica Parker (Carrie Bradshaw)

2009 THE ROAD 2009

A father tries to find a place of safety for his son in a hostile post-apocalyptic world.

THE MAN

I told the boy when you dream about bad things happening, it means you're still fighting and you're still alive. It's when you start to dream about good things that you should start to worry.

Dir: John Hillcoat • Scr: Joe Penhall • Based on a novel by Cormac McCarthy • Cast: Viggo Mortensen (The Man)

2010 ALICE IN WONDERLAND 2010

ALICE

This is impossible.

MAD HATTER

Only if you believe it is.

Dir: Tim Burton • Scr: Linda Woolverton • Based on books by Lewis Carroll • Cast: Mia Wasikowska (Alice), Johnny Depp (Mad Hatter)

The closest reference to this dialogue in Lewis Carroll's novel seems to be Alice's remark that 'Sometimes I've believed as many as six impossible things before breakfast.'

The Wizard of Oz (1939) delighted audiences with its early use of the Technicolor film process.

Daniel Day-Lewis in *Gangs of New York* (2002). Despite accepting relatively few film roles he is the only male actor to have won three Oscars.

Billy Wilder (right), a director noted for his wit both on screen and off, is photographed here with his long-time collaborator, the writer I. A. L. Diamond.

Friends

THE BRIDE OF FRANKENSTEIN

THE MONSTER

Alone, bad. Friend, good.

Dir: James Whale • Scr: William Hurlbut, John L. Balderston • Based on a novel by Mary Shelley • Cast: Boris Karloff (The Monster)

Boris Karloff's costume for the monster was so hot that he sweated off 10kg over the course of the shoot. The actor was so famous at the time that his screen credit was simply his surname.

1940 **THE PHILADELPHIA STORY** **1940**

Tracy Lord needs to get married; tabloid reporter Macaulay Connor chivalrously offers his hand.

MACAULAY

It can't be anything like love, can it?

TRACY

No, no, it can't be.

MACAULAY

Would it be inconvenient?

TRACY

Terribly.

Dir: George Cukor • Scr: Donald Ogden Stewart • Based on a play by Philip Barry • Cast: Katharine Hepburn (Tracy Lord), James Stewart (Macaulay 'Mike' Connor)

George Cukor (1899–1983) was famous both as a sympathetic director of actors and a generous, loyal colleague. During the filming of Cukor's *Camille* (1936), Greta Garbo was confused to notice the same actor taking several different background roles in various scenes. She asked Cukor: 'Who is that big man, and what part is he playing?' The director replied: 'His name is Rex Evans, and he's playing the part of a friend who needs a job.' Evans eventually appeared in ten Cukor pictures.

Despite his renown as a difficult artist who resisted creative discussions with his actors, Cukor candidly confessed: 'Give me a good script, and I'll be a hundred times better.'

1950 **ALL ABOUT EVE** **1950**

An ambitious Broadway producer kids himself – and his colleagues – about his motives.

Directors - even though we all know from the media's portrayal of them that they are men and women of wisdom and artistic vision, masters of the subtle use of symbolism - are more often than not a bunch of insecure assholes.

Understand this: all the sleaze you've heard about Hollywood? All the illiterate scumbags who scuttle down the corridors of power? They are there, all right, and worse than you can imagine.

Goldman reserves particular scorn for the industry's belief that it can predict the public's taste and therefore has the right to dictate all creative decisions. The most famous line from the book is now well established as a salutary warning to all film-makers: 'Nobody knows anything.'

1971 HAROLD AND MAUDE 1971

Introspective teenager Harold finds an inspiring friend in seventy-nine-year-old Maude after meeting her at a funeral.

HAROLD

You sure have a way with people.

MAUDE

Well, they're my species!

Dir: Hal Ashby • Scr: Colin Higgins • Cast: Bud Cort (Harold Parker Chasen), Ruth Gordon (Dame Marjorie 'Maude' Chardin)

1981 RAIDERS OF THE LOST ARK 1981

Two ex-lovers cross paths in a remote bar in Nepal.

MARION

You're not the man I knew ten years ago.

INDIANA

It's not the years, honey. It's the mileage.

Dir: Steven Spielberg • Scr: Lawrence Kasdan, George Lucas, Philip Kaufman • Cast: Harrison Ford (Indiana Jones), Karen Allen (Marion Ravenwood)

Harrison Ford did a good deal of the stunt work himself, including being dragged behind a speeding truck. He sustained several bruised ribs but when asked if he considered the shot dangerous, replied: 'No. If it really was... they would have filmed more of the movie first.'

The sound effects proved an easier assignment: fist-fights were dubbed with the recording of a baseball bat pounding a pile of leather jackets, and the opening of the stone ark was suggested by sliding the lid of a lavatory cistern.

1981 ON GOLDEN POND 1981

> ETHEL
>
> You're my knight in shining armour. Don't you forget it.
> You're gonna get back up on that horse and I'm gonna be right
> behind you holding on tight and away we're gonna go, go, go.
>
> NORMAN
>
> I don't like horses.

She kisses him.

> You are a pretty old dame, aren't you? What are you doing with
> a dotty old son of a bitch like me?
>
> ETHEL
>
> Well, I haven't the vaguest idea.

Dir: Mark Rydell • Ernest Thompson, based on his play • Cast: Katharine Hepburn (Ethel Thayer), Henry Fonda (Norman Thayer Jr)

1982 TOOTSIE 1982

Michael hopes he can still work with Sandy after they split up.

                         MICHAEL

Friends?

                          SANDY

No, we are not friends. I don't take this shit from friends.
Only lovers.

Dir: Sydney Pollack • Scr: Larry Gelbart, Murray Schisgal, Don McGuire •
Cast: Dustin Hoffman (Michael Dorsey/Dorothy Michaels), Teri Garr
(Sandy Lester)

Sydney Pollack was rare among producer/directors in also being an accomplished actor, studying with Sanford Meisner at The Neighborhood Playhouse School of the Theatre before beginning a parallel career behind the camera. After he had taken the lead role in *Tootsie*, Dustin Hoffman refused to proceed unless Pollack himself played his agent. Pollack appeared in forty productions including *The Player*, *Eyes Wide Shut*, *Husbands and Wives* and *Michael Clayton*, and directed thirty-six films, notably *They Shoot Horses, Don't They?*, *Jeremiah Johnson*, *Three Days of the Condor*, *The Firm* and *Out of Africa*.

Hoffman decided to give his female character a Southern accent as he felt it helped him play the voice in a more feminine register; several of the crew said of Hoffman in drag that he was 'much nicer as a woman'.

1989   DO THE RIGHT THING   1989

*Two friends greet each other on the streets of New York's
Brooklyn.*

                     BUGGIN' OUT

You the man.

                       MOOKIE

No, you the man.

                     BUGGIN' OUT

You the man.

                       MOOKIE

No, you the man.

                     BUGGIN' OUT

No. I'm just a struggling black man trying to keep my dick
hard in a cruel and harsh world.

Dir: Spike Lee • Scr: Spike Lee • Cast: Giancarlo Esposito (Buggin' Out),
Spike Lee (Mookie)

Barack Obama has said this was the movie he and his wife went to see on their first date.

Forrest celebrates his love for Jenny, his best friend from high school.

FORREST GUMP

Me and Jenny goes together like peas and carrots.

Dir: Robert Zemeckis • Scr: Eric Roth • Based on a novel by Winston Groom • Cast: Tom Hanks (Forrest Gump)

'DON'T NEVER LET NOBODY MAKE A MOVIE OF YOUR LIFE'S STORY'

Thus begins *Gump & Co.*, the novel Winston Groom wrote following *Forrest Gump*. Frustrated by the way the team who adapted his book twisted the story and censored both language and sex, Groom was further angered when the film received six Oscars but none of the winners thought to mention the original writer in their speeches.

This is a familiar tale in the world of adaptations, although producers who buy the rights to books justify themselves by saying that they are doing the authors a favour; in the case of *Forrest Gump*, the novel sold 30,000 copies on its original appearance but the reprint to accompany the film sold 1.7 million across the world.

In the case of those whose reputations are already established and whose bank balances are perfectly healthy, the arrangement can still be depressing. P. L. Travers, creator of *Mary Poppins*, had a contract with Disney which was supposed to safeguard her much-loved character but the 'script approval' she was promised did little to deflect the changes executives wanted to the book. Travers thought Poppins had been made far less strict than she intended and she hated the animated sequences; what she made of Dick Van Dyke's mangled cockney accent sadly goes unrecorded. Relations between author and studio had become so strained by the time the film was finished that Travers had to beg the producers for a ticket for the première and spent much of the screening in tears. Needless to say, she refused to sell Disney the rights to the rest of the series.

Anthony Burgess was not a man given to tears but his response to the furore surrounding Kubrick's screen version of *A Clockwork Orange* shocked him profoundly. 'The book I am best known for, or only known for, is a novel I am prepared to repudiate: written a quarter of a century ago, a jeu d'esprit knocked off for money in three weeks, it became known as the raw material for a film which seemed to glorify sex and violence. The film made it easy for readers of the book to misunderstand what it was about, and the misunderstanding will pursue me till I die. I should not have written the book because of this danger of misinterpretation.'

Nor was this the only time Kubrick came under fire. Stephen King has had no fewer than thirty-five of his books turned into films, including *The Shawshank Redemption*, *Carrie*, *Misery* and *The Green Mile*, but he felt the director's treatment of *The Shining* was a particular disappointment. 'I'd admired Kubrick for a long time and had great expectations for the project, but I was deeply disappointed in the end result... Kubrick just couldn't grasp the sheer inhuman evil of the Overlook Hotel. So he looked, instead, for evil in the characters and made the film into a domestic tragedy with only vaguely supernatural overtones. That was the basic flaw: because he couldn't believe, he couldn't make the film believable to others.'

Bret Easton Ellis makes a similar complaint: 'I think the problem with *American Psycho* was that it was conceived as a novel, as a literary work with a very unreliable narrator at the centre of it, and the medium of film demands answers... You can be as ambiguous as you want with a movie, but it doesn't matter — we're still looking at it. It's still being answered for us visually. I don't think [the story] is particularly more interesting if you knew that he did it, or think that it all happens in his head. I think the answer to that question makes the book infinitely less interesting.'

Graham Greene, whose novels were adapted by directors as talented as Carol Reed, Otto Preminger, George Cukor and Joseph L. Mankiewicz, put it more succinctly: 'Hollywood made a bad film of nearly every book I did.'

1998 WAKING NED

Speaking at Ned's funeral, Jackie reminds the townsfolk of the pleasures of friendship.

JACKIE

The words that are spoken at a funeral are spoken too late for the man who is dead. What a wonderful thing it would be to visit your own funeral. To sit at the front and hear what was said, maybe say a few things yourself. Michael and I grew old together. But at times, when we laughed, we grew young. If he was here now, if he could hear what I say, I'd congratulate him on being a great man and thank him for being a friend.

Dir: Kirk Jones • Scr: Kirk Jones • Cast: Ian Bannen (Jackie O'Shea)

1999 TOY STORY 2

A toy laments the truth that her owner is growing older.

JESSIE

You never forget kids like Emily or Andy, but they forget you.

Dir: John Lasseter, Ash Brannon, Lee Unkrich • Scr: John Lasseter, Pete Docter, Ash Brannon, Andrew Stanton, Rita Hsiao, Doug Chamberlin, Chris Webb • Cast: Joan Cusack (Jessie, the Yodelling Cowgirl)

2000 ALMOST FAMOUS

A young music journalist on tour with a band strikes up a friendship with one of their groupies.

PENNY

How old are you?

WILLIAM

Eighteen.

PENNY

Me too! How old are we really?

WILLIAM

Seventeen.

PENNY

Me too!

> WILLIAM

Actually, I'm sixteen.

> PENNY

Me too. Isn't it funny? The truth just sounds different.

> WILLIAM

I'm fifteen.

Dir: Cameron Crowe • Scr: Cameron Crowe • Cast: Kate Hudson (Penny Lane), Patrick Fugit (William Miller)

The film features over fifty songs from the 1960s and 1970s and the music licensing budget alone was $3.5 million [$4.7 million].

The actors in the band *Stillwater* rehearsed for six weeks to establish a convincing musical rapport; Peter Frampton gave Billy Crudup guitar coaching, although his actual performances were recorded by *Pearl Jam*'s Mike McCready. Production was complicated by the fact that the young actor Patrick Fugit's voice broke and he grew three inches during filming.

2000 TOGETHER (*TILLSAMMANS*) 2000

A lonely alcoholic calls a plumber who worked for him recently.

> BIRGER

I unscrewed it so you'd come here to fix it and we could talk some more.

Dir: Lukas Moodysson • Scr: Lukas Moodysson • Cast: Sten Ljunggren (Birger)

2001 I AM SAM 2001

Mentally challenged Sam persuades Rita, a lawyer, to help him regain custody of his daughter.

> RITA

I just don't know what to call you: retarded, mentally retarded, mentally handicapped, mentally disabled, intellectually handicapped, intellectually disabled, developmentally disabled...

> SAM

You can call me Sam.

Dir: Jessie Nelson • Scr: Kristine Johnson, Jessie Nelson • Cast: Michelle Pfeiffer (Rita Harrison Williams), Sean Penn (Sam Dawson)

2001   HARRY POTTER AND THE PHILOSOPHER'S STONE   2001

The headmaster of a school for magicians addresses his pupils.

DUMBLEDORE

It takes a great deal of bravery to stand up to your enemies, but a great deal more to stand up to your friends.

Dir: Chris Columbus • Scr: Steve Kloves • Based on a novel by J. K. Rowling • Cast: Richard Harris (Albus Dumbledore)

2002   DIVINE SECRETS OF THE YA-YA SISTERHOOD   2002

Shep helps his daughter Sidda come to terms with the difficulties of her childhood.

SHEP

The road to hell is paved with good intentions.

SIDDA

Well, what about the road back? What's that paved with?

SHEP

Humility.

Dir: Callie Khouri • Scr: Mark Andrus, Callie Khouri • Based on a novel by Rebecca Wells • Cast: James Garner (Shepard 'Shep' Walker), Sandra Bullock (Siddalee 'Sidda' Walker)

2003   THE LORD OF THE RINGS: THE RETURN OF THE KING   2003

Frodo and Sam have vanquished their enemies but realize they will be unable to return home as the world around them destroys itself.

FRODO

I'm glad to be with you, Samwise Gamgee...here at the end of all things.

Dir: Peter Jackson • Scr: Peter Jackson, Fran Walsh, Philippa Boyens • Based on a novel by J. R. R. Tolkien • Cast: Elijah Wood (Frodo Baggins)

The filming of the trilogy had a huge impact on the film and tourist industries in New Zealand. One hundred thousand people turned out for the première in Wellington – almost a quarter of the population.

ALMOST...

Imagine *Brokeback Mountain* directed by Joel Schumacher (*The Phantom of the Opera*, *8mm*) and starring Mark Wahlberg (*Boogie Nights*) and Joaquin Phoenix (*Gladiator*). How about *The Shawshank Redemption* with Rob Reiner at the helm (*Spinal Tap*, *Stand By Me*) and Kevin Costner as Andy Dufresne? Or *Forrest Gump* in the hands of Terry Gilliam (*Fear and Loathing in Las Vegas*, *Jabberwocky*) with John Travolta as Forrest and Tupac Shakur as Bubba? Well, it nearly happened: all of the above were considered for, or expressed an interest in, the roles.

Hardly any projects are conceived and put into production by a fixed director with an actor already attached, and the complexity of scheduling key players further complicates matters. Few directors have so many other projects ready to go that they can afford to bide their time; Spielberg took ten years to persuade Daniel Day-Lewis to play Lincoln in his 2012 biopic. Conversely, when enough key players are in place and a production is slated to start the final pieces of the puzzle have to be found urgently. Kevin Spacey was cast as the killer in *Se7en* only two days before filming began.

One of the most unlikely combinations would surely have been the Beatles' version of *The Lord of the Rings*, not least since they asked Stanley Kubrick to direct it. Even so, when Peter Jackson got the green light for his adaptation, he faced perhaps the greatest casting challenge of his career. A large number of key characters are iconic figures whose presence would need to carry audiences across nine hours split into three films, and whose actors would need to commit to many years of production, re-shoots and dubbing. It seems almost impossible to imagine the result now without Ian McKellen, Christopher Lee and Viggo Mortensen, but it is amusing to bear in mind that the cast might have read as follows:

- Gimli the Dwarf: Bill Bailey

- Elrond, the Elf Lord: David Bowie

- Aragorn: Russell Crowe

- Frodo: Jake Gyllenhaal

- Arwen: Uma Thurman

- Boromir: Bruce Willis

- Saruman: Tim Curry

- Gandalf: Sean Connery

Connery turned the offer down, claiming that he didn't understand the script and hated the idea of spending three years in New Zealand.

Other alternative universes might have given us:

- Shirley MacLaine as Maria and Yul Brynner as Captain von Trapp in *The Sound of Music* (1965)

- Harrison Ford as Benjamin and Ingrid Bergman as Mrs Robinson in *The Graduate* (1967)

- Sissy Spacek as Princess Leia and Bill Murray as Han Solo in *Star Wars* (1977)

- Muhammad Ali as Superman in *Superman* (1978)

- Dustin Hoffman as Deckard in *Blade Runner* (1982)

- Christopher Reeve as Edward and Sarah Jessica Parker as Vivian in *Pretty Woman* (1990)

- Daniel Day-Lewis as Vincent and Jennifer Aniston as Mia in *Pulp Fiction* (1994)

- Macaulay Culkin as Jack and Angelina Jolie as Rose in *Titanic* (1997)

- Will Smith as Neo in *The Matrix* (1999)

- Robin Williams as Hagrid in the *Harry Potter* series (2001-2011)

2008 GRAN TORINO 2008

*An elderly man visits the barber who has cut his hair all his
life.*

MARTIN

There. You finally look like a human being again. You
shouldn't wait so long between haircuts, you cheap son of a
bitch.

WALT

Yeah. I'm surprised you're still around. I was always hoping
you'd die off and they got someone in here that knew what
the hell they were doing. Instead, you're just hanging around
like the doo-wop dago you are.

MARTIN

That'll be ten bucks, Walt.

WALT

Ten bucks? Jesus Christ, Marty. What are you, half Jew or
somethin'? You keep raising the damn prices all the time.

MARTIN

It's been ten bucks for the last five years, you hard-nosed
Polack son of a bitch.

WALT

Yeah, well, keep the change.

MARTIN

See you in three weeks, prick.

WALT

Not if I see you first, dipshit.

Dir: Clint Eastwood • Scr: Nick Schenk, Dave Johannson • Cast: John
Carroll Lynch (Barber Martin), Clint Eastwood (Walt Kowalski)

Dustin Hoffman and Robert Redford proved a formidable combination in *All the President's Men* (1976), the story of the Watergate investigation.

The stunning realism of Kubrick's moon sequences for *2001: A Space Odyssey* (1968) helped fuel conspiracy theories that NASA's lunar landings had been faked in a studio.

'That's funny, that plane's dustin' crops where there ain't no crops.' Cary Grant runs for his life in *North by Northwest* (1959).

Enemies

1933 DUCK SOUP

Wisecracking Rufus T. Firefly is introduced to the gorgeous
dancer Vera Marcal.

RUFUS T. FIREFLY

I could dance with you until the cows come home. On second
thoughts, I'd rather dance with the cows till you come home.

Dir: Leo McCarey • Scr: Bert Kalmar, Harry Ruby, Arthur Sheekman, Nat
Perrin • Cast: Groucho Marx (Rufus T. Firefly)

1939 GONE WITH THE WIND

Desperate not to be abandoned, Scarlett asks Rhett what will
become of her once he is gone.

SCARLETT

Where shall I go? What shall I do?

RHETT

Frankly, my dear, I don't give a damn.

Dir: Victor Fleming • Scr: Sidney Howard • Based on a novel by Margaret
Mitchell • Cast: Vivien Leigh (Scarlett O'Hara), Clark Gable (Rhett
Butler)

Rhett's final line – 'Frankly, my dear, I don't give a damn' – was recently voted the greatest ever
movie quote by the American Film Institute. The Motion Picture Production Code frowned on
profanity and suggested the following substitutes: 'Frankly, my dear, I just don't care'; or 'it
makes my gorge rise'; or 'my indifference is boundless'; or 'I don't give a hoot'; or 'nothing could
interest me less'. At the last moment the Code was amended specifically to let the line stand on
the tenuous grounds that it was taken from a 'literary work'.

Astonishingly, the author's first suggestion for the casting of her male hero was Groucho Marx.

1940 THE SHOP AROUND THE CORNER

Two shop assistants detest each other, only to fall in love as
anonymous pen-pals.

ALFRED

There might be a lot we don't know about each other. You know,
people seldom go to the trouble of scratching the surface of
things to find the inner truth.

KLARA

Well, I really wouldn't care to scratch your surface, Mr Kralik, because I know exactly what I'd find. Instead of a heart, a handbag. Instead of a soul, a suitcase. And instead of an intellect, a cigarette lighter...which doesn't work.

Dir: Ernst Lubitsch • Scr: Samson Raphaelson • Based on a play by Miklós László • Cast: James Stewart (Alfred Kralik), Margaret Sullavan (Klara Novak)

1942 CASABLANCA 1942

Captain Renault, a corrupt official with loyalties to the Nazis, is suspicious of Rick's presence in neutral Casablanca.

CAPTAIN RENAULT

I have often speculated on why you don't return to America. Did you abscond with the church funds? Run off with a senator's wife? I like to think you killed a man. It's the romantic in me.

RICK

It was a combination of all three.

CAPTAIN RENAULT

What in heaven's name brought you to Casablanca?

RICK

My health. I came to Casablanca for the waters.

CAPTAIN RENAULT

The waters? What waters? We're in the desert.

RICK

I was misinformed.

Dir: Michael Curtiz • Scr: Julius J. Epstein, Philip G. Epstein, Howard Koch • Based on a play by Murray Burnett, Joan Alison • Cast: Claude Rains (Captain Louis Renault), Humphrey Bogart (Rick Blaine)

Warner Brothers originally hoped Ronald Reagan would play the part of Rick, but director Michael Curtiz wanted someone tougher. When the producers approached George Raft (*Scarface, Each Dawn I Die*) for the role to play alongside Ingrid Bergman, he replied: 'Whoever heard of Casablanca?', adding 'I don't want to star opposite an unknown Swedish broad.' Humphrey Bogart was the studio's seventh choice for their hero.

Bergman's star quality and beauty were undeniable but her fame did not deter John Gielgud – with whom she appeared in *Murder on the Orient Express* – from remarking: 'Poor Ingrid – she speaks five languages and can't act in any of them.'

1942   THE MAN WHO CAME TO DINNER   1942

Nurse Preen has had enough of her patient's selfishness and bullying.

NURSE PREEN

I am not only walking out on this case, Mr Whiteside, I am leaving the nursing profession. I became a nurse because all my life, ever since I was a little girl, I was filled with the idea of serving a suffering humanity. After one month with you, Mr Whiteside, I am going to work in a munitions factory. From now on anything I can do to help exterminate the human race will fill me with the greatest of pleasure. If Florence Nightingale had ever nursed you, Mr Whiteside, she would have married Jack the Ripper instead of founding the Red Cross.

Dir: William Keighley • Scr: Julius J. Epstein, Philip G. Epstein • Based on a play by George S. Kaufman, Moss Hart • Cast: Mary Wickes (Nurse Preen)

1942   TO BE OR NOT TO BE   1942

Polish actor Joseph Tura pretends to be German Colonel Ehrhardt in order to win the confidence of Nazi agent Siletsky.

TURA

I can't tell you how delighted we are to have you here.

PROFESSOR SILETSKY

May I say, my dear Colonel, that it's good to breathe the air of the Gestapo again. You know, you're quite famous in London, Colonel. They call you 'Concentration Camp Ehrhardt'.

TURA

Ha ha. Yes, yes...we do the concentrating and the Poles do the camping.

Dir: Ernst Lubitsch • Scr: Edwin Justus Mayer • Based on a story by Melchior Lengyel • Cast: Jack Benny (Joseph Tura), Stanley Ridges (Professor Alexander Siletsky)

1944 LAURA   1944

A newspaper columnist considers his fearsome reputation.

LYDECKER

I don't use a pen. I write with a goose quill dipped in venom.

Dir: Otto Preminger • Scr: Jay Dratler, Samuel Hoffenstein, Elizabeth Reinhardt • Based on a novel by Vera Caspary • Cast: Clifton Webb (Waldo Lydecker)

1947 THE LADY FROM SHANGHAI   1947

Arthur tries to evade a killer - his wife - in a carnival hall of mirrors.

ARTHUR

You'd be foolish to fire that gun. With these mirrors, it's difficult to tell. You are aiming at me, aren't you? I'm aiming at you, lover. Of course, killing you is killing myself. It's the same thing. But you know, I'm pretty tired of both of us.

Dir: Orson Welles • Scr: Orson Welles • Based on a novel by Sherwood King • Cast: Everett Sloane (Arthur Bannister)

Welles only agreed to direct the film to get himself out of a financial jam. His Mercury Theatre company was opening a musical version of *Around the World in 80 Days* in Boston and at the eleventh hour the costumes had been impounded. Urgently in need of $55,000 [$575,000] to release them, Welles cabled producer Harry Cohn and told him about the novel on which *The Lady from Shanghai* was based, promising that if he cabled the cash to Boston within two hours Welles would make the film for him. Cohn agreed on the spot.

1949   ADAM'S RIB   1949

Lawyer Amanda Bonner questions an unrepentant defendant.

AMANDA

And after you shot your husband...how did you feel?

DORIS

Hungry.

Dir: George Cukor • Scr: Ruth Gordon, Garson Kanin • Cast: Katharine Hepburn (Amanda Bonner), Judy Holliday (Doris Attinger)

Encouraged by her parents to be ambitious and self-reliant, Katharine Hepburn was known for her outspoken remarks. After shooting *A Bill of Divorcement* (1932), she told her co-star John Barrymore: 'Thank goodness I don't have to act with you any more.' Barrymore reputedly replied: 'I didn't know you ever had, darling.'

1949   WHITE HEAT   1949

Escaping from jail, Cody Jarrett abducts a prisoner who betrayed him earlier.

PARKER

You wouldn't kill me in cold blood, would you?

JARRETT

No, I'll let you warm up a little.

Dir: Raoul Walsh • Scr: Ivan Goff, Ben Roberts • Based on a story by Virginia Kellogg • Cast: Paul Guilfoyle (Roy Parker), James Cagney (Cody Jarrett)

1950   ALL ABOUT EVE   1950

Theatre star Margo Channing takes Eve Harrington, an aspiring actress, under her wing. Throwing a party one night, she realizes her protégée's ambitions threaten her own eminence.

MARGO

Fasten your seatbelts - it's going to be a bumpy night.

Dir: Joseph L. Mankiewicz • Scr: Joseph L. Mankiewicz • Based on a short story by Mary Orr • Cast: Bette Davis (Margo Channing)

Screenwriter Joe Gillis is not happy to see Betty, the studio reader who turned down his latest script.

BETTY

I've been hoping to run into you.

JOE

What for? To recover that knife you stuck in my back?

Dir: Billy Wilder • Scr: Charles Brackett, Billy Wilder, D. M. Marshman Jr • Cast: Nancy Olson (Betty Schaefer), William Holden (Joe Gillis)

'I AM BIG. IT'S THE PICTURES THAT GOT SMALL'

Sunset Boulevard, made when Hollywood's golden age was waning in the face of television's popularity and the influx of bolder European films, attracted keen interest even before it started shooting. Because the story portrays a venal industry, egotistical stars and heartless producers, Wilder and co-writer Charles Brackett gave the project the name 'A Can of Beans' to deflect attention. Fearful of interference from censors and the studio itself, they handed them the script piecemeal as the scenes were finished in the hope that the full impact of the story might be softened.

If its depiction of a fading self-obsessed star were not metaphor enough for the decline of the industry, the production itself was filled with delicious ironies and larger-than-life episodes. Gloria Swanson, a legend in her silent days, was willing to play the role of Norma Desmond, but felt herself too grand to audition; director and friend George Cukor was convinced it would be an extraordinary opportunity, and told her: 'If they want you to do ten screen tests, do ten screen tests. If you don't, I will personally shoot you.'

Down-on-his-luck screenwriter Joe Gillis was played by William Holden, whose career had recently suffered a string of flops and a period of heavy drinking; Erich von Stroheim, a top director and actor from the 1920s, was Max, Desmond's butler, driver and projectionist, and on one occasion screens a picture of his in which Swanson actually starred (*Queen Kelly*, 1929). Even the publicity photos of the young Norma Desmond seen throughout her mansion are genuine stills from Swanson's own career.

Wilder persuaded plenty of other industry figures to play cameos, including Buster Keaton and gossip columnist Hedda Hopper. Cecil B. DeMille, the first great American director, also plays himself in a brief but vital role. He agreed to shoot his scene for $10,000 [$95,000] and a Cadillac, but when Wilder called him back later to get a further close-up DeMille demanded the same fee again.

All of the actors deliver lines bitterly appropriate to their own experiences:

> JOE: Funny how gentle people get with you once you're dead.
>
> NORMA: I am big. It's the pictures that got small.
>
> CECIL B. DEMILLE: A dozen press agents working overtime can do terrible things to the human spirit.

Despite the sensitive personal dynamics on set, Wilder remained his mischievous self. On one occasion, William Holden's wife paid a visit to the studio just as Holden was required to kiss actress Nancy Olson passionately. Wilder knew he had a perfectly good performance on the first take but made them repeat it and refused to call 'Cut!' until Mrs Holden — after several uncomfortable minutes — did so. When Norma Desmond first finds Gillis in her house, she assumes he must be an undertaker who has come to take away her recently deceased pet chimpanzee. Wilder was subsequently asked the meaning of this cryptic encounter and breezily replied: 'Don't you understand? Before Gillis came along, Desmond was fucking the monkey.'

At the end of the film Desmond descends her grand staircase and delivers the famous line 'All right, Mr DeMille, I'm ready for my close-up', mistaking the reporters and policemen for newsreel cameramen and adoring fans. Swanson was so moved by this that when the scene was finished she burst into tears. Wilder remained unimpressed; when interviewers later asked him whether the final dissolve was deliberately ambiguous he replied: 'I have no idea! All I know is that she's meshuggah [crazy], that's all. That's the end.'

The picture was a huge hit, winning three Oscars, and in 1989 was among the first group of films deemed 'culturally, historically, or aesthetically significant' by the Library of Congress.

1952 SINGIN'IN THE RAIN   1952

Actor Don Lockwood does not return his co-star Lina Lamont's affections.

> LINA
>
> Oh Donny! You couldn't kiss me like that and not mean it just a teensy bit!
>
> DON
>
> Meet the greatest actor in the world! I'd rather kiss a tarantula.
>
> LINA
>
> You don't mean that.
>
> DON
>
> I don't? Hey Joe, get me a tarantula.

Dir: Stanley Donen, Gene Kelly • Scr: Adolph Green, Betty Comden • Cast: Jean Hagen (Lina Lamont), Gene Kelly (Don Lockwood)

1952 THE QUIET MAN   1952

A bullying landowner takes against a man who tries to buy a local property.

> 'RED' WILL DANAHER
>
> He'll regret it to his dying day...if he lives that long.

Dir: John Ford • Scr: Frank S. Nugent • Based on a story by Maurice Walsh • Cast: Victor McLaglen ('Red' Will Danaher)

1955   BAD DAY AT BLACK ROCK 1955

A traveller finds himself threatened by the inhabitants of a town with secrets to hide.

> CAFÉ PROPRIETOR
>
> What'll you have?

> MACREEDY
>
> What've you got?

> CAFÉ PROPRIETOR
>
> Chilli and beans.

> MACREEDY
>
> Anything else?

> CAFÉ PROPRIETOR
>
> Chilli without beans.

Dir: John Sturges • Scr: Millard Kaufman, Don McGuire • Based on a story by Howard Breslin • Cast: Spencer Tracy (John J. Macreedy), Walter Sande (Café Proprietor)

1961   WEST SIDE STORY 1961

Maria confronts the Sharks, a neighbourhood gang who killed her boyfriend.

> MARIA
>
> How do you fire this gun, Chino? By pulling this little trigger? How many bullets are left, Chino? Enough for you? Or you? All of you! You all killed him. And my brother. And Riff. Not with bullets and knives - with *hate*. Well, I can kill now too because now I have hate. How many can I kill, Chino? How many - and still have one bullet left for me?

Dir: Jerome Robbins, Robert Wise • Scr: Ernest Lehman, Arthur Laurents • Based on a play by Jerome Robbins, Stephen Sondheim • Cast: Natalie Wood (Maria)

The choreography for the musical numbers was so energetic that the boys' trousers had to be specially sewn with elastic seams. The song 'I Feel Pretty' in the original stage show contains the lyrics 'I feel pretty and witty and bright / And I pity / Any girl who isn't me tonight.' For production reasons the scene could not be shot when it was dark, so the words were changed to 'I feel pretty and witty and gay / And I pity / Any girl who isn't me today.'

The film was the first to win an Academy Award for joint directors.

The Emperor Julius Caesar realizes he is surrounded by traitors.

CAESAR

Infamy, infamy. They've all got it in for me!

Dir: Gerald Thomas • Scr: Talbot Rothwell • Cast: Kenneth Williams (Julius Caesar)

The cheeky historical comedy was shot on the sets left behind from the multimillion-dollar production of *Cleopatra* (1963), starring Elizabeth Taylor and Richard Burton. Adding insult to injury, the producers of *Carry on Cleo* also closely copied the epic's poster design – and were promptly sued.

INCLUDE ME OUT

Producer Samuel Goldwyn (1879–1974) was born in Poland as Schmuel Gelbfisz but on arriving in America aged twenty took the name Samuel Goldfish, a simple translation from the original. Although he was responsible for numerous hits (*The Best Years of Our Lives*, *Wuthering Heights*, *Guys and Dolls*) his greatest fame came as a result of his headstrong outbursts and legendary malapropisms.

Some Goldwynisms have been verifiably documented, others misquoted or misattributed, and in some cases even duplicated. When he bought the rights to *The Well of Loneliness* and a colleague warned him that the book was about lesbians, he was said to have replied: 'That's all right, we'll make them Hungarians.' However, the same story circulates about *The Children's Hour*, with Goldwyn suggesting the lesbians became Armenians.

Goldwyn's claim that 'a verbal contract isn't worth the paper it's written on' is delightful but skewed; what he actually said was: 'his verbal contract is worth more than the paper it's written on'. Charlie Chaplin fought to persuade the world that he, not Goldwyn, once said: 'In two words: im-possible.'

Perhaps the true sign of fame is that the myths loom larger than the truths. When he was told that his eponym had been officially listed in a dictionary, he was furious to discover he had a reputation for putting his foot in it and immediately planted another: 'Goldwynisms? They should talk to Jesse Lasky!'

Whether the following are true or not, who could wish to doubt they were ever really uttered?

- Include me out.

- I'm willing to admit that I may not always be right, but I'm never wrong.

- Anyone who goes to a psychiatrist should have his head examined.

- When you're a star, you have to take the bitter with the sour.

- What we need now is some new, fresh clichés.

- I had a monumental idea this morning, but I didn't like it.

- Flashbacks are a thing of the past.

- I don't care if my pictures never make a dime, so long as everyone keeps coming to see them.

- I'll give you a definite maybe.

- I read part of it all the way through.

- Don't talk to me while I'm interrupting.

- Our comedies are not to be laughed at.

- Tell me, how did you love my picture?

- Don't pay any attention to the critics; don't even ignore them.

- Every director bites the hand that lays the golden egg.

- If I could drop dead right now, I'd be the happiest man alive.

- I never put on a pair of shoes until I've worn them five years.

- The scene is dull. Tell him to put more life into his dying.

- Go see it and see for yourself why you shouldn't see it.

- For your information, I would like to ask a question.

- When I want your opinion, I'll give it to you.

- It's more than magnificent; it's mediocre.

- We want a story that starts out with an earthquake and works its way up to a climax.

- Never make forecasts, especially about the future.

- I don't think anyone should write his autobiography until after he's dead.

- I don't want any yes-men around me. I want everyone to tell me the truth - even though it costs him his job.

- We'd do anything for each other; we'd even cut each other's throats for each other.

- We've all passed a lot of water since then.

- The next time I send a damn fool for something, I'll go myself.

- (On William Wyler's films) I made them - Willy only directed them.

On a more charitable note, these statements contain — for all their clumsiness — more than a grain of truth:

- A wide screen just makes a bad film twice as bad.

- When everybody's happy with the rushes (daily footage), the picture's always a stinker.

- God makes stars. I just produce them.

- A producer shouldn't get ulcers; he should give them.

- I am a rebel. I make a picture to please me. If it pleases me, there is a chance it will please others. But it has to please me first.

- Actors think with their hearts. That's why so many of them die broke.

- It's a mistake to remake a great picture because you can never make it better. Better you should find a picture that was done badly and see what can be done to improve it.

- (On actor Fredric March) I'm overpaying him, but he's worth it.

1966   THE PROFESSIONALS   1966

Rico, a mercenary hired to find Joe's kidnapped wife, realizes Joe has tried to deceive him.

> JOE
>
> You bastard.
>
> RICO
>
> Yes, sir. In my case an accident of birth. But you, sir, you're a self-made man.

Dir: Richard Brooks • Scr: Richard Brooks • Based on a novel by Frank O'Rourke • Cast: Ralph Bellamy (Joe Grant), Lee Marvin (Henry 'Rico' Fardan)

PAPER MOON

Nine-year-old Addie travels with conman Moses - whom she suspects to be her father.

MOSES

I got scruples too, you know. You know what that is? Scruples?

ADDIE

No, I don't know what it is, but if you got 'em it's a sure bet they belong to somebody else.

Dir: Peter Bogdanovich • Scr: Alvin Sargent • Based on a novel by Joe David Brown • Cast: Ryan O'Neal (Moses Pray), Tatum O'Neal (Addie Loggins)

The film is based on the novel *Addie Pray* by Joe David Brown, but director Peter Bogdanovich proposed renaming it *Paper Moon*. Uncertain about his decision, he consulted his great friend Orson Welles who replied: 'That title is so good, you shouldn't even make the picture, just release the title!' Tatum O'Neal remains the youngest-ever Best Actress – at the age of ten – to win an Oscar.

THE WITCHES OF EASTWICK

Alexandra scorns a lover - secretly, the devil in human form - who has mistreated her.

ALEXANDRA

I think - no, I am positive - that you are the most unattractive man I have ever met in my entire life. You know, in the short time we've been together, you have demonstrated every loathsome characteristic of the male personality and even discovered a few new ones. You are physically repulsive, intellectually retarded, you're morally reprehensible, vulgar, insensitive, selfish, stupid, you have no taste, a lousy sense of humour and you smell. You're not even interesting enough to make me sick. Goodbye, Darryl, and thank you for a lovely lunch.

Dir: George Miller • Scr: Michael Cristofer • Based on a novel by John Updike • Cast: Cher (Alexandra Medford)

Amazingly, the genial Bill Murray was originally proposed for the role of Daryl Van Horne, the satanic figure played by Jack Nicholson. Australian director George Miller (*Mad Max*, 1979) was a newcomer to Hollywood and the producers (Warner Brothers and Guber-Peters) proved frustratingly unsupportive. In one scene where Cher had to get into bed with a huge pile of snakes, she asked, 'which one is Jon Peters?'

MISSISSIPPI BURNING

An FBI agent warns his partner not to underestimate the racism of the South.

RUPERT

When I was a little boy there was an old negro farmer lived down the road from us, name of Monroe. And he was, uh - well, I guess he was just a little luckier than my daddy was. He bought himself a mule. That was a big deal around that town. Now, my daddy hated that mule, 'cause his friends were always kiddin' him about oh, they saw Monroe out plowin' with his new mule, and Monroe was gonna rent another field now they had a mule. And one morning that mule just showed up dead. They poisoned the water. And after that there was never any mention about that mule around my daddy. It just never came up. So one time, we were drivin' down the road and we passed Monroe's place and we saw it was empty. He'd just packed up and left, I guess. Gone up north, or somethin'. I looked over at my daddy's face and I knew he'd done it. And he saw that I knew. He was ashamed. I guess he was ashamed. He looked at me and he said: 'If you ain't better than a nigger, son, who are you better than?' He was an old man just so full of hate that he didn't know that bein' poor was what was killin' him.

Dir: Alan Parker • Scr: Chris Gerolmo • Cast: Gene Hackman (Rupert Anderson)

Although fictionalised, the story was inspired by an actual investigation following the murder in 1964 of voting rights activists James Earl Chaney, Mickey Schwerner and Andrew Goodman; the film aroused controversy among those who felt the powerful narrative oversimplified the legally established facts.

POINT BREAK

BEN

You're a real blue flame special, aren't you, son? Young, dumb and full of come, I know. What I don't know is how you got assigned here. Guess we must just have ourselves an asshole shortage, huh?

JOHNNY

Not so far.

Dir: Kathryn Bigelow • Scr: W. Peter Iliff, Rick King • Cast: John C. McGinley (Ben Harp), Keanu Reeves (Johnny Utah)

When Monty, a drug dealer sentenced to seven years in prison, glimpses his reflection in a restroom mirror, he sees the graffiti: 'Fuck You'.

MONTY

Yeah, fuck you too. Fuck me? Fuck you. Fuck you and this whole city and everyone in it. Fuck the panhandlers, grubbing for money, and smiling at me behind my back. Fuck the squeegee men dirtying up the clean windshield of my car - get a fucking job! Fuck the Sikhs and the Pakistanis bombing down the avenues in decrepit cabs, curry steaming out their pores stinking up my day. Terrorists in fucking training. Slow the fuck down! Fuck the Chelsea boys with their waxed chests and pumped-up biceps. Going down on each other in my parks and on my piers, jingling their dicks on my Channel 35. Fuck the Korean grocers with their pyramids of overpriced fruit and their tulips and roses wrapped in plastic. Ten years in the country, still no speaky English? Fuck the Russians in Brighton Beach. Mobster thugs sitting in cafés, sipping tea in little glasses, sugar cubes between their teeth. Wheelin' and dealin' and scheming. Go back where you fucking came from! Fuck the black-hatted Hassidim, strolling up and down 47th Street in their dirty gabardine with their dandruff. Selling South African apartheid diamonds! Fuck the Wall Street brokers. Self-styled masters of the universe. Michael Douglas, Gordon Gekko wannabe mother fuckers, figuring out new ways to rob hard working people blind. Send those Enron assholes to jail for fucking life! You think Bush and Cheney didn't know about that shit? Give me a fucking break! Tyco! Worldcom! Fuck the Puerto Ricans. Twenty to a car, swelling up the welfare rolls, worst fuckin' parade in the city. And don't even get me started on the Dominicans, 'cause they make the Puerto Ricans look good. Fuck the Bensonhurst Italians with their pomaded hair, their nylon warm-up suits, their St Anthony medallions, swinging their Jason Giambi Louisville Slugger baseball bats, trying to audition for *The Sopranos*. Fuck the Upper East Side wives with their Hermès scarves and their fifty-dollar Balducci artichokes. Overfed faces getting pulled and lifted and stretched, all taut and shiny. You're not fooling anybody, sweetheart! Fuck the uptown brothers. They never pass the ball, they don't want to play defence, they take five steps on every lay-up to the hoop. And then they want to turn around and blame everything on the white man. Slavery ended one hundred and thirty-seven years ago. Move the fuck on! Fuck the corrupt cops with their anus-violating plungers and their 41 shots, standing behind a blue wall of silence. You betray our trust! Fuck the priests who put their hands down some innocent child's pants. Fuck the church that protects them, delivering us into evil. And while you're at it, fuck J.C.! He got off easy! A day on the cross, a weekend in hell, and all the hallelujahs of the legioned angels for eternity! Try seven years in fuckin' Otisville, J.! Fuck Osama Bin Laden, al-Qaeda, and backward-ass cave-dwelling fundamentalist assholes everywhere. On the names of innocent thousands murdered, I pray you spend the rest of eternity with your seventy-two whores roasting in a jet-fuel fire in hell. You towel-headed camel jockeys can kiss my royal Irish ass! Fuck Jacob Elinsky. Whining malcontent. Fuck Francis Xavier Slaughtery my best friend, judging me while he stares at my girlfriend's ass. Fuck Naturelle Riviera, I gave her my trust and she stabbed me in the back, sold me up the river, fucking bitch. Fuck my father with his endless grief, standing behind that bar sipping on club sodas, selling whiskey to firemen, and cheering the Bronx Bombers. Fuck this whole city and everyone in it.

Dir: Spike Lee • Scr: David Benioff, based on his novel • Cast: Edward Norton (Monty Brogan)

2008   THE DARK KNIGHT   2008

Realizing that Batman has spared his life, the Joker taunts his rival that their battle will never be over.

THE JOKER

You just couldn't let me go, could you? This is what happens when an unstoppable force meets an immovable object. You truly are incorruptible, aren't you? You won't kill me out of some misplaced sense of self-righteousness. And I won't kill you because you're just too much fun. I think you and I are destined to do this forever.

Dir: Christopher Nolan • Scr: Jonathan Nolan, Christopher Nolan, David S. Goyer • Cast: Heath Ledger (The Joker)

Erica ends her relationship with Mark Zuckerberg, founder of Facebook.

                            ERICA

You are probably going to be a very successful computer
person. But you're going to go through life thinking that
girls don't like you because you're a nerd. And I want you to
know, from the bottom of my heart, that that won't be true.
It'll be because you're an asshole.

Dir: David Fincher • Scr: Aaron Sorkin • Based a book by Ben Mezrich • Cast:
Rooney Mara (Erica Albright)

Mark Zuckerberg was initially reluctant to see a film which painted such an uncompromising
portrait of his company's meteoric success. When he did watch it, he is reported to have said
that it was 'interesting', and that the film-makers got his clothes right.

THOU SHALT NOT

1. LAW DEFEATED
2. INSIDE OF THIGH
3. LACE LINGERIE
4. DEAD MAN
5. NARCOTICS
6. DRINKING
7. EXPOSED BOSOM
8. GAMBLING
9. POINTING GUN
10. TOMMY GUN

An unknown photographer satirizes the advent of the Motion Picture Production Code banning references to sex, violence and alcohol in the early 1930s.

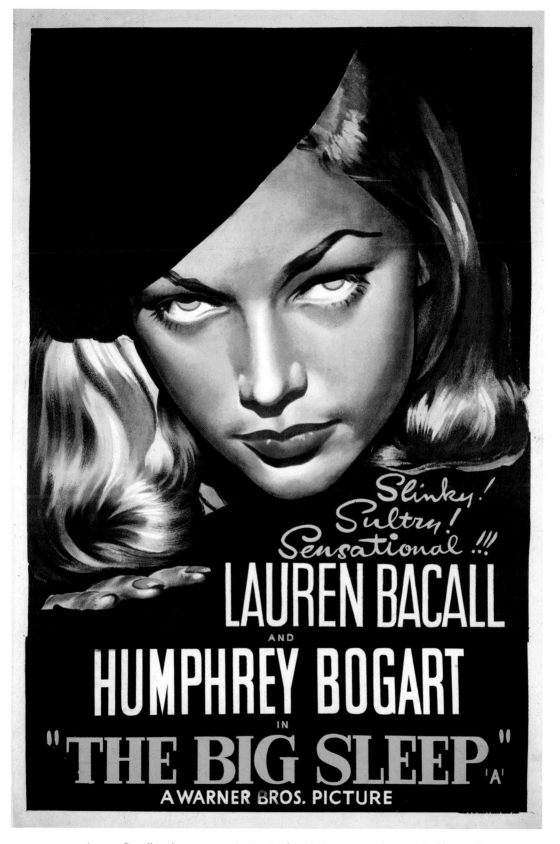

Lauren Bacall is almost as captivating in this 1946 poster as she is in the film itself.

Carrie Ann Moss and Keanu Reaves exploit the 'time slice' photography that was a hallmark of *The Matrix* series (1999–2003).

Partners

1932 TROUBLE IN PARADISE 1932

A millionairess brushes off an eager suitor.

MARIETTE

No, no, François, I tell you, no. You see, François, marriage is a beautiful mistake which two people make together.

Dir: Ernst Lubitsch • Scr: Samson Raphaelson, Grover Jones • Based on a play by Aladár László • Cast: Kay Francis (Madame Mariette Colet)

1940 HIS GIRL FRIDAY 1940

WALTER

You've got an old-fashioned idea divorce is something that lasts forever, 'Till death do us part'. Why, divorce doesn't mean anything nowadays, Hildy, just a few words mumbled over you by a judge.

Dir: Howard Hawks • Scr: Charles Lederer • Based on a play by Ben Hecht and Charles MacArthur • Cast: Cary Grant (Walter Burns)

1941 THE LADY EVE 1941

Colonel Harrington encourages his daughter, also a confidence trickster.

COLONEL HARRINGTON

Let us be crooked, but never common.

Dir: Preston Sturges • Scr: Preston Sturges • Based on a story by Monckton Hoffe • Cast: Charles Coburn (Colonel Harrington)

1944 DOUBLE INDEMNITY 1944

An insurance claims adjuster suspects murder in a case he has paid out on, little knowing one of his own salesmen is the killer.

BARTON

It's beginning to come apart at the seams already. Murder's never perfect. Always comes apart sooner or later, and when two people are involved it's usually sooner. Now we know the Dietrichson dame is in it and somebody else. Pretty soon, we'll know who that somebody else is. He'll show. He's got to show. Sometime, somewhere, they've got to meet. Their emotions are all kicked up. Whether it's love or hate doesn't matter - they can't keep away from each other. They may think it's twice as safe because there's two of them, but it isn't twice as safe.

It's ten times twice as dangerous. They've committed a murder! And it's not like taking a trolley ride together where they can get off at different stops. They're stuck with each other and they got to ride all the way to the end of the line, and it's a one-way trip - and the last stop is the cemetery.

Dir: Billy Wilder • Scr: Billy Wilder, Raymond Chandler • Based on a novella by James M. Cain • Cast: Edward G. Robinson (Barton Keyes)

1945 DETOUR   1945

Two strangers join forces to claim a dead man's inheritance.

VERA

Shut up - you're making noises like a husband.

Dir: Edgar G. Ulmer • Scr: Martin Goldsmith • Cast: Ann Savage (Vera)

Detour was the first B-movie – and the first *film noir* – to be included in the Library of Congress's register of films deemed 'culturally, historically or aesthetically' significant.

1946 NOTORIOUS   1946

A spymaster suspects his female agent is a romantic at heart.

This fog gets me.

DEVLIN

That's your hair in your eyes.

Dir: Alfred Hitchcock • Scr: Ben Hecht • Cast: Ingrid Bergman (Alicia Huberman), Cary Grant (T. R. Devlin)

After working with Hitchcock, Ingrid Bergman said: 'I'd like to know more about his relationships with women. No, on second thoughts, I wouldn't.'

THE SHAKESPEARE OF HOLLYWOOD

Lured to Hollywood by his friend Herman Mankiewicz in 1926, Ben Hecht (1894–1964) won his first Oscar within a year for the screenplay of *Underworld* (*Paying the Penalty*). He won again for *The Scoundrel* in 1935, and as Hollywood's most famous and best-paid scribe wrote or contributed to *Scarface* (1932), *Gone with the Wind* (1939), *Notorious* (1946), *Gilda* (1946) and *Wuthering Heights* (1939).

Often spoken of as the 'Shakespeare of Hollywood', he personified the media's view of the hard-boiled, hard-drinking wordsmith and was famed for delivering drafts in as little as two weeks. In 'Elegy for Wonderland', published in *Esquire* magazine in 1959, he wrote:

> Most of my script-writing friends – I never had more than a handful – took eagerly to the bottle or the analyst's couch, filled their extravagant ménages with threats of suicide, hurled themselves into hysterical amours. And some of them actually died in their forties and fifties. Among these were the witty Herman Mankiewicz and F. Scott Fitzgerald, the fine novelist.

Hecht also penned several Broadway hits, including *The Front Page* (1928), and the fact that this parallel career gave him independent fame may have prompted his diatribes against the film studios who set little store by the notion of authorship:

> The factors that laid low so whooping and puissant an empire as the old Hollywood are many. I can think of a score, including the barbarian hordes of television. But there is one that stands out for me in the post-mortem... The factor

had to do with the basis of movie-making: 'Who shall be in charge of telling the story?' The answer Hollywood figured out for this question was what doomed it. It figured out that writers were not to be in charge of creating stories. Instead, a curious tribe of inarticulate Pooh-Bahs called supervisors and, later, producers were summoned out of literary nowhere and given a thousand sceptres. It was like switching the roles of teacher and pupil in the fifth grade. The result is now history. An industry based on writing had to collapse when the writer was given an errand-boy status.

He was also bitterly sarcastic about Hollywood's prim morality:

Two generations of Americans have been informed nightly that a woman who betrayed her husband (or a husband a wife) could never find happiness; that sex was no fun without a mother-in-law and a rubber plant around; that women who fornicated just for pleasure ended up as harlots or washerwomen; that any man who was sexually active in his youth later lost the one girl he truly loved; that a man who indulged in sharp practices to get ahead in the world ended in poverty and with even his own children turning on him; that any man who broke the laws, man's or God's, must always die, or go to jail, or become a monk, or restore the money he stole before wandering off into the desert. . . For forty years the movies have drummed away on the American character. They have fed it naïveté and bunkum in doses never before administered to any people. They have slapped into the American mind more human misinformation in one evening than the Dark Ages could muster in a decade. One basic plot only has appeared daily in their fifteen thousand theatres – the triumph of virtue and the overthrow of wickedness.

We can only wonder whether his astonishing earnings made his complicity in this intellectual decline more – or less – painful:

I received from each script, whether written in two weeks or (never more than) eight weeks, from $50,000 to $150,000 [$500,000 to $1.5 million]. I worked also by the week. David O. Selznick once paid me $3,500 [$35,000] a day.

Vivian is not happy that Marlowe has been called in to investigate her family's affairs.

VIVIAN

I don't like your manners.

MARLOWE

And I'm not crazy about yours. I didn't ask to see you. I don't mind if you don't like my manners, I don't like them myself. They *are* pretty bad. I grieve over them on long winter evenings.

Dir: Howard Hawks • Scr: William Faulkner, Leigh Brackett, Jules Furthman • Based on a novel by Raymond Chandler • Cast: Lauren Bacall (Vivian Rutledge), Humphrey Bogart (Philip Marlowe)

Bogart and Bacall first worked together on *To Have and Have Not* where they quickly fell in love. Their return to the studio for *The Big Sleep* effectively destroyed Bogart's marriage to his third wife, Mayo Methot, and his subsequent heavy drinking often rendered him unable to shoot. He wed Bacall shortly after the production wrapped and they subsequently starred together in *Dark Passage* and *Key Largo*.

1948   **THE TREASURE OF THE SIERRA MADRE**

An old prospector warns of the perils of teamwork when fortunes are at stake.

HOWARD

That's gold, that's what it makes us. Never knew a prospector yet that died rich. Make one fortune, he's sure to blow it in tryin' to find another. I'm no exception to the rule. Aw sure, I'm a gnawed old bone now, but say, don't you guys think the spirit's gone. I'm all set to shoulder a pickaxe and a shovel anytime anybody's willin' to share expenses. I'd rather go by myself. Going it alone's the best way. But you got to have a stomach for loneliness. Some guys go nutty with it. On the other hand, goin' with a partner or two is dangerous. Murderers always lurkin' about. Partners accusin' each other of all sorts of crimes. Aw, as long as there's no find, the noble brotherhood will last. But when the piles of gold begin to grow, that's when the trouble starts.

Dir: John Huston • Scr: John Huston • Based on a novel by B. Traven • Cast: Walter Huston (Howard)

1951 **THE AFRICAN QUEEN**   **1951**

*A Christian missionary and a dissolute river captain are thrown
together in the African jungle.*

ROSE

Nature, Mr Allnut, is what we are put in this world to rise
above.

Dir: John Huston • Scr: John Huston, James Agee, Peter Viertel, John
Collier • Based on a novel by C. S. Forester • Cast: Katharine Hepburn
(Rose Sayer)

Katharine Hepburn disapproved of the amount of whisky John Huston and Humphrey Bogart
drank on location and made a great show of sticking to water. Her protest led to a severe bout
of dysentery.

1953 **STALAG 17**   **1953**

*American airmen held in a German prison camp suspect one of
their number is an informant.*

PRICE

Are you questioning me?

SEFTON

Getting acquainted. I'd like to make one friend in this
barracks.

PRICE

Well, don't bother, Sefton. I don't like you, I never did, and I
never will.

SEFTON

A lot of people say that, and the first thing you know is
they get married and live happily ever after.

Dir: Billy Wilder • Scr: Billy Wilder, Edwin Blum • Based on a play by
Donald Bevan, Edmund Trzcinski • Cast: Peter Graves (Sergeant Price),
William Holden (Sergeant J. J. Sefton)

Director Wilder kept the identity of the informant a secret from the cast so their genuine
suspicions would influence their performances.

1955   GUYS AND DOLLS   1955

*Sky cautions Adelaide to think hard before walking up the aisle
with Nathan, an inveterate gambler.*

SKY

No matter who you marry, you wake up married to
someone else.

Dir: Joseph L. Mankiewicz • Scr: Joseph L. Mankiewicz, Ben Hecht • Based
on short stories by Damon Runyon and a libretto by Jo Swerling, Abe
Burrows • Cast: Marlon Brando (Sky Masterson)

1956   GIANT   1956

*Towards the end of his life, Bick Benedict reflects on his
enduring friendship with his wife.*

BICK

You want to know something, Leslie? If I live to be ninety,
I'm never going to figure you out.

Dir: George Stevens • Scr: Fred Guiol, Ivan Moffat • Based on a novel by
Edna Ferber • Cast: Rock Hudson (Jordan 'Bick' Benedict Jr)

1957   SWEET SMELL OF SUCCESS   1957

A newspaper magnate cautions an embittered press agent.

J. J. HUNSECKER

Don't remove the gangplank, Sidney - you may want to get back
on board.

Dir: Alexander Mackendrick • Scr: Clifford Odets, Ernest Lehman • Based on a novella by Ernest Lehman • Cast: Burt Lancaster (J. J. Hunsecker)

This film's shoot was filled with macho tensions and at one point the temperamental Burt Lancaster threatened to punch the film's writer, Ernest Lehman. The witty scribe replied: 'Go ahead, I need the money.'

1958 VERTIGO 1958

> SCOTTIE
>
> Don't you think it's sort of a waste for the two of us to...
>
> MADELEINE
>
> Wander separately? Ah, but only one is a wanderer. Two together are always going somewhere.

Dir: Alfred Hitchcock • Scr: Alec Coppel, Samuel A. Taylor • Based on a novel by Pierre Boileau, Thomas Narcejac • Cast: James Stewart (John 'Scottie' Ferguson), Kim Novak (Madeleine Elster)

A tough call among so many outstanding Hitchcock pictures, *Vertigo* was recently voted the greatest film of all time in the British Film Institute's *Sight and Sound* magazine.

1959 SOME LIKE IT HOT 1959

Jerry, a jazz musician, disguises himself as a woman to escape his mobster pursuers but finds he has attracted the attentions of an amorous millionaire.

> JERRY
>
> Oh no you don't! Osgood, I'm gonna level with you. We can't get married at all.
>
> OSGOOD
>
> Why not?
>
> JERRY
>
> Well, in the first place, I'm not a natural blonde.
>
> OSGOOD
>
> Doesn't matter.
>
> JERRY
>
> I smoke! I smoke all the time!

OSGOOD

I don't care.

JERRY

Well, I have a terrible past. For three years now, I've been
living with a saxophone player.

OSGOOD

I forgive you.

JERRY

I can never have children!

OSGOOD

We can adopt some.

JERRY

But you don't understand, Osgood! Ohh...

Jerry gives up and pulls off his wig. His voice is deeper now.

JERRY

I'm a *man*!

Osgood just smiles uncomprehendingly.

OSGOOD

Well, nobody's perfect!

Dir: Billy Wilder • Scr: Billy Wilder, I. A. L. Diamond • Based on a story
by Robert Thoeren, Michael Logan • Cast: Jack Lemmon (Jerry/'Daphne'),
Joe E. Brown (Osgood Fielding III)

There was no love lost between Billy Wilder and Marilyn Monroe on set; as the director
described the shoot, 'We were in mid-flight and there was a nut on the plane.' The star required
forty-seven takes to get 'It's me, Sugar' correct, instead saying either 'Sugar, it's me' or 'It's
Sugar, me'. After take 30, Wilder had the line written on a blackboard. On another occasion,
Monroe had to search some drawers before saying 'Where's the bourbon?' After forty attempts,
including 'Where's the whiskey?', 'Where's the bottle?' or 'Where's the bonbon?', Wilder wrote
the line inside one of the drawers. Even so Monroe could never seem to find the drawer
containing the prompt, so Wilder had it written in every drawer. By the fifty-ninth and final take
Wilder asked Monroe to stand with her back to the camera, giving him the option to overdub
the line if need be.

'I JUST WANT TO BE WONDERFUL'

All stars wax and wane but none, male or female, has achieved
the enduring fame of Marilyn Monroe (born Norma Jeane Mortenson,
1926—62). Although she appeared in classic films including
Gentlemen Prefer Blondes (1953), *The Seven Year Itch* (1955)
and *Some Like It Hot* (1959), she has far outlived the pictures
themselves and the bittersweet story of her own life remains her
true legacy.

Discovered in 1945 by army photographers during a wartime
propaganda photo shoot at the factory where she was working,
she signed with the Blue Book modelling agency where her first
assignment paid $5 [$65]. Over the coming years she changed her
stage name so frequently that when she gave her first autograph
as Marilyn Monroe she had to ask a friend how to spell it. Within
a matter of years she was *Playboy*'s first ever 'Sweetheart of the
Month'; forty years after her death, *People* magazine still voted
her 'Sexiest Woman of the Century'.

While she was universally adored by the public, her reputation
among her peers was less flattering and her habit of turning up
late for work infuriated directors and co-stars. Billy Wilder said:
'She has breasts of granite and a mind like a Gruyère cheese.' Otto
Preminger claimed: 'She's a vacuum with nipples' and Tony Curtis
complained: 'It's like kissing Hitler.'

Her suicide at the age of thirty-six from an overdose of sedatives caused huge controversy as her recent affair with John F. Kennedy had become widely known; rumours quickly spread that her death was in fact ordered by the government to protect the president's image. Startling inconsistencies in the investigation itself and destruction of key evidence were subsequently revealed but no murder charges were ever filed. The inquest was periodically reviewed and on each occasion a verdict of suicide was returned, but the idea of a murderous conspiracy was reignited in 1972 when the home where she died was refurbished and contractors discovered a standard-issue FBI eavesdropping system in every room.

It is widely accepted now that Monroe was a depressive and that the conflict between her desire for fame and the pressures it brought exacerbated her condition. As she said herself:

- I want to be a big star more than anything. It's something precious.

- I'm not interested in money, I just want to be wonderful.

- My problem is that I drive myself... I'm trying to become an artist, and to be true, and sometimes I feel I'm on the verge of craziness, I'm just trying to get the truest part of myself out, and it's very hard. There are times when I think, 'All I have to be is true'. But sometimes it doesn't come out so easily. I always have this secret feeling that I'm really a fake or something, a phony.

After *The Seven Year Itch* (1955) she grew tired of disparaging comments about her acting skills and attended Lee Strasberg's New York's Actors Studio where Marlon Brando and other notable actors had studied. Her next film, *Bus Stop* (1956), gained more respectful reviews and the press was equally surprised by her marriage the same year to leading playwright Arthur Miller. Interviews and tributes from her friends in later life emphasized her desire to gain intellectual credibility, citing her love of poetry, a library filled with books on history, philosophy and literature and an IQ (never actually substantiated) of 168.

Even so, Monroe found it hard to shake off the public image she had already created and the pressures of the industry grew increasingly intolerable. Her later comments are classic cries from the heart:

- My illusions didn't have anything to do with being a fine actress. I knew how third rate I was. I could actually feel my lack of talent, as if it were cheap clothes I was wearing inside. But my God, how I wanted to learn, to change, to improve! No one ever told me I was pretty when I was a little girl. All little girls should be told they're pretty, even if they aren't.

- I knew I belonged to the public and to the world not because I was talented or even beautiful, but because I never had belonged to anything or anyone else.

- I did what they said and all it got me was a lot of abuse. Everyone's just laughing at me. I hate it. Big breasts, big ass, big deal.

- In Hollywood a girl's virtue is much less important than her hairdo. You're judged by how you look, not by what you are. Hollywood's a place where they'll pay you a thousand dollars for a kiss, and fifty cents for your soul. I know, because I turned down the first offer often enough and held out for the fifty.

- Please don't make me a joke. End the interview with what I believe...I want to be an artist, an actress with integrity.

- Dogs never bite me. Just humans.

- People had a habit of looking at me as if I were some kind of mirror instead of a person. They didn't see me, they saw their own lewd thoughts, then they white-masked themselves by calling me the lewd one.

- A sex symbol becomes a thing, I just hate being a thing. But if I'm going to be a symbol of something I'd rather have it [be] sex than some other things we've got symbols of.

- Suicide is a person's privilege. I don't believe it's a sin or a crime, it's your right if you do. Though it doesn't get you anywhere.

Early in the morning of 5 August 1962, Monroe's body was discovered naked in her bed in her Los Angeles home, a telephone in her hand. She left 75 per cent of her estate to Lee Strasberg and the remainder to Marianne Kris, her first psychoanalyst. Even today the licensing of her name and likeness alone nets the Monroe estate about $2 million a year.

1962   THE MANCHURIAN CANDIDATE   1962

*Raymond, unwittingly brainwashed to be a killer, finds it hard
to relax with his lover.*

RAYMOND

My dear girl, have you ever noticed that the human race is
divided into two distinct and irreconcilable groups: those
that walk into rooms and automatically turn television sets
on, and those that walk into rooms and automatically turn
them off. The trouble is that they end up marrying each
other.

Dir: John Frankenheimer • Scr: George Axelrod • Based on a novel by
Richard Condon • Cast: Laurence Harvey (Raymond Shaw)

1964   MARY POPPINS   1964

*On learning that their children have disappeared, George
attempts to calm his distraught wife.*

MR BANKS

Kindly do not attempt to cloud the issue with facts.

Dir: Robert Stevenson • Scr: Bill Walsh, Don DaGradi • Based on a novel by
P. L. Travers • Cast: David Tomlinson (George Banks)

1967   TWO FOR THE ROAD   1967

*A couple on a long journey recall the beginning - and end - of
their marriage.*

MARK

Just wish that you'd stop sniping.

JOANNA

I haven't said a word!

MARK

Just because you use a silencer doesn't mean you're not a
sniper.

Dir: Stanley Donen • Scr: Frederic Raphael • Cast: Albert Finney (Mark
Wallace), Audrey Hepburn (Joanna Wallace)

                    THE KHASI OF KALABAR

May the benevolence of the god Shivoo bring blessings on
your house.

                    SIR SIDNEY RUFF-DIAMOND

And on yours.

                    THE KHASI OF KALABAR

And may his wisdom bring success in all your undertakings.

                    SIR SIDNEY RUFF-DIAMOND

And in yours.

                    THE KHASI OF KALABAR

And may his radiance light up your life.

                    SIR SIDNEY RUFF-DIAMOND

And up yours.

Dir: Gerald Thomas • Scr: Talbot Rothwell • Cast: Kenneth Williams (The
Khasi of Kalabar), Sid James (Sir Sidney Ruff-Diamond)

Perhaps only the British truly delight in the schoolboy humour of the *Carry On…* movies. Foreign
distributors would certainly have had a hard time translating the title: 'Khyber (Pass)' is cockney
rhyming slang for arse.

1972   **LAST TANGO IN PARIS**   1972

Paul mourns his wife's suicide with a mixture of rage and grief.

                    PAUL

Even if a husband lives two hundred fucking years, he'll
never discover his wife's true nature. I may be able to
understand the secrets of the universe, but...I'll never
understand the truth about you. Never.

Dir: Bernardo Bertolucci • Scr: Bernardo Bertolucci, Franco Arcalli,
Agnès Varda • Cast: Marlon Brando (Paul)

1973   **THE LAST DETAIL**   1973

                    MULHALL

You ever been married?

BUDDUSKY

Not so you'd notice.

Dir: Hal Ashby • Scr: Robert Towne • Based on a novel by Darryl Ponicsan • Cast:
Otis Young (Richard 'Mule' Mulhall), Jack Nicholson (Billy 'Badass' Buddusky)

1973 PAT GARRETT AND BILLY THE KID   1973

*Lawman Pat Garrett persuades the reluctant sheriff Kip McKinney
to join him in hunting down Billy the Kid.*

MCKINNEY

I ain't goin'.

GARRETT

You owe it to me.

MCKINNEY

I do? For what?

GARRETT

For not killin' you over at Rosewater, for gettin' you this job,
and not seein' you run outta this territory, for pullin' you
outta that snowdrift up at Shamus, for cold cockin' you over
at Stillwater Saloon last fall, savin' you from Rabbit Owens
bitin' off your ear, and from just puttin' up with you for a
hell of a lot longer than I oughta.

MCKINNEY

MCKINNEY

Yeah...Well, I hope they spell my name right in the paper.

Dir: Sam Peckinpah • Scr: Rudy Wurlitzer • Cast: Richard Jaeckel (Sheriff Kip McKinney), James Coburn (Pat Garrett)

Director Peckinpah, always something of a live wire, frequently argued with Kris Kristofferson, who played Billy the Kid. On one occasion the confrontation escalated and Peckinpah only backed off because he feared Kristofferson – a former Army Airborne Ranger – might actually kill him. When the film was released, Peckinpah so despised the way the studio had recut it that he urinated on the screen.

1979 THE JERK   1979

NAVIN

Now be totally honest. You do have a boyfriend, don't you?

MARIE

Kind of.

NAVIN

I know this is our first date, but do you think the next time you make love to your boyfriend you could think of me?

MARIE

Well, I haven't made love to him yet.

NAVIN

That's too bad. Do you think it's possible that someday you could make love with me and think of him?

MARIE

Who knows? Maybe you and he could make love and you could think of me.

NAVIN

I'd be happy to be in there somewhere.

Dir: Carl Reiner • Scr: Steve Martin, Carl Gottlieb, Michael Elias • Cast: Steve Martin (Navin R. Johnson), Bernadette Peters (Marie Kimble Johnson)

ELWOOD

It's 106 miles to Chicago, we got a full tank of gas, half a
pack of cigarettes, it's dark...and we're wearing sunglasses.

JAKE

Hit it.

Dir: John Landis • Scr: John Landis, Dan Aykroyd • Cast: Dan Aykroyd
(Elwood Blues), John Belushi (Jake Blues)

One hundred and three cars were destroyed for the shoot. Sixty police cruisers were purchased, and a twenty-four-hour body shop set up to perform running repairs after takes; thirteen Bluesmobiles were required for the huge number of stunts. For the sequence in which a Ford Pinto falls from the sky a helicopter dropped the car, which required a certificate of airworthiness from the Federal Aviation Administration.

ROUND UP THE USUAL SUSPECTS

Every screenwriter dreams of penning a line which needs no
introduction, encapsulates an entire story or just takes root in
the popular imagination:

One morning I shot an elephant in my pyjamas. How he got in
my pyjamas, I don't know.
Animal Crackers (1930)

Scr: Morrie Ryskind • Based on a play by George S. Kaufman, Morrie Ryskind, Bert Kalmar, Harry Ruby

It's alive! It's alive!
Frankenstein (1931)
Scr: John L. Balderston, Garrett Fort, Francis Edward Faragoh • Based on a story by Mary Shelley and a play by Peggy Webling

Well, here's another nice mess you've gotten me into!
Sons of the Desert (1933)
Scr: Frank Craven

After all, tomorrow is another day.
Gone with the Wind (1939)
Scr: Sidney Howard • Based on a novel by Margaret Mitchell

Toto, I've got a feeling we're not in Kansas any more.
The Wizard of Oz (1939)
Scr: Noel Langley, Florence Ryerson and eighteen others

Here's looking at you, kid.
Casablanca (1942)
Scr: Julius J. Epstein, Philip G. Epstein, Howard Koch • Based on a play by Murray Burnett, Joan Alison

Badges? We ain't got no badges! We don't need no badges! I don't have to show you any stinking badges!
The Treasure of Sierra Madre (1948)
Scr: John Huston • Based on a novel by B. Traven

A martini. Shaken, not stirred.
Goldfinger (1964)
Scr: Richard Maibaum, Paul Dehn • Based on a novel by Ian Fleming

What we've got here is a failure to communicate.
Cool Hand Luke (1967)
Scr: Donn Pearce, Frank Pierson • Based on a novel by Donn Pearce

Hello, gorgeous.
Funny Girl (1968)
Scr: Isobel Lennart, based on her play

I'm walking here! I'm walking here!
Midnight Cowboy (1969)
Scr: Waldo Salt • Based on a novel by James Leo Herlihy

Love means never having to say you're sorry.
Love Story (1970)
Scr: Erich Segal, based on his novel

Keep your friends close, but your enemies closer.
The Godfather: Part II (1974)
Scr: Francis Ford Coppola, Mario Puzo • Based on a novel by Mario Puzo

Is it safe?
Marathon Man (1976)
Scr: William Goldman, based on his novel

You talkin' to me?
Taxi Driver (1976)
Scr: Paul Schrader

May the Force be with you.
Star Wars (1977)
Scr: George Lucas

STRIKER: Surely you can't be serious!
RUMACK: I am serious...and don't call me Shirley.
Airplane (1980)
Scr: Jim Abrahams, David Zucker, Jerry Zucker

All work and no play makes Jack a dull boy.
Here's Johnny!
The Shining (1980)
Scr: Stephen King, Stanley Kubrick • Based on a novel by Stephen King

They're here!
Poltergeist (1982)
Scr: Steven Spielberg, Michael Grais, Mark Victor

E.T. phone home.
E.T. The Extraterrestrial (1982)
Scr: Melissa Mathison

Say hello to my little friend.
Scarface (1983)
Scr: Oliver Stone

Go ahead, make my day.
Sudden Impact (1983)
Scr: Joseph Stinson, Earl E. Smith, Charles B. Pierce • Based on
characters created by Harry Julian Fink, Rita M. Fink

I'll be back.
The Terminator (1984)
Scr: James Cameron, Gale Anne Hurd

Game over, man! Game Over!
Aliens (1986)
Scr: James Cameron, David Giler, Walter Hill • Based on characters
created by Dan O'Bannon, Ronald Shusett

I feel the need...the need for speed!
Top Gun (1986)
Scr: Jim Cash, Jack Epps Jr. • Based on a magazine article by Ehud
Yonay

If you build it, he will come.
Field of Dreams (1989)
Scr: Phil Alden Robinson • Based on a novel by W. P. Kinsella

I'll have what she's having.
When Harry Met Sally (1989)
Scr: Nora Ephron

Hasta la vista, baby.
Terminator 2: Judgment Day (1991)
Scr: James Cameron, William Wisher Jr.

Mama always said life was like a box of chocolates. You never
know what you're gonna get.
Forrest Gump (1994)
Scr: Eric Roth • Based on a novel by Winston Groom

Houston, we have a problem.
Apollo 13 (1995)
Scr: William Broyles Jr., Al Reinert • Based on a book by Jim Lovell,
Jeffrey Kluger

To Infinity and beyond!

Toy Story (1995)

Scr: John Lasseter, Pete Docter, Andrew Stanton, Joe Ranft, Joss Whedon, Joel Cohen, Alec Sokolow

Show me the money!

Jerry Maguire (1996)

Scr: Cameron Crowe

My precious...

Lord of the Rings: Two Towers (2002)

Scr: Fran Walsh, Philippa Boyens, Stephen Sinclair, Peter Jackson • Based on a novel by J. R. R. Tolkien

1980 **AIRPLANE!** 1980

Airline pilot Clarence Oveur and his flight officers Roger and Victor prepare for take-off.

ROGER MURDOCK

Flight 2-0-9'er, you are cleared for take-off.

CAPTAIN OVEUR

Roger!

                    ROGER MURDOCK

Huh?

                    CONTROL TOWER

L.A. departure frequency 123 point 9'er.

                    CAPTAIN OVEUR

Roger!

                    ROGER MURDOCK

Huh?

                    VICTOR BASTA

Request vector, over.

                    CAPTAIN OVEUR

What?

                    CONTROL TOWER

Flight 2-0-9'er cleared for vector 324.

                    ROGER MURDOCK

We have clearance, Clarence.

                    CAPTAIN OVEUR

Roger, Roger. What's our vector, Victor?

                    CONTROL TOWER

Tower's radio clearance, over!

                    CAPTAIN OVEUR

That's Clarence Oveur. Over.

                    CONTROL TOWER

Over.

                    CAPTAIN OVEUR

Roger.

                    ROGER MURDOCK

Huh?

```
                    CONTROL TOWER
    Roger, over!

                    ROGER MURDOCK
    What?

                    CAPTAIN OVEUR
    Huh?

                    VICTOR BASTA
    Who?
```

Dir: Jim Abrahams, David Zucker, Jerry Zucker • Scr: Jim Abrahams, David
Zucker, Jerry Zucker • Based on the film *Zero Hour!* (1957) by Arthur
Hailey, Hall Bartlett, John C. Champion • Cast: Kareem Abdul-Jabbar
(Roger Murdock), Peter Graves (Captain Clarence Oveur), Unknown (Control
Tower), Frank Ashmore (Victor Basta)

The film parodies many airborne or disaster movies of the time, including *Airport 1975* in which
a stewardess is also forced to pilot a plane after both pilots are incapacitated, a girl needs a
kidney transplant and one of the passengers is also a singing nun. It includes so many direct
references to the unintentionally hilarious *Zero Hour!* ('We have to find someone who can not
only fly this plane, but who didn't have fish for dinner') that the producers had to buy the rights
to the film to avoid charges of plagiarism.

1983 THE BIG CHILL   1983

Meg is frustrated she never seems to meet any suitable men.

```
                    MEG
    They're either married or gay. And if they're not gay,
    they've just broken up with the most wonderful woman in
    the world, or they've just broken up with a bitch who looks
    exactly like me. They're in transition from a monogamous
    relationship and they need more space. Or they're tired of
    space, but they just can't commit. Or they want to commit, but
    they're afraid to get close. They want to get close, you don't
    want to get near them.
```

Dir: Lawrence Kasdan • Scr: Lawrence Kasdan, Barbara Benedek • Cast: Mary
Kay Place (Meg Jones)

1987 HOPE AND GLORY   1987

An old man tells his grandson how his children got their names.

GEORGE

You want to know why they're called Faith, Hope, Grace and Charity?

BILL

Why?

GEORGE

Your Grandmother. She named them after the virtues I lack. That's marriage for you.

Dir: John Boorman • Scr: John Boorman • Cast: Ian Bannen (Grandfather George), Sebastian Rice-Edwards (Bill Rowan)

1992 BITTER MOON 1992

Oscar, who is now in a wheelchair, reminisces about his turbulent relationship with his wife.

OSCAR

She came to see me when I got out of intensive care. She said, there's bad news and there's good news. You're paralysed from the waist down - permanently. Okay, I said, let's have the good news. That was the good news, she said. The bad news is that from now on, I'm taking care of you.

Dir: Roman Polanski • Scr: Roman Polanski, Gérard Brach, John Brownjohn, Jeff Gross • Based on a novel by Pascal Bruckner • Cast: Peter Coyote (Oscar)

1994 PULP FICTION 1994

Two hit-men drink coffee with Jimmie in his kitchen.

JULES

Mmmm...Goddamn, Jimmie! This is some serious gourmet shit. Usually, me and Vince would be happy with some freeze-dried Taster's Choice right, but he springs this serious gourmet shit on us. What flavour is this?

JIMMIE

Knock it off, Julie.

JULES

What?

JIMMIE

I don't need you to tell me how fucking good my coffee is,
okay? I'm the one who buys it. I know how good it is. When
Bonnie goes shopping she buys shit. I buy the gourmet
expensive stuff because when I drink it I want to taste it.
But you know what's on my mind right now? It ain't the coffee
in my kitchen, it's the dead nigger in my garage.

JULES

Oh, Jimmie, don't even worry about that -

JIMMIE

No, no, no - let me ask you a question. When you came pulling
in here, did you notice a sign out in front of my house that
said 'Dead Nigger Storage'?

JULES

Jimmie, you know I ain't seen no...

Jimmie is getting angry now.

JIMMIE

Did you notice a sign out in front of my house that said
'Dead Nigger Storage'?

JULES

No. I didn't.

JIMMIE

You know why you didn't see that sign?

JULES

Why?

JIMMIE

'Cause it ain't there. 'Cause storing dead niggers ain't my fucking business, that's why!

Dir: Quentin Tarantino • Scr: Quentin Tarantino, Roger Avary • Cast: Samuel L. Jackson (Jules Winnfield), Quentin Tarantino (Jimmie Dimmick)

1995 HEAT   1995

Vincent, a detective, and Neil, a bank robber, realize they have met their match in each other.

VINCENT

You know, we're sitting here, you and I, like a couple of regular fellas. You do what you do, and I do what I gotta do. And now that we've been face to face, if I'm there and I gotta put you away, I won't like it. But I tell you, if it's between you and some poor bastard whose wife you're gonna turn into a widow, brother, you are going down.

NEIL

There is a flip side to that coin. What if you do got me boxed in and I gotta put you down? 'Cause no matter what, you will not get in my way. We've been face to face, yeah. But I will not hesitate. Not for a second.

Dir: Michael Mann • Scr: Michael Mann • Cast: Al Pacino (Lieutenant Vincent Hanna), Robert De Niro (Neil McCauley)

Michael Mann originally wrote and directed the story as *L.A. Takedown* (1989), a television pilot which was never commissioned. *Heat* itself, not so much a remake as a revision, was the first film in which Pacino and De Niro acted together (in *The Godfather: Part II* they never actually appeared on screen at the same time).

1997   **THE ICE STORM**   **1997**

*Ben hopes to persuade his fellow dinner guests how solid his
marriage is.*

> BEN
>
> The only big fight we've had in years is about whether to go
> back into couples therapy.

Dir: Ang Lee • Scr: James Schamus • Based on a novel by Rick Moody • Cast:
Kevin Kline (Ben Hood)

1998   **ROUNDERS**   **1998**

*Worm and Petra worry that their friend is in a dead-end
relationship.*

> WORM
>
> She's really got him by the balls.

> PETRA
>
> That's not so bad, is it?

> WORM
>
> It depends on the grip!

Dir: John Dahl • Scr: David Levien, Brian Koppelman • Cast: Edward Norton
(Lester 'Worm' Murphy), Famke Janssen (Petra)

1999   **TOPSY-TURVY**   **1999**

*Librettist Gilbert and composer Sullivan argue over suitable
material for their next production,* The Mikado.

> GILBERT
>
> Every theatrical performance is a contrivance by its very
> nature.

> SULLIVAN
>
> Yes, but this piece consists entirely of an artificial and
> implausible situation.

> GILBERT
>
> If you wish to write a grand opera about a prostitute dying
> of consumption in a garret, I suggest you contact Mr Ibsen in
> Oslo. I am sure he will be able to furnish you with something
> suitably dull.

Dir: Mike Leigh • Scr: Mike Leigh • Cast: Jim Broadbent (W. S. Gilbert), Allan Corduner (Sir Arthur Sullivan)

Gilbert's reference is to Verdi's opera *La Traviata*. His dismissal of Ibsen as 'dull' is somewhat unfair as his play *A Doll's House* was considered deeply risqué and was actually banned in many countries.

AUTHOR, AUTHOR

> I've seen horrors. Horrors that you've seen. But you have no right to call me a murderer. You have a right to kill me. You have a right to do that. But you have no right to judge me...

> We train young men to drop fire on people, but their commanders won't allow them to write 'fuck' on their airplanes because it's obscene...

> Have you ever considered any real freedoms? Freedoms from the opinions of others. Even the opinions of yourself. Did they say why, Willard? Why they wanted to terminate my command?

When Colonel Kurtz (Marlon Brando), half-obscured by lamplight in *Apocalypse Now* (1979), delivers these lines in his final scenes, whose words are we hearing? Are they by:

Joseph Conrad, whose short novel *Heart of Darkness* (1899) about a renegade ivory trader in the African Congo inspired the film's story;

Screenwriter John Milius, who transplanted the narrative to Vietnam in a script originally called 'The Psychedelic Soldier';

Anthropologist James Frazer, whose study *The Golden Bough* (1890) appears as a prop in Kurtz's compound and is a source for many of the cultural themes in the story;

T. S. Eliot, whose poem 'The Hollow Men' (1925) is quoted by Kurtz ('The horror, the horror') and which begins itself with an epigraph from Conrad's *Heart of Darkness*;

Vietnam War reporter Michael Herr, whose book *Dispatches* (1977) was a key reference (Herr also wrote the voice-over narration for the film);

Francis Ford Coppola, who directed the film and rewrote scenes constantly during the shoot;

Marlon Brando, who disliked the draft he was sent and improvised much of his dialogue.

There can, of course, be no real answer — just as it is impossible to determine creative authorship for a jazz recording whose chord sequence is traditional, but whose performance is the result of every player's talents.

What Coppola understood above all is that in the hands of a truly visionary director, 'writing' is a process that transcends the actual words of the shooting script. Every stage he supervises is transformative, from the initial collaboration with (co)writers to discussions with production designers about *mise-en-scène* and the casting of actors who may want to improvise their own dialogue. Film editing of imagery as well as dialogue can radically reshape the way the story unfolds.

Although when credits roll it seems clear who is responsible for the screenplay, the actual truth is often murkier. Phil Alden Robinson (*Field of Dreams*, 1989) warns: 'No one can trust a writing credit. Nobody knows who really wrote the film.' Remarkably few projects are taken from inception to delivery by a sole author; directors, producers and actors (depending on their power) may all contribute to changes in the story, although it is rare for any of them to demand acknowledgement since their job is understood to involve a degree of influence. The process of attribution is trickier when a writer is brought in to make substantial changes to earlier drafts — and trickier still when others are added to the mix.

The opening titles for *The Wizard of Oz* (1939) list the following:

Screenplay: Noel Langley, Florence Ryerson, Edgar Allan Woolf

Adaptation: Noel Langley

Based on the book by: L. Frank Baum

The Internet Movie Database lists a further thirteen uncredited contributing writers, including the poet Ogden Nash and the Oscar-winning Herman J. Mankiewicz; at one point Langley, Nash and Mankiewicz were all working on the film at the same time without knowing the others had been hired. The other two formally credited authors, Ryerson and Woolf, were brought on board much later to bring the other drafts closer to L. Frank Baum's original novel.

Today, the Writers Guild of America has clear guidelines for settling disputes, which affect not only credits but residual payments (royalties) and eligibility for awards. Between 1993 and 1997, they supervised 415 arbitrations — roughly a third of all films submitted.

2000 REMEMBER THE TITANS 2000

An American football coach takes his racially mixed team on a training run to a Civil War battlefield.

HERMAN

Anybody know what this place is? This is Gettysburg. This is where they fought the battle of Gettysburg. Fifty thousand men died right here on this field, fightin' the same fight that we're still fightin' amongst ourselves today. This green field right here, painted red, bubblin' with the blood of young boys. Smoke and hot lead pourin' right through their bodies. Listen to their souls, men. I killed my brother with malice in my heart. Hatred destroyed my family. You listen, you take a lesson from the dead. If we don't come together right now on this hallowed ground, we too will be destroyed just like they were. I don't care if you like each other right now, but you will respect each other. And maybe - I don't know, maybe we'll learn to play this game like men.

Dir: Boaz Yakin • Scr: Gregory Allen Howard • Cast: Denzel Washington (Herman Boone)

2002 CHICAGO 2002

A woman awaiting trial for murder explains how she found her husband's body.

VELMA

My sister Veronica and I had this double act, and my husband
Charlie travelled around with us. Now for the last number in
our act, we did these twenty acrobatic tricks in a row. One,
two, three, four, five, splits, spread-eagles, backflips, flip-
flops, one right after the other. So this one night before the
show, we're down at the Hotel Cicero. The three of us boozin',
having a few laughs. And we ran out of ice, so I go out to
get some. I come back...open the door...and there's Veronica
and Charlie, doing number seventeen: the Spread-eagle. Well, I
was in such a state of shock I completely blacked out, I can't
remember a thing. It wasn't until later when I was washing
the blood off my hands I even knew they were dead.

Dir: Rob Marshall • Scr: Bill Condon • Based on a musical by Bob Fosse,
Fred Ebb and a play by Maurine Dallas Watkins • Cast: Catherine Zeta-
Jones (Velma Kelly)

Renée Zellweger had no singing or dancing training prior to this film; Catherine Zeta-Jones cut
her hair into a bob so her face would always be visible, proving that she never used stand-ins for
the complicated choreography.

2004 BEFORE SUNSET   2004

Jesse tells an old lover how he feels about his marriage.

JESSE

I feel like I'm running a small nursery with someone I used
to date.

Dir: Richard Linklater • Scr: Richard Linklater, Julie Delpy, Ethan
Hawke, Kim Krizan • Cast: Ethan Hawke (Jesse)

2004 CRASH   2004

Graham, an African-American, and Ria, a Latino woman, make love.
The telephone rings. Frustrated, Graham answers the phone.

GRAHAM

Mom, I can't talk to you right now, okay? I'm having sex with a
white woman.

He hangs up. Ria gets out of bed.

GRAHAM

OK, where were we?

RIA

I was white, and you were about to jerk off in the shower.

GRAHAM

Oh, shit. Come on. I would have said you were Mexican, but I don't think it would have pissed her off as much.

RIA

Why do you keep everybody a certain distance, huh? What, you start to feel something and panic?

GRAHAM

Come on, Ria. You're just pissed 'cause I answered the phone.

RIA

That's just where I begin to get pissed. I mean, really, what kind of man speaks to his mother that way, huh?

GRAHAM

Oh, this is about my mother. What do you know about my mother?

RIA

If I was your father, I'd kick your fucking ass.

GRAHAM

OK, I was raised badly. Why don't you take your clothes off, get back into bed, and teach me a lesson?

RIA

You want a lesson? I'll give you a lesson. How 'bout a geography lesson? My father's from Puerto Rico. My mother's from El Salvador. Neither one of those is Mexico.

GRAHAM

Ah. Well then I guess the big mystery is, who gathered all those remarkably different cultures together and taught them all how to park their cars on their lawns?

Dir: Paul Haggis • Scr: Paul Haggis, Robert Moresco • Cast: Don Cheadle (Detective Graham Waters), Jennifer Esposito (Ria)

2004 ETERNAL SUNSHINE OF THE SPOTLESS MIND 2004

Joel tells his girlfriend he fears the spark has disappeared from their relationship.

> JOEL
>
> Are we like couples you see in restaurants? Are we the dining dead?

Dir: Michel Gondry • Scr: Michel Gondry, Charlie Kaufman, Pierre Bismuth • Cast: Jim Carrey (Joel Barish)

The film's title is taken from the poem by Alexander Pope about two devoted lovers, *Eloisa to Abelard*: 'How happy is the blameless vestal's lot! The world forgetting, by the world forgot. Eternal sunshine of the spotless mind! Each pray'r accepted, and each wish resign'd.'

2005 MR & MRS SMITH 2005

A married couple – both contract killers – discover they have both been hired to murder the other.

> JOHN
>
> We have an unusual problem here, Jane. You obviously want me dead, and I'm less and less concerned for your well-being.

Dir: Doug Liman • Scr: Simon Kinberg • Cast: Brad Pitt (John Smith)

2008 IN BRUGES 2008

Two hit-men waiting for an assignment in Bruges find the excitements of the city are quickly exhausted.

> KEN
>
> We shall strike a balance between culture and fun.

> RAY
>
> Somehow, Ken, I believe that the balance shall tip in the favour of culture, like a big fat fucking retarded fucking black girl on a see-saw.

Dir: Martin McDonagh • Scr: Martin McDonagh • Cast: Brendan Gleeson (Ken), Colin Farrell (Ray)

2008 REVOLUTIONARY ROAD   2008

*Frank and April dream of rekindling their passion for life
until Frank confesses he has been unfaithful.*

APRIL

No one forgets the truth, Frank. They just get better at lying.

Dir: Sam Mendes • Scr: Justin Haythe • Based on a novel by Richard
Yates • Cast: Kate Winslet (April Wheeler)

2010 THE KING'S SPEECH   2010

*A speech therapist tries to cure the reluctant king of his
stammer.*

LOGUE

Would I lie to a prince of the realm to win twelve pennies?

GEORGE VI

I have no idea what an Australian might do for that sort of
money.

Dir: Tom Hooper • Scr: David Seidler • Cast: Geoffrey Rush (Lionel Logue),
Colin Firth (King George VI)

The film contains seventeen uses of the word 'fuck' and was originally given a 15 certificate.
The producers wanted a less restrictive rating; after some negotiation the expletives remained
but the certificate was relaxed to 12A with the bizarre warning 'contains strong language in a
speech therapy context'.

The First World War setting of *The African Queen* seems almost peaceful compared with the skirmishes between a gin-swilling Humphrey Bogart and a Bible-toting Katharine Hepburn.

The elegant set and costume design in John Boorman's *Point Blank* (1967) only serve to heighten its icy violence.

The timeless wartime romance of *Casablanca* showed Ingrid Bergman at her most beautiful and Humphrey Bogart in perhaps his tenderest role.

Love

1936   THE PETRIFIED FOREST   1936

> ALAN
>
> Any woman's worth everything that any man has to give: anguish, ecstasy, faith, jealousy, love, hatred, life or death. Don't you see that's the whole excuse for our existence? It's what makes the whole thing possible and tolerable.

Dir: Archie Mayo • Scr: Charles Kenyon, Delmer Daves • Based on a play by Robert E. Sherwood • Cast: Leslie Howard (Alan Squier)

1939   THE WIZARD OF OZ   1939

Dorothy says goodbye to her companions as she returns home to Kansas.

> DOROTHY
>
> Goodbye, Tinman. Oh, don't cry! You'll rust so dreadfully. Here's your oil can.

> TIN MAN
>
> Now I know I've got a heart, 'cause it's breaking.

Dir: Victor Fleming • Scr: Noel Langley, Florence Ryerson, Edgar Allan Woolf • Based on a novel by L. Frank Baum • Cast: Judy Garland (Dorothy Gale), Jack Haley (Tin Man)

1942   CASABLANCA   1942

Rick tries to persuade Ilsa she must flee Casablanca with her husband.

> RICK
>
> Last night we said a great many things. You said I was to do the thinking for both of us. Well, I've done a lot of it since then, and it all adds up to one thing: you're getting on that plane with Victor where you belong.

> ILSA
>
> But, Richard, no, I... I...

> RICK
>
> Now, you've got to listen to me! You have any idea what you'd have to look forward to if you stayed here? Nine chances out of ten, we'd both wind up in a concentration camp. Isn't that true, Louie?

CAPTAIN RENAULT

I'm afraid Major Strasser would insist.

ILSA

You're saying this only to make me go.

RICK

I'm saying it because it's true. Inside of us, we both know you
belong with Victor. You're part of his work, the thing that
keeps him going. If that plane leaves the ground and you're
not with him, you'll regret it. Maybe not today. Maybe not
tomorrow, but soon and for the rest of your life.

ILSA

But what about us?

RICK

We'll always have Paris. We didn't have... we'd lost it until
you came to Casablanca. We got it back last night.

ILSA

When I said I would never leave you.

RICK

And you never will. But I've got a job to do, too. Where I'm going, you can't follow. What I've got to do, you can't be any part of. Ilsa, I'm no good at being noble, but it doesn't take much to see that the problems of three little people don't amount to a hill of beans in this crazy world. Someday you'll understand that.

Ilsa is crying now.

Now, now...

He lifts her face and holds her gaze.

Here's looking at you, kid.

Dir: Michael Curtiz • Scr: Julius J. Epstein, Philip G. Epstein, Howard Koch • Based on a play by Murray Burnett, Joan Alison • Cast: Humphrey Bogart (Rick Blaine), Ingrid Bergman (Ilsa Lund), Claude Rains (Captain Louis Renault)

The Naked Gun (1988) contains a *hommage* to the classic line: 'It's a topsy-turvy world, and maybe the problems of two people don't amount to a hill of beans. But this is our hill. And these are our beans!'

1946   A MATTER OF LIFE AND DEATH (AKA STAIRWAY TO HEAVEN)   1946

A radio operator receives a message from a stricken bomber pilot.

JUNE

Are you receiving me? Repeat, are you receiving me? Request your position. Come in, Lancaster.

PETER

You seem like a nice girl. I can't give you my position, instruments gone, crew gone too - all except Bob here, my sparks, he's dead. The rest all bailed out on my orders, time 03.35. Did you get that?

JUNE

Crew bailed out 03.35.

PETER

Station Warrenden, bomber group A, G George, send them a signal. Got that?

JUNE

Station Warrenden, bomber group A apple, G George.

PETER

They'll be sorry about Bob - we all liked him.

JUNE

Hello, G George, hello G George, are you all right? Are you
going to try to land? Do you want a fix?

PETER

Name's not G George, it's P Peter - Peter D. Carter. D's for
David, Squadron Leader Peter Carter. No, I'm not going to land
- undercarriage is gone, inner port's on fire. I'm bailing out
presently. I'm bailing out.

JUNE

Received your message, we can hear you. Are you wounded?
Repeat, are you wounded? Are you bailing out?

PETER

What's your name?

JUNE

June.

PETER

Yes June, I'm bailing out. I'm bailing out but there's a catch -
I've got no parachute.

JUNE

Hello, hello Peter - do not understand. Hello Peter, can you
hear me?

PETER

Hello June, don't be afraid. It's quite simple, we've had it and
I'd rather jump than fry. After the first thousand feet what's
the difference? I shan't know anything anyway. I say, I hope I
haven't frightened you.

JUNE

No, I'm not frightened.

                    PETER

Good girl.

                    JUNE

Your sparks, you said he was dead - hasn't he got a chute?

                    PETER

Cut to ribbons - cannon shell.

Pause.

June? Are you pretty?

                    JUNE

She sounds surprised.

Not bad, I...

                    PETER

Can you hear me as well as I can hear you?

                    JUNE

Yes.

                    PETER

You've got a good voice. You've got guts too. It's funny, I've
known dozens of girls - I've been in love with some of them, but
it's an American girl whom I've never seen and never shall see
who'll hear my last words - it's funny, it's rather sweet. June,
if you're around when they pick me up, turn your head away -

                    JUNE

Perhaps we can do something, Peter, let me report it.

                    PETER

No, no one can help, only you. Let me do this in my own way. I
want to be alone with you, June. Where were you born?

                    JUNE

Boston.

                    PETER

Mass.?

                    JUNE

Yes.

                    PETER

That's a place to be born, history was made there. Are you in
love with anybody? No, no, don't answer that.

                    JUNE

I could love a man like you, Peter.

                    PETER

I love you, June - you're life, and I'm leaving you. Where do
you live? On the station?

                    JUNE

No, in a big country house about five miles from here - Lee
Wood House.

                    PETER

Old house?

                    JUNE

Yes, very old.

PETER

Good, I'll be a ghost and come and see you. You're not
frightened of ghosts, are you? It would be awful if you were.

JUNE

I'm not frightened.

PETER

What time will you be home?

JUNE

Well, I'm on duty until six. I have breakfast in the mess
and then I have to cycle half an hour. I often go along the
sands... this is such nonsense.

PETER

No it's not, it's the best sense I've ever heard. I was lucky to
get you, June. Can't be helped about the parachute - I'll have
my wings soon anyway, big white ones. I hope they haven't gone
all modern - I'd hate to have a prop instead of wings. What do
you think the next world's like? I've got my own ideas -

JUNE

She interrupts him.

Oh, Peter -

PETER

I think it starts where this one leaves off, or where this one
could leave off if we'd listened to Plato and Aristotle and
Jesus. With all our little earthly problems solved, but with
greater ones worth the solving. I'll know soon enough anyway.
I'm signing off now June, goodbye. Goodbye, June.

Silence.

JUNE

Hello, G for George, hello G George Hello G George, hello -

Dir: Michael Powell, Emeric Pressburger • Scr: Michael Powell, Emeric
Pressburger • Cast: Kim Hunter (June), David Niven (Squadron Leader Peter
Carter)

For the scene where Peter's body is washed up on the beach, cameraman Jack Cardiff breathed
on the lens to create condensation. The appearance of evaporating mist created the perfect
ethereal mood for the shot.

IN A LONELY PLACE

STEELE

I was born when she kissed me. I died when she left me.
I lived a few weeks while she loved me.

Dir: Nicholas Ray • Scr: Andrew Solt, Edmund H. North • Based on a novel by
Dorothy B. Hughes • Cast: Humphrey Bogart (Dixon Steele)

SABRINA

BARON ST FONTANEL

A woman happily in love, she burns the soufflé. A woman
unhappily in love, she forgets to turn on the oven.

Dir: Billy Wilder • Scr: Billy Wilder, Ernest Lehman, Samuel A.
Taylor • Based on a play by Samuel A. Taylor • Cast: Marcel Dalio (Baron St
Fontanel)

BE FUNNY OR THEY'LL KILL YOU

Billy Wilder (1906–2002) is one of only seven men to have won Oscars
for best picture as well as director and screenplay but at heart he
remained, as he had begun, a writer.

Born an Austrian Jew, he moved to Berlin in the late 1920s to work
as a journalist before teaming up with Curt and Robert Siodmak
to write the silent film *Menschen am Sonntag* (*People on Sunday*,
1930). Fleeing Germany as Hitler rose to power, he arrived in
America in 1933 unable to speak a word of English and his work
always reflected an Old World sensibility energized by New World
opportunities. Vincent Canby of the *New York Times* described him as
'the brightest, wittiest, most perceptive, most resourceful' talent
of his generation and noted approvingly that his creations were
like 'sugar laced with acid'.

His private life displayed the same balance of romanticism and
cynicism. When Wilder was pursuing the actress Audrey Young, he
confessed: 'I'd worship the ground you walk on if you lived in a
better neighbourhood'; blessed with an equally robust sense of
humour, she married him.

Throughout his career he remained devoted to the craft of writing,
although he freely admitted: 'It's such an exhausting thing, you
know, facing that empty page in the morning.' His usual solution
to the problem was to work with a partner, and his long-standing
collaborations with Charles Brackett and subsequently I. A. L.
Diamond gave us such classics as *Ninotchka* (1939), *The Lost Weekend*

(1945), *Sunset Boulevard* (1950), *Some Like It Hot* (1959) and *The Apartment* (1960). Despite his wit and urbane manner, his reputation as a co-writer was fearsome; Harry Kurnitz once remarked: 'Billy Wilder at work is actually two people — Mr Hyde and Mr Hyde.' Wilder might well have pleaded guilty, since he once admitted: 'A director must be a policeman, a midwife, a psychoanalyst, a sycophant and a bastard.'

Perhaps surprisingly, his greatest tenderness was reserved for his public:

> An audience is never wrong. An individual member of it may be an imbecile, but a thousand imbeciles together in the dark - that is critical genius.

> Don't be too clever for an audience. Make it obvious. Make the subtleties obvious also.

> In certain pictures I do hope they will leave the cinema a little enriched, but I don't make them pay a buck and a half and then ram a lecture down their throats.

His greatest reverence was for the irreverent:

> In a serious picture you don't hear them being bored, but in a comedy you can hear them not laughing.

> If you're going to tell people the truth, be funny or they'll kill you.

His comment on his craft remains his finest epitaph:

> The best director is the one you don't see.

1955 THE NIGHT OF THE HUNTER   1955

A murderous preacher explains the tattoos on his knuckles.

REVEREND POWELL

Ah, little lad, you're staring at my fingers. Would you like me to tell you the little story of right hand, left hand? The story of good and evil? H-A-T-E! It was with this left hand that old brother Cain struck the blow that laid his brother low. L-O-V-E! You see these fingers, dear hearts? These fingers has veins that run straight to the soul of man. The right hand, friends, the hand of love. Now watch, and I'll show you the story of life. Those fingers, dear hearts, is always a-warring and a-tugging, one agin t'other. Now watch 'em! Old brother left hand, left hand he's a-fighting, and it looks like love's a goner. But wait a minute! Hot dog, love's a-winning! Yes, sirree! It's love that's won, and old left hand hate is down for the count!

Dir: Charles Laughton, Robert Mitchum (uncredited) • Scr: James Agee • Based on a novel by Davis Grubb • Cast: Robert Mitchum (Reverend Harry Powell)

Mitchum, despite other memorable roles in *Out of the Past* (1947), *Cape Fear* (1962) and *Farewell My Lovely* (1975), suffered from none of the self-importance of his actor colleagues. When asked by an interviewer what he looked for in a script, he replied crisply: 'Days off.' Although the film is now considered a *noir* classic and influenced directors as diverse as David Lynch, Martin Scorsese, Terrence Malick and the Coen brothers, it was not well received on its release. Charles Laughton was so disappointed that he never directed a film again.

1966   ALFIE   1966

Jack-the-lad Alfie is not afraid to lie to get what he wants.

ALFIE

I've never told her that I love her - except at those times when you've got to say something for appearance's sake.

Dir: Lewis Gilbert • Scr: Bill Naughton, based on his play • Cast: Michael Caine (Alfie Elkins)

IF...

Rebellious schoolboy Mick still has a romantic streak.

> MICK
>
> There's only one thing you can do with a girl like this. Walk naked into the sea together as the sun sets. Make love once... Then die.

Dir: Lindsay Anderson • Scr: David Sherwin, John Howlett • Cast: Malcolm McDowell (Mick Travis)

The film features the first instance of a full-frontal female nude passed by the British Board of Film Classification.

LOVE AND DEATH

Neurotic intellectual Sonja discusses the nature of love with her equally intense cousin.

> SONJA
>
> To love is to suffer. To avoid suffering one must not love. But then one suffers from not loving. Therefore, to love is to suffer; not to love is to suffer; to suffer is to suffer. To be happy is to love. To be happy, then, is to suffer, but suffering makes one unhappy. Therefore, to be unhappy, one must love or love to suffer or suffer from too much happiness. I hope you're getting this down.

Dir: Woody Allen • Scr: Woody Allen • Cast: Diane Keaton (Sonja)

FELLINI'S CASANOVA (*IL CASANOVA DI FEDERICO FELLINI*)

> CASANOVA
>
> A man who never speaks ill of women does not love them. For, to understand them and to love them one must suffer at their hands. Then and only then can you find happiness at the lips of your beloved.

Dir: Federico Fellini • Scr: Federico Fellini, Bernardino Zapponi • Based on the autobiography of Giacomo Casanova • Cast: Donald Sutherland (Giacomo Casanova)

The film's distributors originally hoped to cast Robert Redford in the lead role but Fellini refused. The director defended his choice of Donald Sutherland thus: 'A sperm-filled waxwork with the eyes of a masturbator; as far removed as you could imagine from an adventurer and seducer like Casanova, but nonetheless a serious, studied, professional actor.'

Lois Lane holds an imaginary conversation with Superman as he flies with her above Metropolis.

LOIS

Can you read my mind? Do you know what it is that you do to me? I don't know who you are. Just a friend from another star. Here I am like a kid out of school. Holding hands with a god. I'm a fool. Will you look at me? Quivering. Like a little girl shivering. You can see right through me. Can you read my mind? Can you picture the things I'm thinking of? Wondering why you are all the wonderful things you are. You can fly! You belong in the sky. You and I could belong to each other. If you need a friend, I'm the one to fly to. If you need to be loved, here I am. Read my mind.

Dir: Richard Donner • Scr: Mario Puzo, David Newman, Leslie Newman, Robert Benton • Based on characters created by Jerry Siegel, Joe Shuster • Cast: Margot Kidder (Lois Lane)

Steven Spielberg was a contender to direct the film but on hearing his salary demands the producers preferred to hedge their bets until they saw how his 'fish movie' (*Jaws*, 1975) performed. The shoot was so complex that at one point there were seven units working on different parts of the story; the credits sequence alone cost more than the budget of an average production at that time. Various approaches were explored to show Superman in flight: a dummy launched from a catapult, a model aircraft carrying a painting of the character and traditional animation. In the end the traditional technique of wire suspension with projected background plates proved most convincing.

NOSFERATU THE VAMPYRE (*NOSFERATU: PHANTOM DER NACHT*)

COUNT DRACULA

The absence of love is the most abject pain.

Dir: Werner Herzog • Scr: Werner Herzog • Based on a novel by Bram Stoker •
Cast: Klaus Kinski (Count Dracula)

In one scene where thousands of grey rats were needed, only the white variety was available: the director ordered them to be painted.

1981 GREGORY'S GIRL 1981

Gregory confides to a classmate that he has fallen for the girl who replaced him on the school football team.

GREGORY

Have you ever been in love? I'm in love.

STEVE

Since when?

GREGORY

This morning. I feel restless and dizzy. I bet I won't get any sleep tonight.

STEVE

Sounds like indigestion.

Dir: Bill Forsyth • Scr: Bill Forsyth • Cast: John Gordon Sinclair
(Gregory Underwood), William Greenlees (Steve)

1986 HANNAH AND HER SISTERS 1986

Mickey used to be married to Hannah but has now wed her sister Lee.

MICKEY

You know, I was talking to your father before, and I
was telling him that it's ironic - I used to always have
Thanksgiving with Hannah, and I never thought that I could
love anybody else. And here it is years later and I'm married
to you and completely in love with you. The heart is a very,
very resilient little muscle, it really is.

Dir: Woody Allen • Scr: Woody Allen • Cast: Woody Allen (Mickey Sachs)

Woody Allen said he was inspired to write the film after rereading Tolstoy's *Anna Karenina*. It took over $40 million [$85 million] at the box office in America alone and a lobby group was formed to propose that the screenplay be eligible for a Pulitzer prize.

IT'S ALL THERE ON THE PAGE

Emma Thompson has won Oscars both as an actor (*Howards End*, 1992) and writer (*Sense and Sensibility*, 1995). In her memoir of the making of the Jane Austen novel she recalls how the producer clarified the distinction between her twin roles on the project: 'Lindsay goes round the table and introduces everyone - making it clear that I am present in the capacity of writer rather than actress, therefore no one has to be too nice to me.' Most actors - on the record, at least - accord the creator of their characters suitable deference:

You don't improvise with a Cameron Crowe script.
Orlando Bloom

I only sound intelligent when there's a good script writer around.
Christian Bale

I see myself as an actor first because writing is what you do when you are ready and acting is what you do when someone else is ready.
Steve Martin

When I'm the one who sits down and looks at the blank page and writes it out all the way, then I'll call it my script.
Edward Norton

You can have a million-dollar, twenty-million-dollar budget or sixty-million-dollar budget and if you don't have a good script, it doesn't mean a thing.
Tippi Hedren

With indies, all they have is their script and it's very important to them. The characters are better drawn, the stories more precise and the experience greater than with studio films where sometimes they fill in the script as they're shooting.
Mark Ruffalo

Well, first of all, you read the script a million times. Because what the script gives you are given circumstances. Given circumstances are all the facts of your character... And then, using my imagination, and then after all that, I have to tackle the scene.
Viola Davis

Every time you say yes to a film there's a certain percentage of your 'yes' that has to do with the director, a certain percentage to do with the story, a certain percentage with the character, the location, etc... I feel I do my best work when it's all there on the page, and I feel that the character is very vivid as I read the script and I'm not having to create stuff and trying to cobble together something. If I have to do that, then I don't entirely trust what I'm doing.
Guy Pearce

A script for an actor is like a bible. You carry it with you, you read it over and over, you go to your passages.
Cameron Diaz

All of the good movies are based on how that story was told. And you cannot do it with a bad script, that's for sure, no matter who.
Javier Bardem

There's a certain arrogance to an actor who will look at a script and feel like, because the words are simple, maybe they can paraphrase it and make it better.
Mary Steenburgen

Not all actors, however, are convinced that a script is a foolproof guide:

Good actors never use the script unless it's amazing writing. All the good actors I've worked with, they all say whatever they want to say.
Jessica Alba

Normally you read a screenplay - and I read a lot of them - and the characters don't feel like people. They feel like plot devices or cliches or stereotypes.
Joseph Gordon-Levitt

I wasn't comfortable in the beginning. But the longer I'm in the business, you see a lot of times these screenplays have been rewritten five times and you're not really offending an author. It's a studio that keeps banging out money having a writer rewrite portions. I've learned that you actually do have some freedom and you're not necessarily stepping on somebody's toes if you come in and say, 'Hey, this thing isn't working for me but I'm still interested in making this film.'
Edward Burns

Laura Linney is open about her intelligent engagement with material she feels is flawed:

> My experience is that's rare that you have a script that is what they call 'film-ready'. These days, many scripts are written to be financed, not to be acted... and so the agenda behind the writing is to explain, as opposed to give cues and hints to an actor to act. You don't have to say things all the time; you can act them. Otherwise, you have a character who doesn't connect to anything because they talk too much.

1987   MOONSTRUCK   1987

Ronny tries to persuade Loretta to abandon her fears and follow his passion.

RONNY

Love don't make things nice, it ruins everything! It breaks your heart, it makes things a mess. We, we aren't here to make things perfect. Snowflakes are perfect, stars are perfect. Not us! Not us! We're here to ruin ourselves and – and to break our hearts and love the wrong people and, and die! I mean that the storybooks are bullshit. Now I want you to come upstairs with me and get in my bed.

Dir: Norman Jewison • Scr: John Patrick Shanley • Cast: Nicolas Cage (Ronny Cammareri)

1989   WHEN HARRY MET SALLY...   1989

HARRY

I love that you get cold when it's seventy-one degrees out; I love that it takes you an hour and a half to order a sandwich; I love that you get a little crinkle above your nose when you're looking at me like I'm nuts; I love that after I spend a day with you I can still smell your perfume on my clothes, and I love that you are the last person I want to talk to before I go to sleep at night. And it's not because I'm lonely, and it's not because it's New Year's Eve. I came here tonight because when you realize you want to spend the rest of your life with somebody, you want the rest of your life to start as soon as possible.

Dir: Rob Reiner • Scr: Nora Ephron • Cast: Billy Crystal (Harry Burns)

PRETTY WOMAN

Vivian, an escort, is weary of always being 'the other woman'.

VIVIAN

When I was a little girl my mama used to lock me in the attic when I was bad, which was pretty often. And I would pretend I was a princess trapped in a tower by a wicked queen. And then suddenly this knight on a white horse with these colours flying would come charging up and draw his sword. And I would wave. And he would climb up the tower and rescue me. But never in all the time...that I had this dream did the knight say to me, 'Come on, baby, I'll put you up in a great condo.'

Dir: Garry Marshall • Scr: J. F. Lawton • Cast: Julia Roberts (Vivian Ward)

When Vivian meets her client Edward at the start of the film they go to see Verdi's *La Traviata*. The opera is about a courtesan who abandons her calling because she falls in love.

THE ENGLISH PATIENT

An adulterous couple share a rare stolen moment together.

ALMÁSY

When were you most happy?

KATHARINE

Now.

ALMÁSY

And when were you least happy?

KATHARINE

Now.

Dir: Anthony Minghella • Scr: Anthony Minghella • Based on a novel by
Michael Ondaatje • Cast: Ralph Fiennes (Count László de Almásy), Kristin
Scott Thomas (Katharine Clifton)

1996 BEAUTIFUL GIRLS   1996

Gina is tired of her male friends' obsession with youthful beauty.

GINA

No matter how perfect the nipple, how supple the thigh,
unless there's some other shit going on in the relationship
besides physical it's going get old, okay? And you guys, as
a gender, have got to get a grip otherwise the future of the
human race is in jeopardy.

Dir: Ted Demme • Scr: Scott Rosenberg • Cast: Rosie O'Donnell (Gina
Barrisano)

1997 THE DEVIL'S ADVOCATE   1997

*Kevin questions Milton, who is actually the Devil disguised as a
New York lawyer.*

KEVIN

What about love?

MILTON

Overrated. Biochemically no different than eating large
quantities of chocolate.

Dir: Taylor Hackford • Scr: Jonathan Lemkin, Tony Gilroy • Based on a
novel by Andrew Neiderman • Cast: Keanu Reeves (Kevin Lomax), Al Pacino
(John Milton)

Lawyer John Milton was named after the seventeenth-century author of *Paradise Lost*. The
poem contains the line 'Better to reign in Hell than serve in Heaven'.

Kathleen writes a heartfelt email to a man she has never even met.

KATHLEEN

I like to start my notes to you as if we're already in the
middle of a conversation. I pretend that we're the oldest
and dearest friends - as opposed to what we actually are,
people who don't know each other's names and met in an 'Over
30' chatroom where we both claimed we'd never been before.
What will NY152 say today, I wonder. I turn on my computer,
I wait impatiently as it boots up. I go on line, and my breath
catches in my chest until I hear three little words: You've
got mail. I hear nothing, not even a sound on the streets of
New York, just the beat of my own heart. I have mail. From you.

Dir: Nora Ephron • Scr: Nora Ephron, Delia Ephron • Based on a play by
Miklós László • Cast: Meg Ryan (Kathleen Kelly)

Nora Ephron adapted her script from *The Shop Around the Corner*, a play by Miklós László in
which the two protagonists fall in love while corresponding by post.

2001   A BEAUTIFUL MIND   2001

*A brilliant mathematician finds himself emotionally awkward
with his lover.*

> NASH
>
> Alicia, does our relationship warrant long-term commitment?
> I need some kind of proof, some kind of verifiable, empirical
> data.

> ALICIA
>
> I'm sorry, just give me a moment to redefine my girlish
> notions of romance.

Dir: Ron Howard • Scr: Akiva Goldsman • Based on a book by Sylvia
Nasar • Cast: Russell Crowe (John Nash), Jennifer Connelly (Alicia Nash)

2002 **THE RULES OF ATTRACTION** 2002

Lauren discovers her partner Sean has slept with her roommate.

> SEAN
>
> I only had sex with her because I'm in love with you.

Dir: Roger Avary • Scr: Roger Avary • Based on a novel by Bret Easton
Ellis • Cast: James van der Beek (Sean Bateman)

2003 **BIG FISH** 2003

*Will suspects his mother may have idealized her relationships
in the past.*

> WILL
>
> I know better than to argue romance with a French woman.

Dir: Tim Burton • Scr: John August • Based on a novel by Daniel
Wallace • Cast: Billy Crudup (Will Bloom)

STARRING

Sean O'Fearna is regularly ranked among the twentieth century's
greatest directors. His collaboration with rising star Marion
Morrison on *Stagecoach* won the Best Picture Oscar in 1940; a screen
legend for over thirty years, Morrison eventually won in the
acting category for *True Grit* (1969). Thomas Mapother IV has been
nominated for three Academy Awards and was Hollywood's highest-
earning star in 2012, while Allan Stewart Konigsberg has won four
from his twenty-three nominations but only attended the ceremony
once. Who would have foreseen Paul Georg Julius Hernreid Ritter von
Wassel-Waldingau would flee Casablanca with Ingrid Bergman, leaving
Humphrey Bogart alone and heartbroken? And who can forget Bernard
Schwartz as a cross-dressing saxophonist consoling Norma Jeane

Mortenson as she complains she always gets 'the fuzzy end of the lollipop'?

Shrewd agents, perhaps. O'Fearna was the birth name of John Ford, Marion Morrison became John Wayne, Mapother is Tom Cruise and Mr Konigsberg is Woody Allen. Herr Wassel-Waldingau is better known as Paul Henreid, Schwartz as Tony Curtis, and Miss Mortenson ended her career worshipped but alone as Marilyn Monroe.

Many talented artists from Europe who fuelled Hollywood's boom through the 1930s were persuaded by immigration officials, studio bosses and plain common sense to give their real names a more user-friendly ring. Some, in a career where identity was increasingly synonymous with brand, just wanted to stand apart. Still others, saddled with a lack of poetry in their birth certificate, just wanted a zippier start.

For some it was easy enough: Ethel Zimmerman shed her youthful Zim to become Ethel Merman, while Frederick Austerlitz dropped Rick and Litz to take off as Fred Astaire. Others found a trim perfectly sufficient: Clint(on) Eastwood, Jr., James (Baum)garner, Walter Matuschanskayasky (Matthau), while the homophonous Dominic Felix Amici (Don Ameche) and Leo Jacoby (Lee J. Cobb) found stardust in spelling. Catherine Jones borrowed a Zeta- before marrying Michael Delaney Dowd, Jr (Michael Douglas, son of Issur Danielovitch — better known as Kirk Douglas).

Mel Columcille Gerard Gibson tactfully buried his middle names, Eldred Gregory Peck abandoned his first and Jennifer Anastassakis (Aniston) seems to have grown bored of hers halfway through. In some cases, professions dictated a certain style: Hulk Hogan may be forgiven for doubting Terry Jene Bollea would look imposing splashed across billboards, and Virginia McMath put a spring in her step to become Ginger Rogers.

The rest hardly need to justify themselves:

- Anne Bancroft: Anna-Maria Louisa Italiano

- Ben Kingsley: Krishna Banji

- Brigitte Bardot: Camille Javal

- Bruce Willis: Walter Willison

- Claudette Colbert: Lily Chauchoin

- Cyd Charisse: Tula Ellice Finklea

- Demi Moore: Demetria Gene Guynes

- Diana Dors: Diana Fluck

- Doris Day: Doris von Kappelhoff

- Edward G. Robinson: Emmanuel Goldenberg

- James Dean: Seth Ward

- Joaquin Phoenix: Joaquin Rafael Bottom

- Judy Garland: Frances Gumm

- Lauren Bacall: Betty Joan Perske

- Michael Caine: Maurice Micklewhite

- Red Buttons: Aaron Chwatt

- Rita Hayworth: Margarita Cansino

- Whoopi Goldberg: Caryn Johnson

For readers who feel cheated by these false identities, the Internet Movie Database lists 139 entries under plain John Smith, although one had actually been persuaded by his agent that a straightforward name was more promising than his former one: Robert Errol Van Orden. The various John Smiths have been responsible for the following credits:

- Actor: *Crazy*

- Actor: *Emergency!*

- Actor: *At Death's Door*

- Producer: *England's Worst Ever Football Team*

- Director: *Bound and Thrashed*

- Transportation Department: *Up in the Air*

- Production Manager: *The Labyrinth of Love*

- Miscellaneous Crew: *Tortoise in Love*

- Composer: *Stuff*

- Self: *The Porn King, the Strippers and The Bent Coppers*

- Self: *The Harlem Globetrotters Popcorn Machine*

- Self: *Super High Me*

- Thanks: *Recalculating*

PRIME MINISTER

Whenever I get gloomy with the state of the world, I think about the arrivals gate at Heathrow Airport. General opinion's starting to make out that we live in a world of hatred and greed, but I don't see that. It seems to me that love is everywhere. Often, it's not particularly dignified or newsworthy, but it's always there - fathers and sons, mothers and daughters, husbands and wives, boyfriends, girlfriends, old friends. When the planes hit the Twin Towers, as far as I know, none of the phone calls from the people on board were messages of hate or revenge - they were all messages of love. If you look for it, I've got a sneaking suspicion... love actually is all around.

Dir: Richard Curtis • Scr: Richard Curtis • Cast: Hugh Grant (David, the Prime Minister)

2004 ANCHORMAN: THE LEGEND OF RON BURGUNDY   2004

Two chauvinistic journalists discuss their hapless love lives.

BRIAN

I think I was in love once.

RON

Really? What was her name?

BRIAN

I don't remember.

RON

That's not a good start, but keep going.

BRIAN

She was Brazilian or Chinese or something weird. I met her in the bathroom of a Kmart and we made out for hours. Then we parted ways, never to see each other again.

RON

I'm pretty sure that's not love.

<pre>
                    LARRY

I'll pay you.

                    ALICE

I don't need your money.

                    LARRY

You have my money.

                    ALICE

Thank you.

                    LARRY

'Thank you.' 'Thank you.' Is that some kind of rule?

                    ALICE

Just being polite.

                    LARRY

Get a lot of grown men crying their guts out, do you?

                    ALICE

Occupational hazard.
</pre>

Dir: Mike Nichols • Scr: Patrick Marber, based on his play • Cast: Clive Owen (Larry Gray), Natalie Portman (Alice Ayres)

<pre>
2005 THE SECRET LIFE OF WORDS   2005
</pre>

Josef tries to persuade Hanna to break free from her fearful, repetitive life.

<pre>
                    JOSEF

I thought, um, you and I, maybe we could go away somewhere.
Together. One of these days. Today. Right now. Come with me.

                    HANNA

No, I don't think that's going to be possible.

                    JOSEF

Why not?
</pre>

HANNA

Because I think that if we go away to someplace together,
I'm afraid that one day, maybe not today, maybe... maybe not
tomorrow either, but one day suddenly, I may begin to cry and
cry so very much that nothing or nobody can stop me and the
tears will fill the room, and I won't be able to breathe and I
will pull you down with me and we'll both drown.

JOSEF

I'll learn how to swim, Hanna. I swear, I'll learn how to swim.

Dir: Isabel Coixet • Scr: Isabel Coixet • Cast: Tim Robbins (Josef), Sarah
Polley (Hanna)

2010 RED   2010

*Secret agent Victoria – Retired, Extremely Dangerous – reveals
her past to her hostage.*

VICTORIA

I was in love with an agent once.

SARAH

What happened?

VICTORIA

Well, I was with MI6 and the relationship wasn't sanctioned.
So when it came to light, my loyalty was questioned and I was
ordered to kill him. It was a test.

SARAH

What did you do?

VICTORIA

I put three bullets in his chest.

Dir: Robert Schwentke • Scr: Jon Hoeber, Erich Hoeber • Based on a graphic
novel by Warren Ellis, Cully Hamner • Cast: Helen Mirren (Victoria),
Mary-Louise Parker (Sarah Ross)

In Bulgaria, the film was distributed under the title *BSP: Besni Strashni Pensii* – which means
'Furious Frightful Pensioners'.

A young woman raised in seclusion by her father encounters other people for the first time.

> HANNA

Are we going to kiss now?

> FELICIANO

Would you like to?

> HANNA

Kissing requires a total of thirty-four facial muscles and a hundred and twelve postural muscles. The most important muscle involved is the orbicularis oris muscle, because it is used to pucker the lips.

Dir: Joe Wright • Scr: David Farr, Seth Lochhead • Based on a story by Seth Lochhead • Cast: Saoirse Ronan (Hanna Heller), Álvaro Cervantes (Feliciano)

A standby prop man on the set of *Dr No* (1962) is surely feeling the heat as he wets down Ursula Andress's costume.

Mischievous as ever, Alfred Hitchcock poses in a publicity shot for *Psycho* (1960) in the chair reserved for Norman Bates's dead mother.

Jane Fonda as Barbarella, epitomizing the sexy exuberance of the science-fiction films of the 1960s.

Libido

1939 NINOTCHKA 1939

LEON

It's midnight. One half of Paris is making love to the other half.

Dir: Ernst Lubitsch • Scr: Charles Brackett, Billy Wilder, Walter
Reisch • Based on a story by Melchior Lengyel • Cast: Melvyn Douglas
(Count Leon d'Algout)

1939 GONE WITH THE WIND 1939

SCARLETT

Rhett, don't. I shall faint.

RHETT

I want you to faint. This is what you were meant for. None of the
fools you've ever known have kissed you like this, have they?

Dir: Victor Fleming • Scr: Sidney Howard • Based on a novel by Margaret
Mitchell • Cast: Vivien Leigh (Scarlett O'Hara), Clark Gable (Rhett Butler)

Gary Cooper turned down the part of Rhett Butler, saying not only '*Gone with the Wind* is going
to be the biggest flop in Hollywood history,' but also 'I'm just glad it'll be Clark Gable who's
falling on his face and not Gary Cooper.' Measured on its US box office receipts and adjusted for
inflation, the film remains the most profitable release in the history of cinema.

1941 BALL OF FIRE 1941

*A mild-mannered lexicographer hopes to learn contemporary slang
from a nightclub performer.*

POTTS

I shall **regret the absence of your keen mind**. Unfortunately,
it is inseparable from an extremely disturbing body.

Dir: Howard Hawks • Scr: Charles Brackett, Billy Wilder, Thomas
Monroe • Cast: Gary Cooper (Bertram Potts)

1942 THE MAJOR AND THE MINOR 1942

OSBORNE

Why don't you get out of that wet coat and into a dry martini?

Dir: Billy Wilder • Scr: Charles Brackett, Billy Wilder • Based on a story
by Fanny Kilbourne and a play by Edward Childs Carpenter • Cast: Robert
Benchley (Mr Albert Osborne)

'WHEN WOMEN GO WRONG, MEN GO RIGHT AFTER THEM'

Mae West (1893—1980) began her career as a child actor before
turning to vaudeville; in 1926 she wrote, directed and starred
in the Broadway play *Sex*. Arrested on charges of obscenity, she
served ten days in jail on Welfare Island where she delighted in
telling reporters she had worn silk underwear throughout her stay.
The controversy ensured her — aged thirty-eight — a contract with
Paramount. During her first film, *Night After Night* (1932), West
insisted on rewriting many of her scenes, prompting her co-star
George Raft to declare: 'she stole everything but the cameras'.

Although a supporter of women's liberation, she never declared
herself a feminist and remained as famous for her sexual innuendo
in real life as on screen. Memorable quips include:

- When women go wrong, men go right after them.

- When caught between two evils I generally pick the one I've
  never tried before.

- When I'm good, I'm very good. But when I'm bad, I'm better.

- Good girls go to heaven. Bad girls go everywhere else.

- I used to be Snow White, but I drifted.

- Ten men waiting for me at the door? Send one of them home, I'm
  tired.

- A hard man is good to find.

- I believe in censorship. After all, I made a fortune out of it.

- I only like two kinds of men: domestic and foreign.

- To err is human, but it feels divine.

- Is that a gun in your pocket or are you just glad to see me?

- Marriage is a great institution, but I'm not ready for an institution yet.

- Sex is emotion in motion.

- Those who are easily shocked should be shocked more often.

- I'm the lady who works at Paramount all day... and Fox all night.

- I always save one boyfriend for a rainy day... and another in case it doesn't rain.

- Sex is an emotion in motion... Love is what you make it and who you make it with.

1945   MILDRED PIERCE   1945

MONTE

In the spring a young man's fancy lightly turns to what he's been thinking about all winter.

Dir: Michael Curtiz • Scr: Ranald MacDougall • Based on a novel by James M. Cain • Cast: Zachary Scott (Monte Beragon)

1946   THE BIG SLEEP   1946

MARLOWE

She tried to sit in my lap while I was standing up.

Dir: Howard Hawks • Scr: William Faulkner, Leigh Brackett, Jules Furthman • Based on a novel by Raymond Chandler • Cast: Humphrey Bogart (Philip Marlowe)

Hawks claims that when producer Jack Warner gave him $50,000 [$600,000] to buy the rights to *The Big Sleep* he paid Chandler $5,000 [$60,000] and kept the rest for himself. Bogart and Bacall argued for years about whose idea it had been for Marlowe to adopt his flustered disguise, conveniently forgetting that Chandler's novel already contained the line: 'I had my horn-rimmed glasses on. I put my voice high and let a bird twitter in it.'

1946 GILDA

Two lovers meet again years after their acrimonious split.

> GILDA
>
> You do hate me, don't you, Johnny?

> JOHNNY
>
> I don't think you have any idea of how much.

> GILDA
>
> Hate is a very exciting emotion. Haven't you noticed? Very
> exciting. I hate you too, Johnny. I hate you so much I think
> I'm going to die from it. Darling...

They kiss passionately.

> I think I'm going to die from it.

Dir: Charles Vidor • Scr: Marion Parsonnet, E. A. Ellington • Cast: Rita
Hayworth (Gilda Mundson Farrell), Glenn Ford (Johnny Farrell)

1955 THE SEVEN YEAR ITCH

*Sherman confesses to his analyst that he is restless in his
marriage.*

> DR BRUBAKER
>
> When something itches, my dear sir, the natural tendency is
> to scratch.

> SHERMAN
>
> Last night I scratched.

Dir: Billy Wilder • Scr: Billy Wilder, George Axelrod • Based on a play by
George Axelrod • Cast: Oskar Homolka (Dr Brubaker), Tom Ewell (Richard
Sherman)

1959 PILLOW TALK

*Jan shares a telephone line with Brad Allen, a relentless
womanizer.*

> JAN
>
> Mr Allen, this may come as a shock to you, but there are some
> men who don't end every sentence with a proposition.

Dir: Michael Gordon • Scr: Stanley Shapiro, Maurice Richlin • Cast: Doris
Day (Jan Morrow)

Lewis, a psychopathic photographer, is interviewed for a job shooting glamour pictures.

MR PETERS

Got a question for you. Which magazines sell the most copies?

MARK

Those with girls on the front covers and no front covers on the girls.

Dir: Michael Powell • Scr: Leo Marks • Cast: Bartlett Mullins (Mr Peters), Karlheinz Böhm (Mark Lewis)

Writer Leo Marks was a noted cryptographer during the Second World War. The thriller explored many of Freud's theories in a sophisticated but shocking manner; censors savaged the released version and the public was outraged by its subject matter. The furore destroyed Powell's hitherto glittering career, although the film is now hailed as a masterpiece. As Powell noted ruefully in his autobiography, 'I make a film that nobody wants to see and then, thirty years later, everybody has either seen it or wants to see it.' *Peeping Tom* remains banned in Finland to this day.

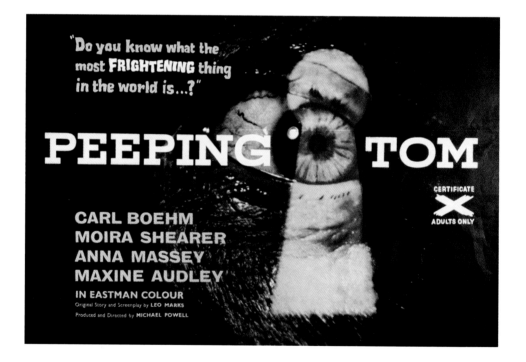

1963   HUD

Ruthless hedonist Hud takes a single-minded approach in matters of love.

HUD

The only question I ever ask any woman is 'What time is your husband coming home?'

Dir: Martin Ritt • Scr: Irving Ravetch, Harriet Frank Jr • Based on a novel by Larry McMurtry • Cast: Paul Newman (Hud Bannon)

1975   ONE FLEW OVER THE CUCKOO'S NEST

McMurphy has been undergoing electroconvulsive therapy against his will.

MCMURPHY

They was giving me ten thousand watts a day, you know, and I'm hot to trot. The next woman takes me on's gonna light up like a pinball machine and pay off in silver dollars!

Dir: Miloš Forman • Scr: Lawrence Hauben, Bo Goldman • Based on a novel by Ken Kesey • Cast: Jack Nicholson (Randle 'Mac' McMurphy)

1983   SCARFACE

Tony dances with Elvira but grows frustrated as she resists his advances.

TONY

Hey baby, what is your problem? Huh, you got a problem? You're good looking, you got a beautiful body, beautiful legs, beautiful face, all these guys in love with you. Only you got a look in your eye like you haven't been fucked in a year.

Dir: Brian De Palma • Scr: Oliver Stone • Based on a 1932 film of the same name, and on a novel by Armitage Trail • Cast: Al Pacino (Tony Montana)

1987   PERSONAL SERVICES

After a raid on her brothel, Christine Painter is interviewed by police.

CHRISTINE

I'm responsible, not the men. You can't expect the men to be responsible. When the balls are full, the brain is empty.

Dir: Terry Jones • Scr: David Leland • Cast: Julie Walters (Christine Painter)

Repressed English laywer Archie finds himself so in love with Wanda that he throws caution to the wind.

ARCHIE

Wanda, do you have any idea what it's like being English? Being so correct all the time, being so stifled by this dread of, of doing the wrong thing, of saying to someone 'Are you married?' and hearing 'My wife left me this morning,' or saying, uh, 'Do you have children?' and being told they all burned to death on Wednesday. You see, Wanda, we're all terrified of embarrassment. That's why we're so... dead. Most of my friends are dead, you know - we have these piles of corpses to dinner. But you're alive, God bless you, and I want to be, I'm so fed up with all this. I want to make love with you, Wanda. I'm a good lover - at least I used to be, back in the early fourteenth century. Can we go to bed?

Dir: Charles Crichton, John Cleese (uncredited) • Scr: John Cleese, Charles Crichton • Cast: John Cleese (Archie Leach)

Cleese named his character Archibald Leach, the real name of screen idol Cary Grant. When an interviewer once offered that 'Everybody would like to be Cary Grant', Grant reputedly replied: 'So would I.' He also decried the many rumours about his reputation, saying: 'Hell, if I'd jumped on all the dames I'm supposed to have jumped on, I'd have had no time to go fishing.'

*Meeting by chance, old acquaintances Harry and Sally seem unsure
how things stand between them.*

HARRY

You realize, of course, that we could never be friends.

SALLY

Why not?

HARRY

What I'm saying is, and this is not a come-on in any way,
shape or form, is that men and women can't be friends because
the sex part always gets in the way.

SALLY

That's not true. I have a number of men friends and there is
no sex involved.

HARRY

No, you don't.

SALLY

Yes, I do.

HARRY

No, you don't.

SALLY

Yes, I do.

HARRY

You only think you do.

SALLY

You say I'm having sex with these men without my knowledge?

HARRY

No, what I'm saying is they all want to have sex with you.

SALLY

They do not.

HARRY

Do too.

SALLY

How do you know?

HARRY

Because no man can be friends with a woman that he finds
attractive. He always wants to have sex with her.

SALLY

So, you're saying that a man can be friends with a woman he
finds unattractive?

HARRY

No. You pretty much want to nail them too.

SALLY

What if they don't want to have sex with you?

HARRY

Doesn't matter, because the sex thing is already out there so
the friendship is ultimately doomed and that's the end of the
story.

SALLY

Well, I guess we're not going to be friends then.

HARRY

I guess not.

SALLY

That's too bad. You were the only person that I knew in New
York.

Dir: Rob Reiner • Scr: Nora Ephron • Cast: Billy Crystal (Harry Burns),
Meg Ryan (Sally Albright)

According to screenwriter Nora Ephron, the infamous 'I'll have what she's having' line was
actually suggested by Billy Crystal.

PRETTY WOMAN

A high-class call girl negotiates her nightly fee with an
attractive client.

                              VIVIAN
    I would have stayed for two thousand.

                              EDWARD
    I would have paid four.

Dir: Garry Marshall • Scr: J. F. Lawton • Cast: Julia Roberts (Vivian
Ward), Richard Gere (Edward Lewis)

The modern Cinderella story struck a chord with many women – but not all. As Laney Boggs
says in *She's All That* (1999): 'I feel just like Julia Roberts in *Pretty Woman*. You know, except
for the whole hooker thing.'

The studio didn't initially want to cast Julia Roberts as Vivian; along the way they considered
Meg Ryan, Kim Basinger, Kathleen Turner, Debra Winger, Geena Davis, Carrie Fisher, Bo Derek,
Kelly McGillis, Melanie Griffith, Sharon Stone, Michelle Pfeiffer, Madonna, Jamie Lee Curtis,
Emma Thompson, Rosanna Arquette, Heather Locklear, Jennifer Jason Leigh, Joan Cusack,
Phoebe Cates, Elisabeth Shue, Tatum O'Neal, Bridget Fonda, Lori Loughlin, Diane Lane and
Justine Bateman.

WILD AT HEART

Romantic Southern outlaw Sailor Ripley has a way with words.

                              SAILOR
    Man, I had a boner with a capital 'O'.

Dir: David Lynch • Scr: David Lynch • Based on a novel by Barry Gifford •
Cast: Nicolas Cage (Sailor Ripley)

A FONT FOR SCHMUCKS

Producer Jack Warner (1892–1978) once dismissively referred to
the staff contracted to work at his studio: 'Actors? Schmucks.
Screenwriters? Schmucks with Underwoods.' (The latter was a famous
brand of manual typewriter.) Warner reputedly demanded his team
deliver a minimum number of pages a week and used to stand outside
the writers' building ready to burst in if he did not hear the
reassuring clack of machinery and the familiar carriage return bell.

It was during Warner's heyday in the 1930s that the screenplay
format took its enduring shape and its conventions remain today.
Fifty years after the widespread acceptance of the electric
typewriter (and thirty years after the personal computer became

commonplace), the typeface used a century ago is still used by the vast majority of film writers.

The original font emulating the manuscript look for printing was designed by Howard Kettler in 1955. Originally named 'Messenger' it was finally christened 'Courier', as Kettler explained: 'A letter can be [from] an ordinary messenger, or it can be [from a] courier, which radiates dignity, prestige, and stability.' His creation endured as the standard typeface for the US State Department until 2004, doubtless lending the font an air of respectability to modern readers.

One of its advantages for the film industry is that it is monospaced — that is, each letter takes up the same width on the page, which regularizes formatting and word counts. The result gives fifty-five average length lines per page, approximating handily to a rule of thumb that each sheet represents a minute of screen time.

A further commonplace is that a one-sentence scene with traditional spacing and numbering takes up an eighth of a page, and thus represents around seven seconds of action. Sometimes writers resent the notion that their work can be mathematically analysed and cheekily compress complicated scenes to frustrate assistant directors. An action-packed war episode might read as follows:

38. DAY EXTERIOR - PEARL HARBOR - QUAYSIDE - (1/8 page)

CIVILIANS race for cover and hundreds of NAVY GUNNERS open fire as the cloudless sky is filled with JAPANESE AIRCRAFT releasing TORPEDOES and BOMBS on the entire US FLEET.

1992 WAYNE'S WORLD 1992

Two teenagers recording a home video introduce a tribute to the model Claudia Schiffer.

                    WAYNE

Schwing!

                    GARTH

Schwing!

—
                    WAYNE

Tent pole! She's a babe!

                    GARTH

She's magically babelicious.

WAYNE

She tested very high on the strokability scale.

Dir: Penelope Spheeris • Scr: Mike Myers, Bonnie Turner, Terry
Turner • Cast: Mike Myers (Wayne Campbell), Dana Carvey (Garth Algar)

1992 BASIC INSTINCT   1992

*Gus worries his detective partner is allowing an attractive
suspect to distract him.*

GUS

Well, she got that magna cum laude pussy on her that done
fried up your brain.

Dir: Paul Verhoeven • Scr: Joe Eszterhas • Cast: George Dzundza (Gus)

Joe Eszterhas claimed to have written the uncommissioned script in thirteen days; a bidding
war between studios raised the price of the screenplay to an unprecedented $3 million [$5
million]. Eszterhas and director Paul Verhoeven fell out several times during production over
the edgy material, and the shoot was picketed by San Francisco's gay community who objected
to the crude depiction of lesbian and bisexual characters. The American public had no such
reservations; the film took $350 million [$580 million] at the box office.

1992 SCENT OF A WOMAN   1992

*A retired US Army Ranger refuses to let his blindness compromise
his passion for life.*

FRANK

Ooh, but I still smell her... Women! What could you say? Who
made 'em? God must have been a fuckin' genius. The hair - they
say the hair is everything, you know. Have you ever buried
your nose in a mountain of curls, just wanted to go to sleep
forever? Or lips - and when they touched yours were like that
first swallow of wine after you just crossed the desert. Tits.
Hoo-hah! Big ones, little ones, nipples starin' right out at
ya, like secret searchlights. Mmm. Legs. I don't care if they're
Greek columns or secondhand Steinways. What's between 'em -
passport to heaven. I need a drink. Yes, Mr Simms, there's only
two syllables in this whole wide world worth hearin': pussy.
Hah! Are you listenin' to me, son? I'm givin' ya pearls here.

Dir: Martin Brest • Scr: Bo Goldman • Based on the film *Profumo di donna* by
Ruggero Maccari, Dino Risi, and on a novel by Giovanni Arpino • Cast: Al
Pacino (Lieutenant Colonel Frank Slade)

1994 NAKED GUN 33⅓ : THE FINAL INSULT 1994

Hapless detective Frank Drebin resists an invitation to a ménage à trois.

FRANK
I like my sex the way I play basketball – one on one, with as little dribbling as possible.

Dir: Peter Segal • Scr: Pat Proft, David Zucker, Robert LoCash • Based on a TV series by Jim Abrahams, David Zucker, Jerry Zucker • Cast: Leslie Nielsen (Lieutenant Frank Drebin)

1997 BOOGIE NIGHTS 1997

A porn film producer discovers a huge new male talent.

JACK
I got a feeling that behind those jeans is something wonderful just waiting to get out.

Dir: Paul Thomas Anderson • Scr: Paul Thomas Anderson • Cast: Burt Reynolds (Jack Horner)

The film opens with an unbroken shot lasting almost three minutes. Although Orson Welles' *A Touch of Evil* (1958) pioneered this technique on a single exterior set, Paul Thomas Anderson's camera move sweeps from a real Los Angeles cityscape through traffic shots and crowds before entering a nightclub where it introduces us to almost every key character in the subsequent story on the packed dance floor.

1988 COLORS   1988

An over-confident young cop offers his wisdom about women.

> DANNY
>
> You don't wanna get laid, man. It leads to kissing and pretty
> soon you gotta talk to 'em.

Dir: Dennis Hopper • Scr: Michael Schiffer • Cast: Sean Penn (Danny McGavin)

The story is set in south-central Los Angeles; the producers hired real gang members as
guardians as well as actors but two of them were shot during filming.

1999 ANALYZE THIS   1999

A Mafia boss forces a psychoanalyst to take him on as a client.

> DR SOBEL
>
> What happened with your wife last night?

> PAUL
>
> I wasn't with my wife, I was with my girlfriend.

> DR SOBEL
>
> Are you having marriage problems?

> PAUL
>
> No.

> DR SOBEL
>
> Then why do you have a girlfriend?

> PAUL
>
> What, are you gonna start moralizing on me?

> DR SOBEL
>
> No, I'm not - I'm just trying to understand. Why do you have a
> girlfriend?

> PAUL
>
> I do things with her I can't do with my wife.

> DR SOBEL
>
> Why can't you do them with your wife?

PAUL

Hey, that's the mouth she kisses my kids goodnight with! What
are you, crazy?

Dir: Harold Ramis • Scr: Kenneth Lonergan, Peter Tolan, Harold
Ramis • Cast: Billy Crystal (Dr Ben Sobel), Robert De Niro (Paul Vitti)

2000 HIGH FIDELITY 2000

*Rob cannot shake the thought that his ex-girlfriend is now with a
new partner.*

ROB

You are as abandoned and noisy as any character in a porn
film, Laura. You are Ian's plaything, responding to his touch
with shrieks of orgasmic delight. No woman in the history of
the world is having better sex than the sex you are having
with Ian... in my head.

Dir: Stephen Frears • Scr: D. V. DeVincentis, Steve Pink, John Cusack,
Scott Rosenberg • Based on a novel by Nick Hornby • Cast: John Cusack (Rob
Gordon)

2002 ABOUT SCHMIDT 2002

*Roberta, mother of the bride-to-be, reassures the groom's father
about their children's future.*

ROBERTA

You already know how famously they get along as friends,
but did you know that their sex life is positively white-
hot? The main reason both of my marriages failed was sexual.
I'm an extremely sexual person, I can't help it, it's just how
I'm wired, you know, even when I was a little girl. I had my
first orgasm when I was six in ballet class. Anyway, the
point is that I have always been very easily aroused and
very orgasmic; Jeannie and I have a lot in common that way.
Clifford and Larry, they were nice guys, but they just could
not keep up with me. Anyway, I don't want to betray Jeannie's
confidence, but let me just assure you that whatever problems
those two kids may run into along the way, they will always
be able to count on what happens between the sheets to keep
them together. More soup?

Dir: Alexander Payne • Scr: Alexander Payne, Jim Taylor • Based on a novel
by Louis Begley • Cast: Kathy Bates (Roberta Hertzel)

2006   BORAT: CULTURAL LEARNINGS OF AMERICA FOR MAKE BENEFIT GLORIOUS NATION OF KAZAKHSTAN 2006

Borat has travelled to the US from Kazakhstan seeking the freedom – and pleasures – of the West.

BORAT

A man yesterday tell me, if I buy a car I must buy one with pussy magnet.

Dir: Larry Charles • Scr: Sacha Baron Cohen, Anthony Hines, Peter Baynham, Dan Mazer • Cast: Sacha Baron Cohen (Borat)

The Kazakh government described *Borat* as 'a concoction of bad taste and ill manners which is incompatible with the ethics and civilized behavior of Kazakhstan's people' and ran a four-page advertisement in the *New York Times* correcting the misperceptions Sacha Baron Cohen had spread. Much of the film was staged as 'reality' and the police were called to the set on ninety-two occasions.

2011 A DANGEROUS METHOD 2011

A psychoanalyst proposes that society has an unhealthy attitude towards sex.

GROSS

It seems to me the measure of the true perversity of the human race is that one of its very few reliably pleasurable activities should be the subject of so much hysteria and repression.

Dir: David Cronenberg • Scr: Christopher Hampton • Based on a play by Christopher Hampton and a book by John Kerr • Cast: Vincent Cassel (Otto Gross)

Chicago, based on Bob Fosse's stage musical, gave the Prohibition era a burst of twenty-first-century energy.

The romance that never was: Bond and Moneypenny embrace in a rare studio portrait from 1962.

A still from the original *Scarface* (1932) before the Motion Picture Production Code clamped down on overt violence and sexuality.

Bruisers

1942   THE PALM BEACH STORY   1942

HACKENSACKER

That's one of the tragedies of this life - that the men who
are most in need of a beating up are always enormous.

Dir: Preston Sturges • Scr: Preston Sturges • Cast: Rudy Vallée (John D.
Hackensacker III)

1947   OUT OF THE PAST   1947

A gangster threatens a private investigator he intends to frame.

WHIT

You're gonna take the rap and play along. You're gonna make
every exact move I tell you. If you don't, I'll kill you. And
I'll promise you one thing: it won't be quick. I'll break you
first. You won't be able to answer a telephone or open a door
without thinking, 'This is it'. And when it comes, it still won't
be quick. And it won't be pretty. You can take your choice.

Dir: Jacques Tourneur • Scr: Daniel Mainwaring • Cast: Kirk Douglas (Whit
Sterling)

1949   KIND HEARTS AND CORONETS   1949

Murderer Louis Mazzini is scrupulous in his professional etiquette.

LOUIS

It is so difficult to make a neat job of killing people with
whom one is not on friendly terms.

Dir: Robert Hamer • Scr: Robert Hamer, John Dighton • Based on a novel by
Roy Horniman • Cast: Dennis Price (Louis Mazzini)

1949   WHITE HEAT   1949

*Cody Jarrett celebrates his escape from jail shortly before he is
killed in a blaze in a chemical plant.*

CODY

Made it, Ma! Top of the world!

Dir: Raoul Walsh • Scr: Ivan Goff, Ben Roberts • Based on a story by
Virginia Kellogg • Cast: James Cagney (Arthur 'Cody' Jarrett)

Jack Dawson (Leonardo DiCaprio) reprises Cagney's line – and triumphant pose – as he yells
from the ship's bow in *Titanic* (1997): 'I'm the king of the world!'

CHEESE

In 2004, British bakery Warburtons celebrated a new line of Cheddar-flavoured crumpets by inviting its customers to nominate the cheesiest movie lines of all time. Here are their top ten:

I'm the king of the world!
Titanic (1997)

Nobody puts Baby in the corner.
Dirty Dancing (1987)

Is it still raining? I hadn't noticed.
Four Weddings and a Funeral (1994)

SAM WHEAT: I love you.
MOLLY JENSEN: Ditto.
Ghost (1990)

You can be my wingman any time.
Top Gun (1986)

I'm just a girl standing in front of a boy asking him to love her.
Notting Hill (1999)

Today we celebrate our Independence Day!
Independence Day (1996)

They may take our lives, but they will not take our freedom!
Braveheart (1995)

You had me at hello.
Jerry Maguire (1996)

BLIND WOMAN: You're a godsend, a saviour.
POSTMAN: No, I'm a postman.
The Postman (1997)

There are plenty of other classics which might have given these winners a run for their money:

One thing's sure. Inspector Clay is dead. Murdered. And somebody's responsible.
Plan 9 From Outer Space (1959)

It makes you kill yourself. Just when you thought there couldn't be any more evil that can be invented.
The Happening (1966)

You know, hot dogs get a bad rap. They got a cool shape, they got protein.
The Happening (1966)

Okay, cocksucker. Fuck with me and we'll see who shits on the sidewalk.
Death Race 2000 (1975)

If Pazuzu comes for you, I will spit a leopard.
Exorcist II: The Heretic (1977)

You have a great body. May I use it?
Saturn 3 (1980)

Flash! I love you, but we only have 14 hours to save the earth!
Flash Gordon (1980)

I eat Green Berets for breakfast. And right now, I'm very hungry!
Commando (1985)

The dingo took my baby!
A Cry in the Dark (1988)

EDWARD: So what happens after he climbs up and rescues her?
VIVIAN: She rescues him right back.
Pretty Woman (1990)

Kenner, just in case we get killed, I wanted to tell you. You have the biggest dick I've ever seen on a man.
Showdown in Little Tokyo (1991)

CRISTAL: You have great tits. They're really beautiful.
NOMI: Thank you.
CRISTAL: I like nice tits. I always have, how about you?
NOMI: I like having nice tits.
Showgirls (1995)

Swoon, I'll catch you.
The English Patient (1996)

You complete me.
Jerry Maguire (1996)

You're why cavemen chiselled on walls.
As Good As It Gets (1997)

I hate to disappoint you, but rubber lips are immune to your charms.
Batman & Robin (1997)

I said, put the bunny back in the box.
Con Air (1997)

It's like looking in a mirror. Only not.
Face/Off (1997)

Did you just have a brain fart?
G.I. Jane (1997)

KITANA: Mother! You're alive!
SINDEL: Too bad. You will die!
Mortal Kombat 2: Annihilation (1997)

He's got space dementia.
Armageddon (1998)

A bird may love a fish, Signore, but where will they live?
Ever After: A Cinderella Story (1998)

Dancing's just a conversation between two people. Talk to me.
Hope Floats (1998)

You better hold on tight, spider-monkey.
Twilight (1998)

While you were still learning how to spell your name, I was being trained to conquer galaxies.
Battlefield Earth: A Saga of the Year 3000 (2000)

God was showing off when he made you.
Keeping the Faith (2000)

This is Walker. We need to get those planes fuelled and loaded right now!... I think World War Two has just hit us.
Pearl Harbor (2001)

Well, you might be a cunning linguist, but I am a master debater.
Austin Powers in Goldmember (2002)

I'm really wired. What do you say I take you home and eat your pussy?
Shark Attack 3: Megalodon (2002)

I don't like sand. It's coarse and rough and irritating, and it gets everywhere.
Star Wars: Episode II - Attack of the Clones (2002)

You know what happens when a toad gets struck by lightning? The same thing that happens to everything else.
X-Men (2002)

It's turkey time. Gobble gobble.
Gigli (2003)

Are you a Mexican or a Mexi-can't?
Once Upon a Time in Mexico (2003)

Are you sure you saw what you think you thought you saw?
Hellbreeder (2004)

I've always been standing in your doorway.
Spider-Man 2 (2004)

BRENDA: I know Tai Kwon Do!
MADEA: And I know 'Whoop Your Ass'!
Diary of a Mad Black Woman (2005)

Hold me, like you did by the lake on Naboo.
Star Wars: Episode III — Revenge of the Sith (2005)

Forgive my lips. They find joy in the most unusual places.
A Good Year (2006)

It's a pressure valve. It won't open unless there's tremendous pressure.
Poseidon (2006)

Spartans! Ready your breakfast and eat hearty. For tonight, we dine in hell!
300 (2006)

Not the bees!
The Wicker Man (2006)

1950   **THE ASPHALT JUNGLE**   1950

Crooked lawyer Emmerich finds it easy to forgive himself.

EMMERICH

Crime is only a left-handed form of human endeavour.

Dir: John Huston • Scr: Ben Maddow, John Huston • Based on a novel by W. R. Burnett • Cast: Louis Calhern (Alonzo D. Emmerich)

1951   ACE IN THE HOLE   1951

Lorraine is puzzled by the motives of an unscrupulous journalist.

> LORRAINE
>
> I met a lot of hard-boiled eggs in my life, but you - you're twenty minutes.

Dir: Billy Wilder • Scr: Billy Wilder, Lesser Samuels, Walter Newman • Cast: Jan Sterling (Lorraine Minosa)

1953   THE WILD ONE   1953

A young woman questions a Hell's Angel who has ridden into town.

> MILDRED
>
> Hey Johnny, what are you rebelling against?

> JOHNNY
>
> Whadda you got?

Dir: László Benedek • Scr: John Paxton • Based on a story by Frank Rooney • Cast: Peggy Maley (Mildred), Marlon Brando (Johnny Strabler)

Triumph, manufacturers of the motorcycle Brando rides, were not happy to be associated with the film until they realized it had substantially boosted sales.

Crime boss Brewster plans to eliminate one of his partners.

> BREWSTER
>
> Fairfax is dead. He just doesn't know it yet.

Dir: John Boorman • Scr: Alexander Jacobs, David Newhouse, Rafe Newhouse • Based on a novel by Donald E. Westlake (as Richard Stark) • Cast: Carroll O'Connor (Brewster)

US Marshal Rooster Cogburn suspects Ned Pepper is harbouring the man he is pursuing.

> ROOSTER
>
> When's the last time you saw Ned Pepper?

> EMMETT
>
> I don't remember any Ned Pepper.

> ROOSTER
>
> Short feisty fella, nervous and quick, got a messed-up lower lip.

> EMMETT
>
> That don't bring nobody to mind. A funny lip?

> ROOSTER
>
> Wasn't always like that, I shot him in it.

> EMMETT
>
> In the lower lip? What was you aiming at?

> ROOSTER
>
> His upper lip.

Dir: Henry Hathaway • Scr: Marguerite Roberts • Based on a novel by Charles Portis • Cast: John Wayne (Reuben J. 'Rooster' Cogburn), Jeremy Slate (Emmett Quincy)

Between 1926 and 1976 John Wayne starred in over 170 films; this was the only one that won him an Oscar.

1971 GET CARTER 1971

Small-time crook Jack Carter hears Cliff Brumby has been trying to get rid of him.

BRUMBY

Listen, I don't like it when some tough nut comes pushing his way in and out of my house in the middle of the night! Bloody well tell me who sent you.

CARTER

You're a big man, but you're in bad shape. With me it's a full-time job. Now behave yourself.

Dir: Mike Hodges • Scr: Mike Hodges • Based on a novel by Ted Lewis • Cast: Bryan Mosley (Cliff Brumby), Michael Caine (Jack Carter)

1972 THE GODFATHER 1972

MICHAEL

Well, when Johnny was first starting out, he was signed to a personal services contract with this big-band leader. And as his career got better and better, he wanted to get out of it. But the band leader wouldn't let him. Now, Johnny is my father's godson. So my father went to see this band leader and offered him $10,000 to let Johnny go, but the band leader said no. So the next day, my father went back, only this time with Luca Brasi. Within an hour, he had a signed release for a certified check of $1,000.

KAY

How did he do that?

MICHAEL

My father made him an offer he couldn't refuse.

KAY

What was that?

MICHAEL

Luca Brasi held a gun to his head, and my father assured him that either his brains or his signature would be on the contract.

Dir: Francis Ford Coppola • Scr: Francis Ford Coppola, Mario Puzo • Based on a novel by Mario Puzo • Cast: Al Pacino (Michael Corleone), Diane Keaton (Kay Adams)

'DON'T QUIT. MAKE THEM FIRE YOU'

It's easy to look back on *The Godfather* and believe it sprang fully formed from the talents of Mario Puzo, Francis Ford Coppola and their stellar cast. Who else could have delivered the screen-searing power of Don Corleone but Marlon Brando? Try these names for size, Paramount's original suggestions: Ernest Borgnine, Edward G. Robinson, Orson Welles, Danny Thomas, Richard Conte, Anthony Quinn and George C. Scott. Even Coppola himself first wanted Laurence Olivier for the role.

The studio hated Coppola's second choice of Brando and offered him the minimum fee permitted by the Screen Actors Guild; one of the producers later said the star received $50,000 [$275,000] plus a percentage of the profits, which he sold back to the studio to pay for an expensive divorce. The film went on to make $135 million [$740 million] in its US theatrical release alone.

During pre-production the film received numerous threats from the Mafia, who controlled the 'teamsters' — drivers and labourers for the film industry. One of the producers eventually met with Joseph Colombo, boss of one of New York's Five Families organization, and agreed that if the mobsters permitted the production to go ahead undisturbed the script would not include the terms 'Mafia' or 'Cosa Nostra'.

The early days of the project were so dogged by arguments and setbacks that Coppola returned from a location scout to find a telegram from his agent, urging him: 'Don't quit. Make them fire you.' His persistence paid off, although he said afterwards: 'Every film creates its own identity and it's possible to rivet the audience without the obvious tools. I was more surprised than anyone that this picture seemed to work the way it did.'

The Godfather won Oscars for Best Picture, Best Screenplay and Best Actor. Even the ceremony itself had its memorable clashes: three other cast members (James Caan as Sonny, Robert Duvall as Tom Hagen and Al Pacino as Michael Corleone) were all nominated for Best Supporting Actor but Pacino boycotted the awards as he calculated his 'secondary' role had more screentime than Brando's; Brando refused to collect his own Oscar, sending instead rights activist Sacheen Littlefeather to deliver a speech about the film industry's mistreatment of Native American Indians.

1972 CHATO'S LAND 1972

Whitmore's men grow restless as he leads them deeper into hostile territory.

CAPTAIN WHITMORE

For a thirsty man in a dry land, you gotta lotta talk.

Dir: Michael Winner • Scr: Gerald Wilson • Cast: Jack Palance (Captain Quincey Whitmore)

1974 BRING ME THE HEAD OF ALFREDO GARCIA 1974

Bennie hopes to claim the bounty on a wanted man who is already dead.

BENNIE

There ain't nothing sacred about a hole in the ground - or the man that's in it.

Dir: Sam Peckinpah • Scr: Sam Peckinpah, Gordon T. Dawson • Cast: Warren Oates (Bennie)

Although Peckinpah was reportedly desperate, drunk and depressed while directing the film, many consider it his finest work. Banned in many countries on its release and panned by the *Wall Street Journal* as being 'grotesque, sadistic, irrational, obscene and incompetent', the film was hailed by Roger Ebert as 'some kind of bizarre masterpiece'.

1974 BLAZING SADDLES 1974

Hedley Lamarr recruits a gang of thugs to evict the townsfolk of Rock Ridge.

TAGGART

What do you want me to do, sir?

HEDLEY

I want you to round up every vicious criminal and gunslinger in the West. Take this down.

Taggart looks for a pen and paper while Hedley talks.

I want rustlers, cut-throats, murderers, bounty hunters, desperadoes, mugs, pugs, thugs, nitwits, halfwits, dimwits, vipers, snipers, conmen, Indian agents, Mexican bandits, muggers, buggerers, bushwhackers, hornswogglers, horse thieves, bull dykes, train robbers, bank robbers, ass-kickers, shit-kickers and Methodists!

Taggart finally finds a pen and paper.

TAGGART

Could you repeat that, sir?

Dir: Mel Brooks • Scr: Mel Brooks, Norman Steinberg, Andrew Bergman, Richard Pryor, Alan Uger • Cast: Slim Pickens (Taggart), Harvey Korman (Hedley Lamarr)

1974 CHINATOWN   1974

Private investigator Jake Gittes is under no illusion about the integrity of his profession.

EVELYN

Hollis seems to think you're an innocent man.

JAKE

Well, I've been accused of a lot of things before, Mrs Mulwray, but never that.

Dir: Roman Polanski • Scr: Robert Towne • Cast: Faye Dunaway (Evelyn Mulwray), Jack Nicholson (Jake Gittes)

Jack Nicholson is a devoted LA Lakers fan and was persistently late for filming because he was following their games on TV in his trailer. After one heated argument, director Polanski smashed the television set with a mop.

1975 NIGHT MOVES   1975

Private investigator Harry Moseby quizzes a reluctant suspect.

HARRY

What happened to your face?

QUENTIN

I won second prize in a fight.

Dir: Arthur Penn • Scr: Alan Sharp • Cast: Gene Hackman (Harry Moseby),
James Woods (Quentin)

As a struggling actor Hackman had jobs as a doorman, furniture mover, soda jerk and pharmacy
assistant. During his rise to fame he turned down the lead role in *Jaws*, *Close Encounters of
the Third Kind*, *Raiders of the Lost Ark* and *One Flew Over the Cuckoo's Nest*. He later said: 'I was
trained to be an actor, not a star. I was trained to play roles, not to deal with fame and agents
and lawyers and the press.'

1975 JAWS   1975

*Quint, a local fisherman, interrupts a town meeting about a man-
eating shark terrorizing their beach.*

QUINT

Y'all know me. Know how I earn a livin'. I'll catch this bird
for you, but it ain't gonna be easy. Bad fish. Not like going
down the pond chasin' bluegills and tommycods. This shark,
swallow you whole. Little shakin', little tenderizin', an' down
you go. And we gotta do it quick, that'll bring back your
tourists, put all your businesses on a payin' basis. But it's
not gonna be pleasant. I value my neck a lot more than three
thousand bucks, chief. I'll find him for three, but I'll catch
him, and kill him, for ten. But you've gotta make up your
minds. If you want to stay alive, then ante up. If you want
to play it cheap, be on welfare the whole winter. I don't want
no volunteers, I don't want no mates, there's just too many
captains on this island. $10,000 for me by myself. For that
you get the head, the tail, the whole damn thing.

Dir: Steven Spielberg • Scr: Carl Gottlieb, Peter Benchley • Based on a
novel by Peter Benchley • Cast: Robert Shaw (Quint)

1976 TAXI DRIVER   1976

A disturbed Vietnam vet takes a job as a New York taxi driver.

                          TRAVIS

    All the animals come out at night - whores, skunk pussies,
    buggers, queens, fairies, dopers, junkies. Sick, venal. Someday
    a real rain'll come and wash all this scum off the streets. I
    go all over. I take people to the Bronx, Brooklyn, I take 'em
    to Harlem. I don't care. Don't make no difference to me. It does
    to some. Some won't even take spooks. Don't make no difference
    to me.

Dir: Martin Scorsese • Scr: Paul Schrader • Cast: Robert De Niro (Travis
Bickle)

Bizarrely, one of the studios who read the script suggested Neil Diamond for the lead role.
The famous scene where Travis Bickle talks to himself was ad-libbed by Robert De Niro. The
screenplay just read: 'Travis looks in the mirror.'

1971 SHAFT   1971

*Private investigator John Shaft warns a suspect not to interrupt
him.*

                          SHAFT

    Don't let your mouth get your ass in trouble.

Dir: Gordon Parks • Scr: Ernest Tidyman, John D. F. Black • Based on a
novel by Ernest Tidyman • Cast: Richard Roundtree (John Shaft)

1983 SCARFACE   1983

*Drug lord Tony Montana is determined to safeguard his empire
on his own terms.*

                          TONY

    All I have in this world is my balls and my word, and I don't
    break them for no one.

Dir: Brian De Palma • Scr: Oliver Stone • Based on a 1932 film of the same
name, and on a novel by Armitage Trail • Cast: Al Pacino (Tony Montana)

When Saddam Hussein set up a front company to launder money from various illegal
enterprises, he named it Montana Management after the main character in the film.

'STICKS NIX HICK PIX'

One of the most famous media headlines ever printed, this terse 1935 splash in *Variety* announces that films about country life do not play well with rural audiences — proof, perhaps, that the Hollywood dream of fleeing a small-town existence for the bright lights of the big city had already taken root. Further epigrammatic utterances include:

- Cocktail: Cruise Boozer Brews Snooze (1988: audiences are finding Tom Cruise's *Cocktail* less than thrilling)

- A Wing-Ding for the King (2004: *The Lord of the Rings: The Return of the King* proves a success at the box office)

- Bay's Bots Rock Box (2007: director Michael Bay's *Transformers* is a hit in cinemas).

Variety was first published in 1905 as a trade magazine for the entertainment industry and soon formulated its own shorthand for familiar aspects of the business. Its 'Slanguage Dictionary' includes the following terms to deal with movies and their production:

- Ankle - a classic (and enduring) *Variety* term meaning to quit or be dismissed from a job, without necessarily specifying which; instead, it suggests walking; 'Alan Smithee has ankled his post as production prexy at U.'

- Aud - audience; 'Liza Minnelli has always had a special rapport with her aud.'

- Biopic - a *Variety* coinage meaning biographical film; '*Coal Miner's Daughter*, about Loretta Lynn, is one of the most successful biopics ever produced.'

- Boff (also boffo, boffola) - outstanding (usually refers to box office performance); '*My Best Friend's Wedding* has been boffo at the B.O.' (See also socko, whammo)

- Chopsocky - a martial arts film; 'Chopsocky star Chuck Norris will make a guest appearance on *Seinfeld* this season.'

- Click - a hit; 'Disney click *The Lion King* is slated to air on ABC this season.'

- Crix - critics; 'While the director's last film was a flop with auds, the crix were in his corner.'

- Gotham - New York City; 'Film production in Gotham has been on the rise for the past several years.'

- Horse opera - Western film; 'John Carradine appeared in numerous horse operas throughout his career.'

- Hotsy - strong performance at the box office; '*The Devil's Advocate* made a hotsy bow last weekend.'

- Huddle - (v.) to have a meeting; (n.) a meeting; 'The exec was in a huddle and was not available for comment.'

- Legs - stamina at the box office; 'The film opened big but rival distribs are dubious about its legs.'

- Lense - to film a motion picture; 'The project will lense in Rome and New York.'

- Meller - melodrama; 'The company is in pre-production on a meller about a blind woman held hostage on a New York City subway.'

- Moppet - child, especially child actor; 'Elizabeth Taylor is one of the few moppets who made the transition to adult star.'

- Mouse (also Mouse House) - the Walt Disney Co. or any division thereof, a reference to the company's most famous animated character, Mickey Mouse; 'The Mouse's music division is reuniting with talent manager Alan Smithee on a joint-venture label.'

- (The) o.o. - the once-over; to examine something; 'Sylvester Stallone gave the script the o.o. before passing on it.'

- Pen - (v.) to write; 'Alan Smithee has been inked to pen the biopic about Abraham Lincoln.'

- Percenter (also tenpercenter) - agent; 'Mike Ovitz was a percenter before becoming a talent manager.'

- Pour - cocktail party; 'Universal held a pour for the press in New York to promote its upcoming release.'

- Praiser - publicist; 'A praiser for the star had no comment on the deal.'

- Preem - (n.) an opening-night or première performance; (v.) to show a completed film for the first time; 'Several of the pic's

stars were on hand for the preem' or 'The pic will preem Dec.
18.'

- Prexy (also prez) – president; 'The studio has no plans to fill
  the prexy post in the wake of the exec's resignation.'

- Shingle – a small business, often set up by an actor or
  established player at a larger company; 'Tom Green has
  launched production shingle Tom Green Films.'

- Solon – an authority; someone in the know; from the ancient
  Greek wise man, Solon; 'Solons say the deal is likely to go
  down by the end of the week.'

- Sprocket opera – film festival; 'The actor plans to attend the
  annual Sundance sprocket opera next year.'

- Tentpole – Movie expected by a studio to be its biggest
  grossing blockbuster of the season, usually summer. Often
  the pic is the start of, or an instalment in, a franchise;
  '*Armageddon* was a successful tentpole in 1998.'

- Topline – to star; to be billed above the title of a show or
  film; 'Julia Roberts will topline the director's next pic.'

- Turnaround – no longer active; a project put into 'turnaround'
  has been abandoned by one studio and may be shopped to
  another.

- Unspool – to screen a film; 'More than 30 films are set to
  unspool at the upcoming festival.'

- Wrap – to finish production; 'The picture will wrap in the next
  two weeks.'

1987 BARFLY   1987

A dissolute bohemian defends his lifestyle.

HENRY

Some people never go crazy. What truly horrible lives they
must lead.

Dir: Barbet Schroeder • Scr: Charles Bukowski • Cast: Mickey Rourke (Henry
Chinaski)

More famous for his novels than his screenplays, Bukowski was hailed by *Time Magazine* as a 'laureate of American lowlife'. His stories and films are shocking and touching in equal measure, but rarely lack his characteristic dark humour. The script contains several other bitter gems:

'It's hatred. It's the only thing that lasts.'

'So you hired a dick to find an asshole?'

'I'd hate to be you if I were me.'

'Don't be sorry, just put on some new underwear.'

1987   THE UNTOUCHABLES   1987

Veteran Chicago patrolman Malone warns Federal agent Ness he will have to abandon his scruples if he hopes to bring Al Capone to justice.

MALONE

You said you wanted to get Capone. Do you really wanna get him? You see what I'm saying is, what are you prepared to do?

NESS

Anything within the law.

MALONE

And then what are you prepared to do? If you open the can on these worms you must be prepared to go all the way. Because they're not gonna give up the fight, until one of you is dead.

NESS

I want to get Capone! I don't know how to do it.

MALONE

You wanna know how to get Capone? They pull a knife, you pull a gun. He sends one of yours to the hospital, you send one of his to the morgue. That's the Chicago way. And that's how you get Capone. Now, do you want to do that? Are you ready to do that? I'm offering you a deal. Do you want this deal?

NESS

I have sworn to capture this man with all legal powers at my disposal and I will do so.

MALONE

Well, the Lord hates a coward.

He reaches out a hand. Ness shakes it.

MALONE

Do you know what a blood oath is, Mr Ness?

NESS

Yes.

MALONE

Good, 'cause you just took one.

Dir: Brian De Palma • Scr: David Mamet • Based on a book by Oscar Fraley, Eliot Ness • Cast: Sean Connery (Jim Malone), Kevin Costner (Eliot Ness)

1988 **MISSISSIPPI BURNING** 1988

FBI agent Anderson warns his younger colleague Ward not to underestimate the determination of the Ku Klux Klan.

WARD

Some things are worth dying for.

ANDERSON

Down here, things are different. Here, they believe some things are worth killing for.

Dir: Alan Parker • Scr: Chris Gerolmo • Cast: Willem Dafoe (Alan Ward), Gene Hackman (Rupert Anderson)

1988 THEY LIVE

Nada seeks out aliens who have colonized the planet disguised as humans.

NADA

I've come here to chew bubblegum and kick ass... and I'm all out of bubblegum.

Dir: John Carpenter • Scr: John Carpenter • Based on a short story by Ray Nelson • Cast: Roddy Piper (Nada)

1989 LICENCE TO KILL

James Bond confronts drugs lord Sanchez.

BOND

In my business you prepare for the unexpected.

SANCHEZ

And what business is that?

BOND

I help people with problems.

SANCHEZ

Problem solver?

BOND

More of a problem eliminator.

Dir: John Glen • Scr: Michael G. Wilson, Richard Maibaum • Based on characters created by Ian Fleming • Cast: Timothy Dalton (James Bond), Robert Davi (Franz Sanchez)

Putting a dampener on 007's swashbuckling style, the US credits for the film feature a tobacco warning from the United States Surgeon-General. The writers had originally intended the story to be set in the heroin-producing Golden Triangle, with sequences including a motorcycle chase along the Great Wall of China and a fight scene in the museum of the Terracotta Warriors, but the Chinese authorities vetoed the script.

The film was the first to use a title not directly taken from one of Ian Fleming's James Bond novels, although the phrase 'licence to kill' occurs frequently with reference to 007's powers. *Octopussy* (1983), *The Living Daylights* (1987) and *Quantum of Solace* (2008) all took their names from short stories featuring Bond. Remaining unadapted titles include 'Property of a Lady', '007 In New York', 'Risico' and 'The Hildebrand Rarity'.

A mobster recalls the moment of his arrest.

                          HENRY

For a second I thought I was dead, but when I heard all the noise
I knew they were cops. Only cops talk that way. If they had been
wiseguys, I wouldn't have heard a thing. I would've been dead.

Dir: Martin Scorsese • Scr: Nicholas Pileggi, Martin Scorsese • Based on a
book by Nicholas Pileggi • Cast: Ray Liotta (Henry Hill)

1994 PULP FICTION

*Butch has just liberated Marsellus from being sodomized by two
hillbillies, who now lie prostrate on the floor.*

                          BUTCH

You okay?

                        MARSELLUS

Naw man. I'm pretty fuckin' far from okay.

                          BUTCH

What now?

                        MARSELLUS

What now? Let me tell you what now. I'm a call a coupla hard,
pipe-hittin' niggers who'll go to work on the homies here with
a pair of pliers and a blow torch.

He turns to the rapists.

You hear me talkin', hillbilly boy? I ain't through with you
by a damn sight. I'm a get medieval on your ass.

Dir: Quentin Tarantino • Scr: Quentin Tarantino, Roger Avary • Cast: Bruce
Willis (Butch Coolidge), Ving Rhames (Marsellus Wallace)

Quentin Tarantino (with Roger Avary) wrote many of the roles with specific actors in mind:
Harvey Keitel as The Wolf, Amanda Plummer and Tim Roth as Honey Bunny and Pumpkin, and
Samuel L. Jackson as Jules. Daniel Day-Lewis reportedly agreed to play Vincent but Tarantino
overlooked him in favour of John Travolta; the film returned Travolta to major star status after
several years of unremarkable roles. Tarantino, who plays Jimmie, had originally intended to take
the part of drug dealer Lance but decided he would prefer to give his full attention as director
in the scene where Mia (Uma Thurman) overdoses; the shot where Vincent tries to revive Mia
with a shot of adrenaline was filmed in reverse to avoid harming the actress with the needle.
The film, with its abundant references to earlier *noir* classics, was described by some critics as a

masterpiece of post-modernism. Tarantino explained that his idea was simply 'to take the oldest chestnuts that you've ever seen when it comes to crime stories... and then purposely having them run awry.'

1997 GROSSE POINTE BLANK 1997

A professional hit-man attends his high school reunion but finds it hard to explain what he has been doing since he graduated.

                    DEBI

    You're a psychopath.

                    MARTIN

    No, no. Psychopaths kill for no reason. I kill for money.
    It's a job.

Dir: George Armitage • Scr: Tom Jankiewicz, D. V. DeVincentis, Steve Pink, John Cusack • Cast: Minnie Driver (Debi Newberry), John Cusack (Martin Q. Blank)

Martin later elucidates: 'I killed the president of Paraguay with a fork. How have you been?'

1999 FIGHT CLUB 1999

Tyler Durden founds an anarchic self-help group where members fight one another to vent their anger against a conformist, consumerist world.

TYLER

Welcome to Fight Club. The first rule of Fight Club is: you
do not talk about Fight Club. The second rule of Fight Club
is: you do not talk about Fight Club. The third rule of Fight
Club: someone yells stop, goes limp, taps out, the fight is
over. The fourth rule: only two guys to a fight. The fifth
rule: one fight at a time, fellas. The sixth rule: no shirts,
no shoes. The seventh rule: fights will go on as long as they
have to. And the eighth and final rule: if this is your first
night at Fight Club, you have to fight.

Dir: David Fincher • Scr: Jim Uhls • Based on a novel by Chuck Palahniuk •
Cast: Brad Pitt (Tyler Durden)

When Tyler first sleeps with Marla, she was supposed to shock him with the line: 'I want to have
your abortion.' The studio objected, so director David Fincher agreed to change it provided the
executives made no further comment. They agreed, so Fincher had Marla say: 'I haven't been
fucked like that since grade school [primary school].' Author Chuck Palahniuk said he thought
the film better than his novel.

2000 THE CONTENDER   2000

Republican Congressman Shelly Runyon challenges Democrat
President Evans over the appointment of a new vice president.

SHELLY

We're both sticking to our guns. The difference is, mine are
loaded.

Dir: Rod Lurie • Scr: Rod Lurie • Cast: Gary Oldman (Shelly Runyon)

2001 HEIST   2001

Two gold thieves have fallen out over how to divide the spoils.

MICKEY

Don't you want to hear my last words?

JOE

I just did.

Dir: David Mamet • Scr: David Mamet • Cast: Danny DeVito (Mickey Bergman),
Gene Hackman (Joe Moore)

BEND OVER

David Mamet (b. 1947) rose to fame as a playwright, winning a Pulitzer Prize for Drama with *Glengarry Glen Ross* in 1984. Hollywood studios soon wooed him, hoping his terse, intelligent dialogue and tight plotting would translate into Oscar successes for their movies. The producers he worked with were soon to discover that his uncompromising working methods and dislike of leaving his home town Chicago made for a distinctly un-Californian partnership. His thoughts on the film industry are as lively as his screenplays:

> Working as a screenwriter, I always thought that 'Film is a collaborative business' only constituted half of the actual phrase. From a screenwriter's point of view the correct rendering should be 'Film is a collaborative business: bend over'.

> Life in the movie business is like the beginning of a new love affair: it's full of surprises, and you're constantly getting fucked.

> Thank God Hollywood people don't have souls so they don't have to suffer through their lives.

> Hollywood is like cocaine. You cannot understand its attraction until you are doing it. And when you are doing it, you are insane.

Nevertheless his Oscar nominations for *The Verdict* (1982) and *Wag the Dog* (1997) and his success with *The Postman Always Rings Twice* (1981) and *The Untouchables* (1987) have kept him in fierce demand. Many of his statements in interviews have become mantras for screenwriters:

> We respond to a drama to that extent to which it corresponds to our dream life.

> Every scene should be able to answer three questions: 'Who wants what from whom? What happens if they don't get it? Why now?'

> People may or may not say what they mean, but they always say something designed to get what they want.

He often uses the fees he earns from uncredited rewriting on troubled projects to fund his own directorial efforts. These include *House of Games* (1987), *State and Main* (2000) and *Heist* (2001). The latter film contains much of his famous 'Mamet-speak', as well as some outstanding dark humour:

PINKY: My motherfucker is so cool, when he goes to bed, sheep count him.

BERGMAN: Everybody needs money. That's why they call it money.

BERGMAN: Do you want to tell me what made you a criminal?
JOE MOORE: What made *you* a criminal?
BERGMAN: Nothing made me a criminal. I *am* a criminal.

JOE MOORE: She could talk her way out of a sunburn.

BOBBY BLANE: There's nothing wrong with prayer. We knew this firefighter, this trooper, who always carried a bible next to his heart. We used to mock him, but that bible stopped a bullet.
JIMMY: No shit.
BOBBY BLANE: Hand of God, that bible stopped a bullet, would of ruined that fucker's heart. And had he had another bible in front of his face, that man would be alive today.

D.A. FRECCIA: You're a pretty smart fellow.
JOE MOORE: Ah, not that smart.
D.A. FRECCIA: If you're not that smart, how'd you figure it out?
JOE MOORE: I tried to imagine a fellow smarter than myself. Then I tried to think, 'what would he do?'

2008 IN BRUGES   2008

Ray goes to make a surprising confession.

PRIEST
Why did you murder someone, Raymond?

RAY
For money, father.

PRIEST
For money? You murdered someone for money?

                            RAY
Yes, father. Not out of anger. Not out of nothing. For money.

                           PRIEST
Who did you murder for money, Raymond?

                            RAY
You, father.

                           PRIEST
I'm sorry?

                            RAY
I said you, father. What are you, deaf?

He raises a pistol.
                            RAY
Harry Waters says hello.

Dir: Martin McDonagh • Scr: Martin McDonagh • Cast: Ciarán Hinds (Priest),
Colin Farrell (Ray)

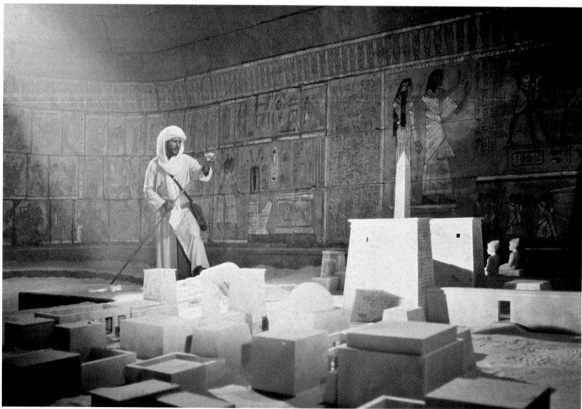

Daredevil archeologist Dr Indiana Jones takes us back to the days of the Saturday matinée adventure movie in *Raiders of the Lost Ark* (1981).

Michael Cimino's *Heaven's Gate* was a critical and financial disaster but offered stunning performances and photography.

Sharon Stone in her most controversial role in *Basic Instinct* (1992) – the perfect pin-up for the glossy 1990s.

Vamps

1930 HELL'S ANGELS   1930

Helen exchanges her fur wrap for a dressing gown.

HELEN

Would you be shocked if I put on something more comfortable?

Dir: Howard Hughes • Scr: Howard Estabrook, Marshall Neilan, James
Moncure March, Harry Behn • Cast: Jean Harlow (Helen)

1932 THE CABIN IN THE COTTON   1932

After asking Marvin out on a date, Madge finds herself bashful.

MADGE

I'd like to kiss you, but I just washed my hair.

Dir: Michael Curtiz • Scr: Paul Green • Based on a novel by Harry Harrison
Kroll • Cast: Bette Davis (Madge Norwood)

Davis claimed in an interview after she retired that this was her all-time favourite movie line. Her
reputation as a competitive actress caused Vincent Sherman to say of her and Miriam Hopkins,
who co-starred in *Old Acquaintance* (1930): 'I didn't direct them, I refereed.'

'EXCESSIVE OR LUSTFUL KISSING'

The Cinematograph Act of 1909 was introduced largely to protect the
public from the hazards of highly flammable nitrate prints but the
authorities quickly realized that the content of a motion picture
could also be incendiary.

Although we tend to look back on the earliest surviving films as
charming echoes of a bygone era, we should remember that some of the
pioneers — Eisenstein, Griffith and Chaplin — were trying to tell
stories as sophisticated as those of their literary peers. Crude
technologies may have hampered them, but they dealt with controversial
subjects such as racism, revolution and sexual desire. As early as
1906 some American cities passed local laws regulating content,
but most forms of censorship proved unwieldy and unenforceable.
Meanwhile, directors grew bolder and stars more smouldering.

At the same time, audiences were growing at an astonishing rate; by
1930 two thirds of Americans were going to the movies at least once
a week. Governments remained slow to react to this new influence on
their citizens and were forced to invoke outdated laws regulating
obscenity, blasphemy and libel as guidelines; religious groups were
far quicker to show outrage at themes they considered unsuitable
for their congregations.

Incensed by the further danger of talking pictures, Daniel Lord, a leading American Catholic, wrote: 'Silent smut had been bad. Vocal smut cried to the censors for vengeance.' Some states tried to enact legislation but with little effect, so Lord and his Jesuit brother-in-arms Martin Quigley took their crusade directly to Hollywood.

Producers, aware that the vast majority of their customers were under twenty-five, feared that unless they joined forces to regulate their own output the business would destroy itself. They agreed to Lord and Quigley's proposals and on 19 February 1930 *Variety* published the Motion Picture Production Code. Will Hays, a Presbyterian Republican and President of the Motion Picture Producers and Distributors of America, was chosen to be its head of enforcement.

The Hays Code, as it became known, was widely ridiculed for its moralizing tone and was initially impossible to implement. Under the section 'The Don'ts and Be Carefuls', it stipulated:

> Those things which are included in the following list shall not appear in pictures produced by the members of this Association, irrespective of the manner in which they are treated:

- Pointed profanity - by either title or lip - this includes the words God, Lord, Jesus, Christ (unless they be used reverently in connection with proper religious ceremonies), hell, damn, Gawd, and every other profane and vulgar expression however it may be spelled;

- Any licentious or suggestive nudity, in fact or in silhouette;

- Any inference of sex perversion (homosexuality);

- White slavery;

- Miscegenation (sex relationships between the white and black races);

- Children's sex organs;

- Ridicule of the clergy.

It further advised that:

- Special care be exercised in the manner in which the following subjects are treated:

- Theft, robbery, safe-cracking, and dynamiting of trains, mines, buildings, etc. (having in mind the effect which a too-detailed description of these may have upon the moron);

- Brutality and possible gruesomeness;

- First-night scenes (one-night stands);

- Man and woman in bed together;

- Deliberate seduction of girls;

- The institution of marriage;

- Excessive or lustful kissing, particularly when one character or the other is a 'heavy'.

1933 DUCK SOUP   1933

Rufus (Groucho Marx) encourages his brothers to defend Mrs Teasdale.

RUFUS T. FIREFLY

Remember, you're fighting for this woman's honour, which is probably more than she ever did.

Dir: Leo McCarey • Scr: Bert Kalmar, Harry Ruby • Cast: Groucho Marx (Rufus T. Firefly)

1933 I'M NO ANGEL

Jack has fallen in love with Tira, a circus lion-tamer.

JACK

You were wonderful tonight.

TIRA

Yeah, I'm always wonderful at night.

JACK

Tonight you were especially good.

TIRA

Well, when I'm good, I'm very good. But when I'm bad, I'm better.

Dir: Wesley Ruggles • Scr: Mae West • Cast: Cary Grant (Jack Clayton), Mae West (Tira)

1944 TO HAVE AND HAVE NOT

Slim Browning and Harry 'Steve' Morgan settle their differences with a kiss.

SLIM

You know you don't have to act with me, Steve. You don't have to say anything, and you don't have to do anything. Not a thing. Oh, maybe just whistle. You know how to whistle, don't you, Steve? You just put your lips together and... blow.

Dir: Howard Hawks • Scr: Jules Furthman, William Faulkner • Based on a novel by Ernest Hemingway • Cast: Lauren Bacall (Marie 'Slim' Browning)

All great lines invite parody. In *Dead Men Don't Wear Plaid* (1982), the heroine purrs: 'If you need me, just call. You know how to dial, don't you? You just put your finger in the hole and make tiny little circles.'

1946 THE BIG SLEEP

VIVIAN

Speaking of horses, I like to play them myself. But I like to see them work out a little first, see if they're front-runners or come from behind, find out what their whole card is, what makes them run.

MARLOWE

Find out mine?

VIVIAN

I think so.

MARLOWE

Go ahead.

VIVIAN

I'd say you don't like to be rated. You like to get out in front, open up a little lead, take a little breather in the backstretch, and then come home free.

MARLOWE

You don't like to be rated yourself.

VIVIAN

I haven't met anyone yet that can do it. Any suggestions?

MARLOWE

Well, I can't tell till I've seen you over a distance of ground. You've got a touch of class, but I don't know how far you can go.

VIVIAN

A lot depends on who's in the saddle.

Dir: Howard Hawks • Scr: William Faulkner, Leigh Brackett, Jules Furthman • Based on a novel by Raymond Chandler • Cast: Lauren Bacall (Vivian Rutledge), Humphrey Bogart (Philip Marlowe)

1946 NOTORIOUS 1946

Alicia, fond of both drink and men, falls for the man who has recruited her as a spy.

DEVLIN

Don't you need a coat?

ALICIA

You'll do.

Dir: Alfred Hitchcock • Scr: Ben Hecht • Cast: Cary Grant (T. R. Devlin), Ingrid Bergman (Alicia Huberman)

Director Hitchcock claimed the FBI had him under surveillance during the shoot as the film dealt with uranium, a component of nuclear weapons. The famous sequence where Cary Grant and Ingrid Bergman kiss, only to separate and then resume, was designed to circumvent the Hays Code ruling that a screen embrace should last no more than three seconds.

1949   WHITE HEAT   1949

Verna tries to persuade her gangster husband to buy her a present.

> VERNA
>
> I'd look good in a mink coat, honey.

> CODY
>
> You'd look good in a shower curtain.

Dir: Raoul Walsh • Scr: Ivan Goff, Ben Roberts • Based on a story by Virginia Kellogg • Cast: Virginia Mayo (Verna Jarrett), James Cagney (Arthur 'Cody' Jarrett)

In the days before 'squibs' – tiny explosive charges detonated by special effects teams – gunfights were recreated using trained marksmen to fire actual low-velocity bullets. Cagney, a fearless performer of many of his own stunts, was nearly hit on several occasions. Despite his huge box office success he remained remarkably modest, saying: 'I hate the word superstar... You don't hear them speak of Shakespeare as a superpoet. You don't hear them call Michelangelo a superpainter. They only apply the word to this mundane market.'

1950   ALL ABOUT EVE   1950

Margo Channing, a famous actress, has lost none of her pride as she grows older.

> MARGO
>
> I'll admit I may have seen better days, but I'm still not to be had for the price of a cocktail, like a salted peanut.

Dir: Joseph L. Mankiewicz • Scr: Joseph L. Mankiewicz • Based on a story by Mary Orr • Cast: Bette Davis (Margo Channing)

1951   AN AMERICAN IN PARIS   1951

> JERRY
>
> That's quite a dress you almost have on.

> MILO
>
> Thanks.

What holds it up?

MILO

Modesty.

Dir: Vincente Minnelli • Scr: Alan Jay Lerner • Cast: Gene Kelly (Jerry
Mulligan), Nina Foch (Milo Roberts)

1953 GENTLEMEN PREFER BLONDES   1953

The wealthy Mr Esmond is suspicious of Lorelei's love for his son.

LORELEI

Don't you know that a man being rich is like a girl being
pretty? You wouldn't marry a girl just because she's pretty,
but my goodness, doesn't it help?

Dir: Howard Hawks • Scr: Charles Lederer • Based on the musical by Joseph
Fields and a novel and play by Anita Loos • Cast: Marilyn Monroe (Lorelei Lee)

Criminal mastermind Auric Goldfinger has asked one of his associates to take care of his prisoner James Bond.

> PUSSY

My name is Pussy Galore.

> BOND

I must be dreaming.

Dir: Guy Hamilton • Scr: Richard Maibaum, Paul Dehn • Based on a novel by Ian Fleming • Cast: Honor Blackman (Pussy Galore), Sean Connery (James Bond)

KEEPING THE BRITISH END UP

James Bond, commander in the Royal Naval Reserve but employed by the Secret Intelligence Service under the code name 007, first appeared in *Casino Royale* in 1952. Its opening sentence read: 'The scent and smoke and sweat of a casino are nauseating at three in the morning.'

Fleming — who had been involved in intelligence work during the Second World War — intended to portray the life of a secret agent in its full seamy, cynical reality. Of his creation he once said: 'Exotic things would happen to and around him but he would be a neutral figure — an anonymous blunt instrument wielded by a Government Department... Apart from the fact that he wears the same clothes that I wear, he and I really have little in common. I do rather envy him his blondes and his efficiency, but I can't say I much like the chap.'

Bond's sexual innuendo, more a hallmark of the films than of the original novels, echoes Fleming's own chauvinism: 'Men want a woman whom they can turn on and off like a light switch.' Ten years after 007's literary début, his creator admitted: 'The target of my books lay somewhere between the solar plexus and the upper thigh.'

Screenwriters, directors and actors for fifty years have responded to the challenge of portraying this enigmatic figure, yet audiences remain determined to champion a man whose humour remains as dry as his martinis:

> BOND: It's just the right size - for me, that is.
> *From Russia With Love* (1963)

> BOND: Something big's come up.
> *Goldfinger* (1964)

BOND: I'm afraid you've caught me with more than my hands up.
Diamonds Are Forever (1971)

PLENTY O'TOOLE: Hi, I'm Plenty.
BOND: But of course you are.
PLENTY O'TOOLE: Plenty O'Toole.
BOND: Named after your father perhaps?
Diamonds Are Forever (1971)

BOND: Miss Anders! I didn't recognize you with your clothes on.
The Man with the Golden Gun (1974)

BOND: Just keeping the British end up.
The Spy Who Loved Me (1977)

BOND: When one is in Egypt, one should delve deeply into its treasures.
The Spy Who Loved Me (1977)

MINISTER OF DEFENCE: My God, what's Bond doing?
Q: I think he's attempting re-entry, sir.
Moonraker (1979)

BOND: You appear tense... That's too bad. Going down, one should always be relaxed.
Never Say Never Again (1983)

FATIMA BLUSH: Oh, how reckless of me. I made you all wet.
BOND: Yes, but my martini is still dry. My name is James.
Never Say Never Again (1983)

BOND: Well my dear, I take it you spend quite a lot of time in the saddle.
JENNY FLEX: Yes, I love an early morning ride.
BOND: Well, I'm an early riser myself.
A View to a Kill (1985)

XENIA ONATOPP: You don't need the gun, Commander.
BOND: Well, that depends on your definition of safe sex.
GoldenEye (1995)

MISS MONEYPENNY: You know, this sort of behaviour could qualify as sexual harassment.
BOND: Really. What's the penalty for that?
MISS MONEYPENNY: Someday, you'll have to make good on your innuendos.
GoldenEye (1995)

BOND: I always enjoyed learning a new tongue.
MONEYPENNY: You always were a cunning linguist, James.
Tomorrow Never Dies (1997)

BOND: I was wrong about you.
CHRISTMAS JONES: Yeah, how so?
BOND: I thought Christmas only comes once a year.
The World Is Not Enough (1999)

1965 DARLING   1965

Robert has fallen in love with headstrong model Diana but is
frustrated that she continues to have affairs.

ROBERT

Your idea of fidelity is not having more than one man in bed
at the same time.

Dir: John Schlesinger • Scr: Frederic Raphael • Cast: Dirk Bogarde (Robert
Gold)

1967 THE GRADUATE   1967

An older woman tries to seduce her daughter's boyfriend.

MRS ROBINSON

Sit down, Benjamin.

BENJAMIN

If you don't mind my saying so - this conversation is getting
a little strange. Now I'm sure that Mr Robinson will be here
any minute and -

MRS ROBINSON

No.

BENJAMIN

What?

MRS ROBINSON

My husband will be back quite late.

She makes her meaning clearer:

He should be gone for several hours.

She moves towards him.

                    BENJAMIN

Oh my God.

                    MRS ROBINSON

Pardon?

                    BENJAMIN

Oh no, Mrs Robinson, oh no.

                    MRS ROBINSON

What's wrong?

                    BENJAMIN

Mrs Robinson, you didn't - I mean you didn't expect -

                    MRS ROBINSON

What?

                    BENJAMIN

I mean - you didn't really think that I would do something
like that.

                    MRS ROBINSON

Like what?

                    BENJAMIN

What do you think?

                    MRS ROBINSON

Well, I don't know.

                    BENJAMIN

For God's sake, Mrs Robinson, here we are, you've got me into
your house. You give me a drink. You put on music, now you
start opening up your personal life to me and tell me your
husband won't be home for hours.

                    MRS ROBINSON

So?

                    BENJAMIN

Mrs Robinson - you *are* trying to seduce me.

He hesitates. She holds his gaze.

    Aren't you?

Dir: Mike Nichols • Scr: Calder Willingham, Buck Henry • Based on a novel
by Charles Webb • Cast: Anne Bancroft (Mrs Robinson), Dustin Hoffman
(Benjamin Braddock)

Mel Brooks had already cast Dustin Hoffman in his upcoming film *The Producers* and only
let Hoffman audition for *The Graduate* because he was convinced the actor would never be
right for the role of Benjamin. Hoffman got the part, and was bemused to find himself starring
opposite Anne Bancroft – Mel Brooks's wife.

1970 MYRA BRECKINRIDGE   1970

*Leticia, a libidinous seventy-year-old, runs a casting agency 'for
leading men'.*

LETICIA

How tall are you, son?

ACTOR

Ma'am, I'm six feet seven inches.

LETICIA

Never mind about the six feet. Let's talk about the seven
inches.

Dir: Michael Sarne • Scr: Michael Sarne, David Giler • Based on a novel by
Gore Vidal • Cast: Mae West (Leticia Van Allen), Cal Bartlett (Actor)

1970 BEYOND THE VALLEY OF THE DOLLS   1970

*Porn star Ashley St Ives takes a shine to the manager of a rock
band.*

ASHLEY

You're a groovy boy. I'd like to strap you on sometime.

Dir: Russ Meyer • Scr: Russ Meyer, Roger Ebert • Cast: Edy Williams
(Ashley St Ives)

Director Russ Meyer trained as a cameraman in the US Army and some of the footage he shot
during the Second World War can be seen in *Patton* (1970). He hoped to pursue a career as a
cinematographer in Hollywood but strict union rules debarred him from membership, so he
turned his hand to directing and developed a cult following for his cheerfully sleazy pictures.
Defending his reputation as a salacious storyteller, he said: 'Nothing is obscene providing it is
done in bad taste.'

1977 LOOKING FOR MR GOODBAR   1977

A bartender shares his views on drinking with a customer.

BARTENDER

Confidentially, with me... one's too many and a million's not
enough.

THERESA

I got the same problem with men.

Dir: Richard Brooks • Scr: Richard Brooks • Based on a novel by Judith
Rossner • Cast: Eddie Garrett (Bartender), Diane Keaton (Theresa Dunn)

1979 ALL THAT JAZZ   1979

Two showgirls commiserate after an open casting call.

DANCER BACKSTAGE 1

Fuck him! He never picks me!

DANCER BACKSTAGE 2

Honey, I did fuck him and he never picks me either.

Dir: Bob Fosse • Scr: Robert Alan Aurthur, Bob Fosse • Cast: uncredited

1980 DRESSED TO KILL   1980

*Call girl Liz finds herself attracted to a psychiatrist who may
hold the answer to an unsolved murder.*

LIZ

Do you want to fuck me?

DR ELLIOTT

Oh, yes.

LIZ

Then why don't you?

DR ELLIOTT

Because I'm a doctor and...

LIZ

Fucked a lot of doctors.

DR ELLIOTT

... and I'm married.

LIZ

Fucked a lot of them, too.

Dir: Brian De Palma • Scr: Brian De Palma • Cast: Nancy Allen (Liz Blake),
Michael Caine (Dr Robert Elliott)

1981 BODY HEAT   1981

NED

Maybe you shouldn't dress like that.

MATTY

This is a blouse and a skirt. I don't know what you're talking
about.

NED

You shouldn't wear that body.

Dir: Lawrence Kasdan • Scr: Lawrence Kasdan • Cast: William Hurt (Ned
Racine), Kathleen Turner (Matty Walker)

William Hurt and Kathleen Turner wanted to make sure the crew didn't feel bashful when they
filmed their love scenes, so to break the ice they introduced themselves to everyone on the set
– naked.

1983 GORKY PARK 1983

A Moscow black marketeer is accused of providing prostitutes for visitors.

GOLODKIN

Girls like screwing foreigners, don't they? It's almost as good as travel.

Dir: Michael Apted • Scr: Dennis Potter • Based on a novel by Martin Cruz Smith • Cast: Alexei Sayle (Golodkin)

1983 NOSTALGIA (*NOSTALGHIA*) 1983

Eugenia is unsure why she feels attracted to her married colleague Andrei.

EUGENIA

You're the kind of man I'd sleep with rather than explain why I don't feel like it.

Dir: Andrei Tarkovsky • Scr: Tonino Guerra, Andrei Tarkovsky • Cast: Domiziana Giordano (Eugenia)

Tarkovsky's first film shot outside the Soviet Union had to be awarded a special prize at the Cannes Festival in 1983 because the Soviet authorities had forbidden him to accept the prestigious Palme D'Or.

1988 WHO FRAMED ROGER RABBIT? 1988

Despite her curvaceous figure, cartoon character Jessica Rabbit knows how to sound bashful.

JESSICA RABBIT

I'm not bad. I'm just drawn that way.

Dir: Robert Zemeckis • Scr: Jeffrey Price, Peter S. Seaman • Based on a novel by Gary K. Wolf • Cast: Kathleen Turner (voice of Jessica Rabbit)

Bob Hoskins (starring opposite Jessica Rabbit) had to act with cut-outs and dummies representing the cartoon characters who had yet to be drawn for the film. He studied his young daughter to learn how to interact with imaginary friends but found the whole experience so disorienting that he began to suffer hallucinations.

The film offers cameos for many of cinema's most memorable animated characters, including Mickey Mouse, Minnie Mouse, Pluto, Donald Duck, Goofy, the Three Little Pigs and the Big Bad Wolf, Snow White and all seven dwarfs, Pinocchio and Jiminy Cricket, Dumbo, Bambi, Chicken Little, Peter and the Wolf, Tinker Bell from *Peter Pan*, the penguins from *Mary Poppins*, Bugs Bunny, Daffy Duck, Porky Pig, Tweety, Sylvester, Yosemite Sam, Foghorn Leghorn, Road Runner, Wile E. Coyote, Speedy Gonzales, Betty Boop and Woody Woodpecker.

AS SOON AS I GET THE REWRITE

Awarding the 2003 Oscar for Best Adapted Screenplay, Steve Martin quipped: 'I handed in a script last year and the studio didn't change one word. The word they didn't change was on page eighty-seven.' Screenwriters may be the unsung heroes of their own jokes but they are under no illusion about the way their talents are viewed by the industry:

Did you hear about the dumb but ambitious starlet?
She slept with the screenwriter.

The screenwriter of a Frank Capra comedy was watching a
TV interview with the great director. An awestruck female
reporter was heaping praise on a passage from the writer's
script, and Frank explained the scene's charm by saying:
'That's the Capra touch.' The reporter continued to praise
scenes in many other Capra movies. In each case the director's
comment was: 'That's the Capra touch.' The writer responsible
for the script couldn't take it any more so he stuffed 120
blank sheets of paper in an envelope and sent the package to
the director with the note: 'Put the Capra touch on this.'

Q. How many screenwriters does it take to screw in a light bulb?
A. Does it really need to be changed?

Q. How many development executives does it take to change a
light bulb?
A. One – but does it have to be a light bulb?

Q. How many screenwriters does it take to change a light bulb?
A. Ten.

1st draft: Hero changes light bulb.

2nd draft: Villain changes light bulb.

3rd draft: Hero stops villain from changing light bulb. Villain falls to
death.

4th draft: Cut the light bulb.

5th draft: Reinstate light bulb. Fluorescent instead of tungsten.

6th draft: Villain breaks bulb, uses it to kill hero's mentor.

7th draft: Fluorescent not working. Back to tungsten.

8th draft: Hero forces villain to eat light bulb.

9th draft: Hero laments loss of light bulb. Doesn't change it.

10th draft: Hero changes light bulb.

Q. How many agents does it take to screw in a light bulb?
A. Three - one to screw it in, and two to hold down the screenwriter.

A screenwriter dies and is given the choice of going to heaven or to hell, so she decides to visit each place first. As she enters the satanic realms she sees a thousand writers shackled to their typewriters in a fiery furnace being lashed by overseers.

Shocked, she leaves and sets out to inspect heaven. There, she discovers another thousand writers chained to the same typewriters and receiving the same whipping. Turning to an angel, she says in surprise: 'But this is just the same as hell!'

The angel replies: 'Sure, but here your script goes into production.'

Two development execs meet in the hallway. One says, 'Hey, what's cooking?' The second one, extremely excited, replies, 'I just bought this script. It's the most perfect piece of writing I've ever seen. Characters, story, everything about it is A1. Academy Award time.'

'That's fantastic,' says the first one, dripping with envy. 'So when do you go into production?'

'As soon as I get the rewrite.'

1988   BULL DURHAM   1988

A baseball groupie confesses she likes to read poetry to her lovers.

ANNIE

A guy'll listen to anything if he thinks it's foreplay.

Dir: Ron Shelton • Scr: Ron Shelton • Cast: Susan Sarandon (Annie Savoy)

1988   WORKING GIRL   1988

Tess is determined to stay true to herself in a tough corporate world.

TESS

I have a head for business and a bod for sin. Is there anything wrong with that?

Dir: Mike Nichols • Scr: Kevin Wade • Cast: Melanie Griffith (Tess McGill)

Lula makes no attempt to hide her passion for her lover.

LULA

Uh oh... Baby, you'd better get me back to that hotel. You got me hotter than Georgia asphalt.

Dir: David Lynch • Scr: David Lynch • Based on a novel by Barry Gifford • Cast: Laura Dern (Lula Pace Fortune)

1994   **THE LAST SEDUCTION**

When Linda first meets Mike she makes her wishes crystal clear.

BRIDGET

You're my designated fuck.

MIKE

Designated fuck? Do they make cards for that? What if I want to be more than your designated fuck?

BRIDGET

Then I'll designate someone else.

Dir: John Dahl • Scr: Steve Barancik • Cast: Linda Fiorentino (Bridget Gregory), Peter Berg (Mike Swale)

DANGEROUS BEAUTY

A courtesan in sixteenth-century Venice defends herself against the hypocrisy of her interrogators.

VERONICA

I confess that as a young girl I loved a man who would not marry me for want of a dowry. I confess I had a mother who taught me a different way of life, one I resisted at first but learned to embrace. I confess I became a courtesan, traded yearning for power, welcomed many rather than be owned by one. I confess I embraced a whore's freedom over a wife's obedience. I confess I find more ecstasy in passion than in prayer. Such passion *is* prayer. I confess I pray still to feel the touch of my lover's lips, his hands upon me, his arms enfolding me... Such surrender has been mine. I confess I pray still to be filled and inflamed. To melt into the dream of us, beyond this troubled place, to where we are not even ourselves. To know that always, this is mine. If this had not been mine - if I had lived any other way - a child to her husband's will, my soul hardened from lack of touch and lack of love... I confess such endless days and nights would be a punishment far greater than you could ever mete out. You, all of you, you who hunger so for what I give, yet cannot bear to see that kind of power in a woman. You call God's greatest gift - ourselves, our yearning, our need to love - you call it filth and sin and heresy... I repent there was no other way open to me. I do not repent my life.

Dir: Marshall Herskovitz • Scr: Jeannine Dominy • Based on a book by Margaret Rosenthal • Cast: Catherine McCormack (Veronica Franco)

2001   *Y TU MAMÁ TAMBIÉN*   2001

A young woman encourages her lover to approach her tenderly.

LUISA

You have to make the clitoris your best friend.

TENOCH

What kind of friend is always hiding?

Dir: Alfonso Cuarón • Scr: Alfonso Cuarón, Carlos Cuarón • Cast: Maribel Verdú (Luisa Cortés), Diego Luna (Tenoch Iturbide)

The Mexican film was released in most countries with its original title. Its literal translation (*And Your Mother Too*) fails to convey its common usage as a retort to a wide range of insults.

Katie leaves her summer camp admirer in no doubt about his prospects as her boyfriend.

KATIE

Listen, Coop. Last night was really great. You were incredibly romantic and heroic, no doubt about it. And that's great. But I've thought about it, and my thing is this. Andy is really hot. And don't get me wrong, you're cute too, but Andy is like, cut. From marble. He's gorgeous. He has this beautiful face and this incredible body, and I genuinely don't care that he's kinda lame. I don't even care that he cheats on me. And I like you more than I like Andy, Coop, but I'm sixteen. And maybe it'll be a different story when I'm ready to get married, but right now, I am entirely about sex. I just wanna get laid. I just wanna take him and grab him and fuck his brains out, ya know? So that's where my priorities are right now. Sex. Specifically with Andy and not with you.

Dir: David Wain • Scr: David Wain, Michael Showalter • Cast: Marguerite Moreau (Katie)

This unusual portrait of Hannibal Lecter and FBI agent Clarice Starling in *Silence of the Lambs* (1991) echoes their ambivalent relationship on screen.

Peter O'Toole as T. E. Lawrence. The actor's good looks and the ambiguous sexuality of his character caused some wits to dub David Lean's 1962 epic 'Florence of Arabia'.

The crazed scientist and his monster enjoy a break on the set of James Whale's *Bride of Frankenstein* (1935).

Monsters

DRACULA

I am Dracula. I bid you welcome.

Dir: Tod Browning • Scr: Garrett Fort • Based on a play by Hamilton Deane,
John L. Balderston, adapted from the novel by Bram Stoker • Cast: Bela
Lugosi (Count Dracula)

No cosmetic modifications were made to Bela Lugosi's teeth for the film; his Dracula has no fangs. Cinematographer Karl Freund intensified the monster's piercing gaze by highlighting each eye with an individual keylight. Sound was still a recent innovation in films and the studio feared audiences would be confused by 'invisible' orchestral accompaniment, so the only time we hear music is during the title sequence and when Dracula meets Mina outside a theatre.

1932 ISLAND OF LOST SOULS   1932

*A scientist obsessed by evolution struggles to control the half-
human creatures he has bred from wild animals.*

DR MOREAU

What is the law?

SAYER OF THE LAW

Not to eat meat, that is the law. Are we not men?

BEASTS

Are we not men!

DR MOREAU

What is the law?

SAYER OF THE LAW

Not to go on all fours, that is the law. Are we not men?

BEASTS

Are we not men!

DR MOREAU

What is the law?

SAYER OF THE LAW

Not to spill blood, that is the law. Are we not men?

BEASTS

Are we not men!

Dir: Erle C. Kenton • Scr: Waldemar Young, Philip Wylie • Based on a novel
by H. G. Wells • Cast: Charles Laughton (Dr Moreau), Bela Lugosi (Sayer of
the Law)

1933   KING KONG   1933

*King Kong's captor Denham pays wistful tribute as the giant
ape is killed.*

POLICE LIEUTENANT

Well, Denham, the airplanes got him.

DENHAM

Oh no, it wasn't the airplanes - it was beauty killed the
beast.

Dir: Merian C. Cooper (uncredited), Ernest B. Schoedsack
(uncredited) • Scr: James Ashmore Creelman, Ruth Rose, Merian C.
Cooper • Based on a story by Edgar Wallace • Cast: Unknown (Police
Lieutenant), Robert Armstrong (Carl Denham)

Merian Cooper and Ernest Schoedsack jointly directed the film but were also its producers, only
taking the screen credit as the latter. Conveniently they had both been wrestlers and were able
to act out the fight between Kong and the Tyrannosaurus Rex to help the animators.

1938   ANGELS WITH DIRTY FACES 1938

Recently released from a reformatory, Rocky is keen to make an impression on his old neighbourhood associates.

ROCKY

Morning, gentlemen. Nice day for a murder.

Dir: Michael Curtiz • Scr: Rowland Brown, John Wexley, Warren Duff • Cast: James Cagney (Rocky Sullivan)

1939   THE WIZARD OF OZ 1939

WICKED WITCH OF THE WEST

Oh, you cursed brat! Look what you've done. I'm melting! Melting! Oh, what a world! What a world! Who would have thought a good little girl like you could destroy my beautiful wickedness?

Dir: Victor Fleming • Scr: Noel Langley, Florence Ryerson, Edgar Allan Woolf • Based on a novel by L. Frank Baum • Cast: Margaret Hamilton (Wicked Witch of the West)

1946   BEAUTY AND THE BEAST (*LA BELLE ET LA BÊTE*) 1946

THE BEAST

Belle, you must not look into my eyes. You need not fear. You will never see me except each evening at seven when you will dine, and I will come to the great hall. And never look into my eyes.

Dir: Jean Cocteau • Scr: Jean Cocteau • Based on a story by Jeanne-Marie Leprince de Beaumont • Cast: Jean Marais (The Beast)

1957   THE SEVENTH SEAL (*DET SJUNDE INSEGLET*) 1957

A wandering knight seeks the help of a witch in his struggle for faith.

ANTONIUS

Have you met the devil? I want to meet him too.

WITCH

Why do you want to do that?

ANTONIUS

I want to ask him about God. He must know. He, if anyone.

Dir: Ingmar Bergman • Scr: Ingmar Bergman, based on his play • Cast: Max von Sydow (Antonius Block), Maud Hansson (Witch)

The iconic shot of figures dancing behind Death on a distant hilltop was nearly abandoned because most of the actors had left for the day. Bergman only managed to complete it with the help of passing tourists.

1960 PSYCHO 1960

A shy motel owner tries to reassure a guest that the argument she has overheard is nothing to worry about.

NORMAN

It's not like my mother is a maniac or a raving thing. She just goes a little mad sometimes. We all go a little mad sometimes. Haven't you?

MARION

Yes. Sometimes just one time can be enough.

Dir: Alfred Hitchcock • Scr: Joseph Stefano • Based on a novel by Robert Bloch • Cast: Anthony Perkins (Norman Bates), Janet Leigh (Marion Crane)

Hitchcock was so keen to keep the ending a secret that after he secured the rights to the novel he tried to buy up all unsold copies to stop word spreading. Rumours circulated that he shot the film in black and white because the blood in the shower scene would be too shocking in colour, but later he said he was just curious to see if he could make a success of a production shot like a low-budget B-movie.

A BODY IN THE COACH

A 2007 poll of critics in the *Daily Telegraph* hailed Alfred Hitchcock (1899–1980) as 'Unquestionably the greatest filmmaker to emerge from these islands, [he] did more than any director to shape modern cinema...His flair was for narrative, cruelly withholding crucial information (from his characters and from us) and engaging the emotions of the audience like no one else.'

The American magazine *MovieMaker* was more succinct, declaring him 'The most influential filmmaker of all time'.

Recurring themes of suspicion, anxiety and a mistrust of authority clearly have their roots in his upbringing. Born in the East End of London, he was educated by strict Jesuits, and his own father once sent him — at the age of five — to the local police station with a note asking the officer to lock him in a cell for five minutes as a punishment for bad behaviour.

Before finding his first film employment as a designer of title cards, he wrote short stories which further reflected his macabre, voyeuristic interests and fondness for surprising narrative twists. 'Gas' (1919) tells of a woman who dreams she is being assaulted, only to discover she has been hallucinating under the influence of a dentist's anaesthetic. 'And There Was No Rainbow' (1920) offers us a young man in search of a brothel who mistakenly seeks out the house of his best friend's girl.

Hitchcock's body of film work is remarkably consistent in its preoccupations and style. He worked from meticulous storyboards and avoided unnecessary extra angles or takes in order to prevent his producers from changing his vision during subsequent editing.

Unsurprisingly, his comments about his work and the industry itself are self-aware and slyly humorous:

- I am a type(cast) director. If I made *Cinderella*, the audience would immediately be looking for a body in the coach.

- One of television's great contributions is that it brought murder back into the home, where it belongs.

- Give them pleasure – the same pleasure they have when they wake up from a nightmare.

- Blondes make the best victims. They're like virgin snow that shows up the bloody footprints.

- Reality is something that none of us can stand, at any time.

- Man does not live by murder alone. He needs affection, approval, encouragement and, occasionally, a hearty meal.

- In the documentary the basic material has been created by God, whereas in the fiction film the director is a God; he must create life.

- I enjoy playing the audience like a piano.

- If it's a good movie, the sound could go off and the audience would still have a perfectly clear idea of what was going on.

- The length of a film should be directly related to the endurance of the human bladder.

- I deny I ever said that actors are cattle. What I said was, 'Actors should be treated like cattle'.

- When an actor comes to me and wants to discuss his character, I say, 'It's in the script'. If he says, 'But what's my motivation?', I say, 'Your salary'.

Hitchcock, however, was bested in a debate about his technique during the shoot of *Lifeboat* (1944) when he told the composer Hugo Friedhofer it would be inappropriate to have a musical score as the characters were adrift on the open sea. After all, where could the sound of an orchestra possibly come from? Undeterred, Friedhofer is reported to have replied: 'The same place the camera came from, Mr Hitchcock.'

1962   CAPE FEAR   1962

Lawyer Sam Bowden has shot Max Cady – the murderer and former client who has been terrorizing his family – and readies himself to fire again.

CADY

Go ahead. I just don't give a damn.

BOWDEN

No. No! That would be letting you off too easy, too fast. Your words – do you remember? Well, I do. No, we're gonna take good care of you. We're gonna nurse you back to health. And you're strong, Cady. You're gonna live a long life... in a cage! That's

where you belong and that's where you're going. And this time
for life! Bang your head against the walls. Count the years -
the months - the hours...until the day you rot!

Dir: J. Lee Thompson • Scr: James R. Webb • Based on a novel by John D.
MacDonald • Cast: Robert Mitchum (Max Cady), Gregory Peck (Sam Bowden)

The film was remade in 1991 by Martin Scorsese and writer Wesley Strick with Robert De Niro as
the terrifying Cady, Nick Nolte as Sam Bowden and Jessica Lange as his wife Leigh. Interestingly,
the final lines of their screenplay are a voice-over from Danielle, the teenage daughter of the
family Cady menaces (played by Juliette Lewis):

DANIELLE: We never spoke about what happened, at least not to each other. Fear, I
suppose, that to remember his name and what he did would mean letting him into our
dreams. And me, I hardly dream about him any more. Still, things won't ever be the way
they were before he came. But that's all right because if you hang onto the past you die
a little every day. And for myself, I know I'd rather live. (*she whispers*) The end.

1962   THE EXTERMINATING ANGEL (*EL ÁNGEL EXTERMINADOR*)   1962

RITA

I believe the common people, the lower class people, are less
sensitive to pain. Haven't you ever seen a wounded bull? Not a
trace of pain.

Dir: Luis Buñuel • Scr: Luis Buñuel • Cast: Patricia Morán (Rita Ugalde)

1968   2001: A SPACE ODYSSEY   1968

*An astronaut is barred from re-entering his spacecraft by its
central computer.*

DAVE

Hello, HAL. Do you read me, HAL?

HAL

Affirmative, Dave. I read you.

DAVE

Open the pod bay doors, HAL.

HAL

I'm sorry, Dave. I'm afraid I can't do that.

DAVE

What's the problem?

                              HAL

I think you know what the problem is just as well as I do.

                              DAVE

What are you talking about, HAL?

                              HAL

This mission is too important for me to allow you to
jeopardize it.

                              DAVE

I don't know what you're talking about, HAL.

                              HAL

I know that you and Frank were planning to disconnect me,
and I'm afraid that's something I cannot allow to happen.

Dave feigns innocence.
                              DAVE

Where the hell did you get that idea, HAL?

                              HAL

Dave, although you took very thorough precautions in the pod
against my hearing you, I could see your lips move.

                              DAVE

All right, HAL. I'll go in through the emergency airlock.

                              HAL

Without your space helmet, Dave? You're going to find that
rather difficult.

                              DAVE

HAL, I won't argue with you any more! Open the doors!

                              HAL

Dave, this conversation can serve no purpose any more.
Goodbye.

Dir: Stanley Kubrick • Scr: Stanley Kubrick, Arthur C. Clarke • Cast: Keir
Dullea (Dave Bowman), Douglas Rain (voice of HAL)

Chicago Sun-Times critic Roger Ebert re-evaluated the film in 1997: '*2001: A Space Odyssey* is in many respects a silent film... The genius is not in how much Stanley Kubrick does in [it] but in how little. This is the work of an artist so sublimely confident that he doesn't include a single shot simply to keep our attention. He reduces each scene to its essence, and leaves it onscreen long enough for us to contemplate it, to inhabit it in our imaginations. Alone among science fiction movies, *2001* is not concerned with thrilling us, but with inspiring our awe.'

'YOU AIN'T HEARD NOTHIN' YET!'

Although some directors, including D. W. Griffith, had incorporated audio recording into their productions during the 1920s, it was largely for musical accompaniment and ambient sound effects. The kind of synchronized dialogue we now take for granted was first used in a full-length feature in *The Jazz Singer* (1927) when Al Jolson, dubbed 'The World's Greatest Entertainer', delivered his trademark line: 'Wait a minute, wait a minute, you ain't heard nothin' yet!'

The recording technology was temperamental, expensive and bulky and its use added further complications to the process of capturing a scene. Cameras now had to run at precise speeds to match the tape machines but were so loud they had to be soundproofed — often in boxes big enough to enclose the operator and assistant as well. Before the stages themselves were soundproofed, much filming had to be done at night to avoid traffic noise. On one occasion, a canny but penniless bit-player hired for a single scene brought a box of crickets and released them on the set. Production was halted; five days — and five pay cheques later — the crew were still hunting them down.

Many stars were sceptical of the invention as they had grown used to being icons, not actors. They now had to focus on all aspects of performance and an unfortunate number discovered they had been hired for their looks rather than their speaking voice — or, indeed, their actual acting abilities. Many Europeans had their studio contracts cancelled when their accents proved unpalatable to audiences, and many household names, including Lillian Gish, Buster Keaton, John Gilbert, Gloria Swanson, Douglas Fairbanks and Mary Pickford, all realized their heyday was over.

Directors also resented the fact that actors now had unprecedented freedom since it was no longer possible to shout comments at them during takes. One hated this loss of control so much that he devised a low voltage electrical system through which he could issue signals to guide his cast's performance while the camera was rolling. Much as perfectionists such as Tarkovsky, Hitchcock and Kubrick might regret it, this invention never took off but the public embraced the advent of sound unhesitatingly and by 1929 all major studios had stopped making silent pictures.

CHITTY CHITTY BANG BANG

Vulgaria's most feared official smells something amiss in a puppet workshop.

CHILDCATCHER

I don't trust a man who makes toys in a land where children are forbidden.

Dir: Ken Hughes • Scr: Roald Dahl, Ken Hughes, Richard Maibaum • Based on a novel by Ian Fleming • Cast: Robert Helpmann (Childcatcher)

BARBARELLA

Fugitive scientist Durand-Durand has invented a weapon with which he threatens Earth.

DURAND-DURAND

I'll do things to you that are beyond all known philosophies! Wait until I get my devices!

Dir: Roger Vadim • Scr: Terry Southern, Roger Vadim and five others • Based on stories in *Barbarella* comics by Jean-Claude Forest, Claude Brulé • Cast: Milo O'Shea (Durand-Durand)

A CLOCKWORK ORANGE

A violent thug with a fondness for Beethoven picks up a couple of girls in a record shop.

ALEX

What you got back home, little sister, to play your fuzzy warbles on? I bet you got little save pitiful, portable picnic players. Come with uncle and hear all proper! Hear angel trumpets and devil trombones. You are invited.

Dir: Stanley Kubrick • Scr: Stanley Kubrick • Based on a novel by Anthony Burgess • Cast: Malcolm McDowell (Alex)

Anthony Burgess originally sold the rights to his novel to Mick Jagger for $500 [$3,000] because he was short of cash; Jagger had wanted his fellow Rolling Stones to play the droogs, the story's thuggish anti-heroes. Ken Russell was initially slated to direct; both Tim Curry and Jeremy Irons were approached to play the lead role of Alex but turned it down. Kubrick later said of the final casting that if Malcolm McDowell had not been available he would not have made the film.

1972 DELIVERANCE

Two violent hillbillies humiliate the hikers they find in their territory.

> MOUNTAIN MAN
>
> What do you want to do now?

> TOOTHLESS MAN
>
> He got a real pretty mouth, ain't he?

> MOUNTAIN MAN
>
> That's the truth.

He turns to their victim.

> TOOTHLESS MAN
>
> You gonna do some prayin' for me, boy. And you better pray good.

Dir: John Boorman • Scr: James Dickey, based on his novel • Cast: Bill McKinney (Mountain Man), Herbert Coward (Toothless Man)

1973 THE EXORCIST

A demon possessing Regan, a young girl, turns his attention to the priest who hopes to exorcize her.

> DEMON
>
> What an excellent day for an exorcism.

> FATHER KARRAS
>
> You would like that?

> DEMON
>
> Intensely.

> FATHER KARRAS
>
> But wouldn't that drive you out of Regan?

> DEMON
>
> It would bring us together.

FATHER KARRAS

You and Regan?

DEMON

You and us.

Dir: William Friedkin • Scr: William Peter Blatty, based on his novel •
Cast: Mercedes McCambridge (Demon), Jason Miller (Father Damian Karras)

Author William Peter Blatty could only afford to take time off to write the novel after winning
$10,000 [$50,000] on *You Bet Your Life*, a game show hosted by Groucho Marx. When the film
was banned by several local authorities in Britain, enterprising travel companies set up special
'Exorcist Bus Trips' to unaffected cinemas.

1978 DAWN OF THE DEAD   1978

*One of the survivors of a zombie attack explains why the corpses
have risen.*

PETER

When there's no more room in hell, the dead will walk the
Earth.

Dir: George A. Romero • Scr: George A. Romero • Cast: Ken Foree (Peter)

*Crew members of the Nostromo, an interstellar cargo ship with
an alien predator on board, discover their colleague Ash is an
android.*

> RIPLEY

Ash, can you hear me? Ash?

*Ash's head has been torn from his body. His voice sounds
electronic now.*

> ASH

Yes, I can hear you.

> RIPLEY

What was your special order?

> ASH

You read it. I thought it was clear.

> RIPLEY

What was it?

> ASH

Bring back life form. Priority One. All other priorities
rescinded.

> PARKER

The damn company. What about our lives, you son of a bitch?

> ASH

I repeat, all other priorities are rescinded.

> RIPLEY

How do we kill it, Ash? There's gotta be a way of killing it.
How? How do we do it?

> ASH

You can't.

> PARKER

That's bullshit.

ASH

You still don't understand what you're dealing with, do you?
A perfect organism. Its structural perfection is matched only
by its hostility.

LAMBERT

You admire it.

ASH

I admire its purity. A survivor...unclouded by conscience,
remorse, or delusions of morality.

PARKER

I've heard enough of this, and I'm asking you to pull the
plug.

Ripley moves to shut Ash down.

ASH

Last word.

RIPLEY

What?

ASH

I can't lie to you about your chances, but...you have my
sympathies.

Dir: Ridley Scott • Scr: Dan O'Bannon, Ronald Shusett • Cast: Sigourney
Weaver (Ripley), Ian Holm (Ash), Yaphet Kotto (Parker), Veronica
Cartwright (Lambert)

1980   THE SHINING   1980

*Jack, caretaker of a lonely hotel, has been driven insane by its
supernatural inhabitants. Wendy, his wife, tries to escape him.*

WENDY

Stay away from me.

JACK

Why?

WENDY

I just wanna go back to my room!

JACK

Why?

WENDY

Well, I'm very confused, and I just need time to think things over.

JACK

You've had your whole fucking life to think things over, what good's a few minutes more gonna do you now?

WENDY

Please! Don't hurt me!

JACK

I'm not gonna hurt you.

WENDY

Stay away from me!

JACK

Wendy? Darling? Light of my life, I'm not gonna hurt you. You didn't let me finish my sentence. I said, I'm not gonna hurt you. I'm just going to bash your brains in. Gonna bash 'em right the fuck in!

Dir: Stanley Kubrick • Scr: Stanley Kubrick, Diane Johnson • Based on a novel by Stephen King • Cast: Shelley Duvall (Wendy Torrance), Jack Nicholson (Jack Torrance)

1981   TIME BANDITS   1981

A malevolent sorcerer seeks a cosmic map which will allow him to travel through time.

EVIL GENIUS

When I have the map I will be free and the world will be different, because I have understanding...of digital watches. And soon I shall have understanding of videocassette recorders and car telephones. And when I have understanding of them, I shall have understanding of computers. And when I have understanding of computers, I shall be the Supreme Being! God isn't interested in technology. He knows nothing of the potential of the microchip or the silicon revolution.

Look how He spends His time! Forty-three species of parrots!
Nipples for men! Slugs! He created slugs. They can't hear!
They can't speak! They can't operate machinery! I mean, are we
not in the hands of a lunatic? If I were creating a world, I
wouldn't mess about with butterflies and daffodils. I would
have started with lasers, eight o'clock, day one!

He presses a button, unleashing the beam. An assistant screams.

Sorry.

Dir: Terry Gilliam • Scr: Michael Palin, Terry Gilliam • Cast: David
Warner (Evil Genius)

As a joke to help with the casting of other main characters, Gilliam had written in the script:
'The warrior (Agamemnon) takes off his helmet, revealing someone who looks exactly like Sean
Connery, or an actor of equal but cheaper stature.' To the director's surprise, someone gave
Connery a copy. He liked it, and signed up.

1986 THE FLY   1986

*Scientist Seth Brundle tries to persuade a stranger to help with
his teleportation experiments but his colleague Veronica knows
it is too dangerous.*

TAWNY

I'm afraid.

SETH

Don't be afraid.

VERONICA

No! Be afraid. Be very afraid.

Dir: David Cronenberg • Scr: David Cronenberg, Charles Edward
Pogue • Based on a story by George Langelaan • Cast: Joy Boushel (Tawney),
Jeff Goldblum (Seth Brundle), Geena Davis (Veronica Quaife)

When Jeff Goldblum's character delivers the line 'I'm an insect who dreamed he was a man
and loved it, but now that dream is over and the insect is awake,' he is referring to Franz
Kafka's *The Metamorphosis* (1915), in which the narrator discovers he has been transformed
into a cockroach. Cronenberg's original conception featured several other biological mutations
including an ape/cat hybrid and a child born with butterfly wings, but they were omitted from his
final cut. Although a film's end credits typically give the director top billing, Cronenberg broke
with precedent and listed Chris Walas first for his groundbreaking work in creating the special
effects make-up for the creature. Walas duly won the Academy Award. Over twenty years later
Cronenberg teamed up with the film's composer, Howard Shore, to create an opera based on
the story. It had its first showing at the prestigious Théâtre du Châtelet in Paris in 2008.

MISERY

A writer is wounded in a car accident and held helpless by his rescuer, a woman obsessed by his work.

ANNIE

There's nothing to worry about. You're going to be just fine - I'm your number one fan.

Dir: Rob Reiner: • Scr: William Goldman • Based on a novel by Stephen King • Cast: Kathy Bates (Annie Wilkes)

THE SILENCE OF THE LAMBS

A serial killer renowned for cannibalism taunts an FBI agent who seeks his help.

LECTER

A census taker once tried to test me. I ate his liver with some fava beans and a nice Chianti.

Dir: Jonathan Demme • Scr: Ted Tally • Based on a novel by Thomas Harris • Cast: Anthony Hopkins (Dr Hannibal Lecter)

The pattern on the moth's body in the poster was changed to echo Salvador Dalí's *In Voluptas Mors*, which shapes seven naked women into the image of a skull. The Tobacco horn worm moths used in the film received five-star treatment, being flown first-class in special carriers and kept in a climate-controlled room before being costumed in special body shields bearing a skull and crossbones.

SCHINDLER'S LIST

SS officer Amon Goeth rallies his troops before a raid to eliminate the Jewish ghetto in Krakow.

GOETH

Today is history. Today will be remembered. Years from now the young will ask with wonder about this day. Today is history and you are part of it. Six hundred years ago when elsewhere they were footing the blame for the Black Death, Casimir the Great - so called - told the Jews they could come to Krakow. They came. They trundled their belongings into the city. They settled. They took hold. They prospered in business, science, education, the arts. With nothing they came and with nothing they flourished. For six centuries there has been a Jewish Krakow. By this evening those six centuries will be a rumour. They never happened. Today is history.

Dir: Steven Spielberg • Scr: Steven Zaillian • Based on a novel by Thomas Keneally • Cast: Ralph Fiennes (Amon Goeth)

SE7EN

A serial killer exacts revenge on the detective pursuing him.

JOHN DOE

I visited your home this morning after you'd left. I tried to play husband. I tried to taste the life of a simple man. It didn't work out, so I took a souvenir: her pretty head.

Dir: David Fincher • Scr: Andrew Kevin Walker • Cast: Kevin Spacey (John Doe)

THE USUAL SUSPECTS

A crippled conman describes the elusive criminal mastermind responsible for the deaths of his colleagues.

VERBAL

Who is Keyser Söze? He is supposed to be Turkish. Some say his father was German. Nobody believed he was real. Nobody ever saw him or knew anybody that ever worked directly for him, but to hear Kobayashi tell it, anybody could have worked for Söze. You never knew. That was his power. The greatest trick the Devil ever pulled was convincing the world he didn't exist. And like that, poof. He's gone.

Dir: Bryan Singer • Scr: Christopher McQuarrie • Cast: Kevin Spacey (Roger 'Verbal' Kint)

The quote about the devil is by French poet Charles Baudelaire, although the film-makers were unaware of its origin. Strangely, a similar remark appears in *End of Days* (1999), also starring Gabriel Byrne and Kevin Pollak.

'WHO IS KEYSER SÖZE?'

Although filled with compelling characters and memorable dialogue, *The Usual Suspects* is a rare example of a thriller whose construction feels almost purely intellectual. Through flashbacks, contradiction, ambiguity and visual sleight-of-hand it draws the audience into a world where facts are unreliable and the very concept of 'writing' is shown to be a kind of game.

Director Bryan Singer's inspiration was the line in *Casablanca* where Captain Renault tells his men to 'round up the usual suspects'; Singer's subsequent conception consisted simply of five criminals who meet in a police line-up. When he asked writer Christopher McQuarrie what could have drawn the men together, McQuarrie remembered a true story he had read about a man who murdered his family and disappeared for decades. As McQuarrie began writing in lunch breaks at the law firm where he worked he was distracted by a cluttered notice board and decided to use it as a motif for the story. From these fragments they created a journey that was to be as immersive for its cast as for its audience.

In the line-up and interrogation scenes, shot before the rest of the film, McQuarrie fed the cast questions off-camera and they improvised answers. From the start of the process, the 'criminals' seemed to be united against the authorities (the film-makers), refusing to take the shooting seriously and constantly trying to make each other laugh. When Singer upbraided them, they ignored him; in the end he was forced to use the takes where they cracked up, and the editor put the scenes together in a way that showed the men were — quite genuinely — forging relationships with one another.

McQuarrie gave the suspects names from staff members at the law firm and this method of purely random invention became a key part of his storytelling. By the end of the film we realize that 'Verbal' Kint's statement to the detectives has been entirely fabricated using haphazard details from the police station where he is interrogated to provide 'evidence' and corroborative detail for his confession.

Singer used a similar trick to ensure realism in the actors' performances: because the police investigation revolves around exactly who criminal mastermind Keyzer Söze is, the director refused to give any of his cast the answer. Kevin Spacey revealed later that Singer had managed to persuade all the main players that they themselves were the anti-hero. When the film was first screened for the cast Gabriel Byrne (as Dean Keaton) was so shocked to discover he was not the central figure that he fled to the parking lot where he yelled at Singer for an hour. Debate still rages in internet movie chat rooms, where fans who have watched the film dozens of times offer their conclusions: most claim Kint is Söze (his surname means 'verbal' in Turkish) while others suggest the lawyer Kobayashi is the only character with enough knowledge to mastermind the entire story. Other aficionados insist Kobayashi himself is a fiction — just a name Kint saw on a detective's coffee mug.

Five different actors were used to play Söze as their conflicting viewpoints are explored, and the whole film initially seems to be an impenetrable construction of interlocking fictions. On repeated viewing, however, it displays a masterful confidence in its deceptions and once the truth is revealed a multitude of details prove that a careful observer might have followed the plot without distraction. As if to prove how much he enjoyed baffling us along the way, writer McQuarrie has a cameo as a police officer at the end when he just turns to the camera and laughs.

1997 THE DEVIL'S ADVOCATE 1997

Satan - in the form of a New York lawyer - warns that God will not save the human race from its own greed and selfishness.

MILTON

You sharpen the human appetite to the point where it can split atoms with its desire. You build egos the size of cathedrals. Fibre-optically connect the world to every ego impulse. Grease even the dullest dreams with these dollar-green, gold-plated fantasies until every human becomes an aspiring emperor, becomes his own god. Where can you go from there? And as we're scrambling from one deal to the next, who's got his eye on the planet? As the air thickens, the water sours. Even the bees' honey takes on the metallic taste of radioactivity - and it just keeps coming, faster and faster...And then it hits home: you gotta pay your own way, Eddie. It's a little late in the game to buy out now. Your belly's too full, your dick is sore, your eyes are bloodshot, and you're screaming for someone to help. But guess what? There's no one there.

Dir: Taylor Hackford • Scr: Jonathan Lemkin, Tony Gilroy • Based on a novel by Andrew Neiderman • Cast: Al Pacino (John Milton)

1997 DECONSTRUCTING HARRY 1997

The Devil offers his view on life.

THE DEVIL

It's like Vegas. You're up, you're down, but in the end the
house always wins.

Dir: Woody Allen • Scr: Woody Allen • Cast: Billy Crystal (The Devil)

1999 AUSTIN POWERS: THE SPY WHO SHAGGED ME 1999

Dr Evil explains to his son why he abandoned him.

DR EVIL

You're semi-evil. You're quasi-evil. You're the margarine of evil.
You're the Diet Coke of evil. Just one calorie, not evil enough.

Dir: Jay Roach • Scr: Mike Myers, Michael McCullers • Cast: Mike Myers
(Dr Evil)

2000 AMERICAN PSYCHO 2000

A jaded killer hires two prostitutes to amuse him.

PATRICK

Do you like Phil Collins? I've been a big Genesis fan ever
since the release of their 1980 album, *Duke*. Before that, I

really didn't understand any of their work. Too artsy, too intellectual. It was on *Duke* where Phil Collins' presence became more apparent. I think *Invisible Touch* was the group's undisputed masterpiece. It's an epic meditation on intangibility. At the same time, it deepens and enriches the meaning of the preceding three albums. Christy, take off your robe. Listen to the brilliant ensemble playing of Banks, Collins and Rutherford. You can practically hear every nuance of every instrument. Sabrina, remove your dress. In terms of lyrical craftsmanship, the sheer songwriting, this album hits a new peak of professionalism. Sabrina, why don't you, uh, dance a little. Take the lyrics to 'Land of Confusion'. In this song, Phil Collins addresses the problems of abusive political authority. 'In Too Deep' is the most moving pop song of the 1980s, about monogamy and commitment. The song is extremely uplifting. Their lyrics are as positive and affirmative as anything I've heard in rock. Christy, get down on your knees so Sabrina can see your asshole. Phil Collins' solo career seems to be more commercial and therefore more satisfying, in a narrower way. Especially songs like 'In the Air Tonight' and 'Against All Odds'. Sabrina, don't just stare at it, eat it. But I also think Phil Collins works better within the confines of the group than as a solo artist, and I stress the word artist. This is 'Sussudio': a great, great song, a personal favourite.

Dir: Mary Harron • Scr: Mary Harron, Guinevere Turner • Based on a novel by Bret Easton Ellis • Cast: Christian Bale (Patrick Bateman)

2005 THE DEVIL'S REJECTS   2005

A murderous kidnapper confronts his victims.

DRIFTWOOD

I am the devil, and I am here to do the devil's work.

Dir: Rob Zombie • Scr: Rob Zombie • Cast: Bill Moseley (Otis B. Driftwood)

2006 THE DEVIL WEARS PRADA   2006

The haughty, impatient editor of a fashion magazine upbraids her assistant.

MIRANDA

Details of your incompetence do not interest me. Tell Simone I'm not going to approve that girl that she sent me for the Brazilian layout. I asked for clean, athletic, smiling. She sent me dirty, tired and paunchy. And RSVP 'yes' to Michael

Kors' party - I want the driver to drop me off at 9:30 and pick me up at 9:45 sharp. Call Natalie at Glorious Foods and tell her no for the fortieth time. No! I don't want dacquoise, I want tortes filled with warm rhubarb compote. Then call my ex-husband and remind him that the parent-teacher conference is at Dalton tonight. Then call my husband, ask him to meet me for dinner at that place I went to with Massimo. Tell Richard I saw the pictures that he sent for that feature on the female paratroopers and they're all so deeply unattractive. Is it impossible to find a lovely, slender, female paratrooper? Am I reaching for the stars here? Not really. Also, I need to see all the things that Nigel has pulled for Gwyneth's second cover try. I wonder if she's lost any of that weight yet.

Dir: David Frankel • Scr: Aline Brosh McKenna • Based on a novel by Lauren Weisberger • Cast: Meryl Streep (Miranda Priestly)

The character of Miranda in the book is widely held to be a portrait of Anna 'Nuclear' Wintour, editor of the New York edition of *Vogue*. It was also reported that Wintour told fashion designers who had been approached to play cameo roles that if they accepted, their collections would never again appear in her publication. Despite being a portrait of the fashion world, the film is rarely mentioned in the magazine.

2007 NO COUNTRY FOR OLD MEN   2007

Anton Chigurh, a hired killer, stops at a gas station but realizes the owner may be able to identify him.

CHIGURH

How much?

He points to a bag of nuts.

PROPRIETOR

Sixty-nine cents.

CHIGURH

This. And the gas.

PROPRIETOR

Y'all getting any rain up your way?

CHIGURH

What way would that be?

PROPRIETOR

I seen you was from Dallas.

CHIGURH

What business is it of yours where I'm from, friendo?

PROPRIETOR

I didn't mean nothing by it.

CHIGURH

Didn't mean nothing.

PROPRIETOR

I was just passing the time. If you don't wanna accept that,
I don't know what else to do for you. Will there be something
else?

CHIGURH

I don't know. Will there?

PROPRIETOR

Is something wrong?

                    CHIGURH

With what?

                    PROPRIETOR

With anything?

                    CHIGURH

Is that what you're asking me? Is there something wrong with
anything?

The proprietor sounds afraid.

                    PROPRIETOR

Will there be anything else?

                    CHIGURH

You already asked me that.

                    PROPRIETOR

Well...I need to see about closing.

                    CHIGURH

See about closing.

                    PROPRIETOR

Yessir.

                    CHIGURH

What time do you close?

                    PROPRIETOR

Now. We close now.

                    CHIGURH

Now is not a time. What time do you close?

Dir: Ethan Coen, Joel Coen • Scr: Ethan Coen, Joel Coen • Based on a novel by
Cormac McCarthy • Cast: Javier Bardem (Anton Chigurh), Gene Jones (Proprietor)

Directors Joel and Ethan Coen based Chigurh's bizarre hairdo on a 1979 photograph they found
of a man visiting a brothel. When the normally suave Javier Bardem saw the results of the styling,
he complained to the Coens: 'Now I won't get laid for the next two months.' The brothers just
high-fived each other.

2008 THE DARK KNIGHT

Alfred warns Bruce Wayne (aka Batman) not to query their adversary's motives.

ALFRED

Some men just want to watch the world burn.

Dir: Christopher Nolan • Scr: Jonathan Nolan, Christopher Nolan • Cast: Michael Caine (Alfred Pennyworth)

When Heath Ledger, playing the Joker, first appeared in a scene with Michael Caine, his performance was so frightening that Caine forgot his lines.

2010 SHUTTER ISLAND

Two US Marshals investigate a murder in a mental hospital on a remote island.

TEDDY

You know, this place makes me wonder.

CHUCK

Yeah, what's that, boss?

TEDDY

Which would be worse - to live as a monster? Or to die as a good man?

Dir: Martin Scorsese • Scr: Laeta Kalogridis • Based on a novel by Dennis Lehane • Cast: Leonardo DiCaprio (Teddy Daniels), Mark Ruffalo (Chuck Aule)

De Niro's career has provided stand-out performances and awards in equal measure: here he plays the young Vito Corleone in *The Godfather: Part II* (1974).

Terry Jones as Simon the Holy Man attempts to save wardrobe costs in Monty Python's *Life of Brian* (1979).

Orson Welles and his groundbreaking cinematographer Gregg Toland on the set of *Citizen Kane* (1941).

Power

Kane admits the newspaper he owns is an expensive folly.

KANE

You're right, I did lose a million dollars last year. I expect to lose a million dollars this year. I expect to lose a million dollars next year. You know, Mr Thatcher, at the rate of a million dollars a year, I'll have to close this place in ...sixty years.

Dir: Orson Welles • Scr: Herman J. Mankiewicz, Orson Welles • Cast: Orson Welles (Charles Foster Kane)

Citizen Kane topped *Sight and Sound* magazine's poll as best film for over fifty years from 1962 to 2012, but was so unpopular on its release that at the 1941 Oscars it was booed every time one of its nine nominations was announced.

YOUR ONLY COMPETITION IS IDIOTS

Herman J. Mankiewicz (1897—1953) was one of cinema's most talented writers, responsible for seventy-eight films including *Citizen Kane*, *It's a Wonderful World* and *The Pride of St Louis*. Shortly after moving to Los Angeles, he cabled his journalist friend Ben Hecht (*Scarface*, *Notorious*, *Wuthering Heights*): 'Will you accept $300 per week to work for Paramount? All expenses paid. $300 is peanuts. Millions are to be grabbed out here and your only competition is idiots. Don't let this get around.'

Writers have always had a conflicted relationship with film; for many, it feels like a choice between money and integrity. Many start out as acclaimed playwrights, novelists or journalists and resent the fact that in the world of screenplays their freedom diminishes in inverse proportion to the size of their pay cheque. As Harry Zimm says in *Get Shorty* (1995): 'I once asked this literary agent what kind of writing paid the best. He said, "Ransom notes".'

Mankiewicz probably didn't spend much time pondering this dilemma, since within a month of beginning his new career he was earning $400 [$5,000] a week. Hecht was similarly rewarded, with the additional advantage that he turned in his work with startling speed; he delivered *Scarface* (1932) in nine days.

At the time this new breed of writer was arriving on the West Coast the industry was still in upheaval following the advent of sound and it was the perfect opportunity to transform film from a medium of mute spectacle into a more sophisticated art form. Mankiewicz already had a reputation as the cleverest, funniest man in New York — Hecht famously described him as 'the Central Park West Voltaire' — and his style was perfectly suited to giving audiences the blend of fast-paced, intelligent and gritty humour we now associate with that era.

Perhaps the one aspect of cinema that didn't change once sound had become universally accepted was its hierarchy of talent. In the theatre, a successful playwright will have a higher billing than the director: the work is essentially his. But the legacy of silent films meant that audiences paid primarily to see the actors. They might remember the studio and the director's name, but the idea of going to the pictures on the basis of who had written the film remained largely irrelevant.

Mankiewicz was well aware he would never be as famous as the films he wrote, although he never lost his sense of humour about the way the industry operated:

> In a novel the hero can lay ten girls and marry a virgin for the finish. In a movie this is not allowed. The villain can lay anybody he wants, have as much fun as he wants cheating and stealing, getting rich and whipping the servants. But you have to shoot him in the end. When he falls with a bullet in his forehead, it is advisable that he clutch at the Gobelin tapestry on the wall and bring it down over his head like a symbolic shroud. Also, covered by such a tapestry, the actor does not have to hold his breath while being photographed as a dead man.

Not surprisingly, his outspoken manner caused plenty of battles with his paymasters. Pauline Kael recounts of one lost screenplay:

> When a studio attempted to punish him for his customary misbehaviour by assigning him to a *Rin Tin Tin* picture, he rebelled by turning in a script that began with the craven dog frightened by a mouse and reached its climax with a house on fire and the dog taking a baby into the flames.

Sometimes, it seemed, he longed for a quieter life, settling down with one of the leading ladies from his films. Even then, his tongue remained firmly in his cheek:

> Barbara Stanwyck is my favorite. My God, I could just sit and dream of being married to her, having a little cottage out in the hills, vines around the door. I'd come home from the office tired and weary, and I'd be met by Barbara, walking through the door holding an apple pie she had cooked herself. And wearing no drawers.

1941 MAJOR BARBARA   1941

Undershaft is not afraid to tell his daughter what he feels about his money.

UNDERSHAFT

My religion? My dear, I'm a millionaire. That's my religion.

Dir: Gabriel Pascal • Scr: George Bernard Shaw, based on his play • Cast: Robert Morley (Andrew Undershaft)

1942 THE MAN WHO CAME TO DINNER   1942

Whiteside terrorizes everyone in the house where he stays as a guest.

WHITESIDE

Now will you all leave quietly, or must I ask Miss Cutler to pass among you with a baseball bat?

Dir: William Keighley • Scr: Julius J. Epstein, Philip G. Epstein • Based on a play by George S. Kaufman, Moss Hart • Cast: Monty Woolley (Sheridan Whiteside)

1951 THE DAY THE EARTH STOOD STILL   1951

Klaatu, a visitor from outer space, brings a message to all humanity.

KLAATU

Now, we do not pretend to have achieved perfection, but we do have a system, and it works. I came here to give you these facts. It is no concern of ours how you run your own planet, but if you threaten to extend your violence, this Earth of yours will be reduced to a burned-out cinder. Your choice is simple: join us and live in peace, or pursue your present course and face obliteration. We shall be waiting for your answer. The decision rests with you.

Dir: Robert Wise • Scr: Edmund H. North • Based on a story by Harry Bates • Cast: Michael Rennie (Klaatu)

1951 STRANGERS ON A TRAIN 1951

Barbara seems at ease with the political world her family inhabits.

BARBARA

Oh, Daddy doesn't mind a little scandal. He's a senator.

Dir: Alfred Hitchcock • Scr: Raymond Chandler, Czenzi Ormonde, Whitfield Cook • Based on a novel by Patricia Highsmith • Cast: Patricia Hitchcock (Barbara Morton)

Raymond Chandler, one of the screenwriters, did not enjoy his collaboration with Hitchcock. As the director arrived for one story meeting, Chandler yelled out of the window: 'Look at the fat bastard trying to get out of his car!'

1956 THE TEAHOUSE OF THE AUGUST MOON 1956

After the war, American troops are sent to Okinawa to teach the locals democracy.

COLONEL PURDY

You'll need an interpreter.

CAPTAIN FISBY

I can study the language.

COLONEL PURDY

No need. We won the war.

Dir: Daniel Mann • Scr: John Patrick, adapted from his play • Based on a book by Vern J. Sneider • Cast: Paul Ford (Colonel Purdy), Glenn Ford (Captain Fisby)

1957 SWEET SMELL OF SUCCESS   1957

Musician Jimmy is furious that his expensive publicity
agent is not advancing his career.

JIMMY

It's a dirty job, but I pay clean money for it.

Dir: Alexander Mackendrick • Scr: Clifford Odets, Ernest Lehman • Based on
a novella by Ernest Lehman • Cast: Unknown (Jimmy Weldon)

1957 12 ANGRY MEN   1957

Twelve jurors deliberate their verdict in a murder trial.

JUROR #3

You're talking about a matter of seconds. Nobody can be that
accurate.

JUROR #8

Well, I think that testimony that can put a boy into the
electric chair *should* be that accurate.

Dir: Sidney Lumet • Scr: Reginald Rose • Cast: Lee J. Cobb (Juror #3),
Henry Fonda (Juror #8)

Henry Fonda, at that time a huge star, was asked by United Artists to make the film and he acted as producer as well as leading man; he personally chose Sidney Lumet to direct. The process was intense, as Lumet insisted on long rehearsals in which the cast remained in the jurors' room without respite to create the feeling of a group under relentless pressure. Although the film failed to make a profit on its initial release, Fonda maintained it was one of the three pictures he made of which he was most proud.

The film lasts ninety-six minutes, of which ninety-three take place in the room where the jurors congregate; the set was a mere sixteen by twenty-four feet. As the story progresses, Lumet gradually increased the focal length of the camera's lenses and lowered the angle of the shots to intensify his portraits of the characters and emphasize the claustrophobia of their surroundings.

1958 TOUCH OF EVIL   1958

VARGAS

A policeman's job is only easy in a police state.

Dir: Orson Welles • Scr: Orson Welles • Based on a novel by Whit
Masterson • Cast: Charlton Heston (Miguel 'Mike' Vargas)

JUDGMENT AT NUREMBERG

An American judge passes sentence on a German counterpart accused of war crimes.

JUDGE HAYWOOD

Janning, to be sure, is a tragic figure. We believe he loathed the evil he did. But compassion for the present torture of his soul must not beget forgetfulness of the torture and death of millions by the government of which he was a part. Janning's record and his fate illuminate the most shattering truth that has emerged from this trial. If he and the other defendants were all depraved perverts - if the leaders of the Third Reich were sadistic monsters and maniacs - these events would have no more moral significance than an earthquake or other natural catastrophes. But this trial has shown that under the stress of a national crisis, men - even able and extraordinary men - can delude themselves into the commission of crimes and atrocities so vast and heinous as to stagger the imagination. No one who has sat through this trial can ever forget. The sterilization of men because of their political beliefs, the murder of children - how easily that can happen. There are those in our country today, too, who speak of the 'protection' of the country. Of 'survival'. The answer to that is: survival as what? A country isn't a rock. And it isn't an extension of one's self. It is what it stands for - when standing for something is the most difficult. Before the people of the world - let it now be noted in our decision here that this is what we stand for: justice, truth - and the value of a single human being.

Dir: Stanley Kramer • Scr: Abby Mann • Cast: Spencer Tracy (Judge Dan Haywood)

Many of the cast worked for less than their usual salary because they believed the subject matter was so important. Some of the court scenes feature actual footage from the concentration camps.

KNIFE IN THE WATER (*NÓŻW WODZIE*)

Andrzej and a mysterious traveller become antagonistic on a sailing trip.

ANDRZEJ

If two men are on board, one is the skipper.

Dir: Roman Polanski • Scr: Jakub Goldberg, Roman Polanski, Jerzy Skolimowski • Cast: Leon Niemczyk (Andrzej)

1964 MY FAIR LADY 1964

Pickering has offered to pay for Eliza Doolittle's elocution lessons, but Eliza's father demands a share of his generosity too.

> PICKERING
>
> Have you no morals, man?

> DOOLITTLE
>
> Nah, can't afford 'em. Neither could you, if you were as poor as me.

Dir: George Cukor • Scr: Alan Jay Lerner • Based on a play by George Bernard Shaw • Cast: Wilfrid Hyde-White (Colonel Hugh Pickering), Stanley Holloway (Alfred P. Doolittle)

1966 A MAN FOR ALL SEASONS 1966

Cromwell, a minister of Henry VIII, applies political pressure to Sir Thomas More.

> SIR THOMAS MORE
>
> You threaten like a dockside bully.

> CROMWELL
>
> How should I threaten?

> SIR THOMAS MORE
>
> Like a minister of state. With justice.

> CROMWELL
>
> Oh, justice is what you're threatened with.

> SIR THOMAS MORE
>
> Then I am not threatened.

Dir: Fred Zinnemann • Scr: Robert Bolt, based on his play • Cast: Paul Scofield (Sir Thomas More), Leo McKern (Thomas Cromwell)

Writer Robert Bolt took the title for his play from this contemporaneous description of the statesman: 'More is a man of an angel's wit and singular learning; I know not his fellow. For where is the man of that gentleness, lowliness and affability? And, as time requireth, a man of marvellous mirth and pastimes, and sometime of as sad gravity: a man for all seasons.'

Cool Hand Luke meets Carr, his prison warder.

CARR

Them clothes got laundry numbers on them. You remember your
number and always wear the ones that has your number. Any
man forgets his number spends a night in the box. These here
spoons you keep with you. Any man loses his spoon spends
a night in the box. There's no playing grab-ass or fighting
in the building. You got a grudge against another man, you
fight him Saturday afternoon. Any man playing grab-ass or
fighting in the building spends a night in the box. First
bell's at five minutes of eight when you will get in your
bunk. Last bell is at eight. Any man not in his bunk at
eight spends the night in the box. There is no smoking in

the prone position in bed. To smoke you must have both legs
over the side of your bunk. Any man caught smoking in the
prone position in bed... spends a night in the box. You get
two sheets. Every Saturday, you put the clean sheet on the
top...the top sheet on the bottom... and the bottom sheet you
turn in to the laundry boy. Any man turns in the wrong sheet
spends a night in the box. No one'll sit in the bunks with
dirty pants on. Any man with dirty pants on sitting on the
bunks spends a night in the box. Any man don't bring back
his empty pop bottle spends a night in the box. Any man
loud talking spends a night in the box. You got questions,

you come to me. I'm Carr, the floor walker. I'm responsible for order in here. Any man don't keep order spends a night in...

                              LUKE

...the box.

                              CARR

I hope you ain't going to be a hard case.

Dir: Stuart Rosenberg • Scr: Frank Pierson, Donn Pearce • Based on a novel by Donn Pierce • Cast: Clifton James (Carr), Paul Newman (Luke Jackson)

1968 THE LION IN WINTER   1968

Eleanor of Aquitaine begs her sons to settle the succession to their father's throne without bloodshed.

                              ELEANOR

We are the origins of war. Not history's forces, nor the times, nor justice, nor the lack of it, nor causes, nor religions, nor ideas, nor kinds of government nor any other thing! We are the killers; we breed war. We carry it, like syphilis, inside. Dead bodies rot in field and stream because the living ones are rotten. For the love of God, can't we love each other just a little? That's how peace begins. We have so much to love each other for. We have such possibilities, my children; we could change the world.

Dir: Anthony Harvey • Scr: James Goldman, based on his play • Cast: Katharine Hepburn (Eleanor of Aquitaine)

1968 IF...   1968

Mick rebels against his conservative, repressive schooling.

                              MICK

One man can change the world with a bullet in the right place.

Dir: Lindsay Anderson • Scr: David Sherwin, John Howlett • Cast: Malcolm McDowell (Mick Travis)

A WORD TO THE WISE

Producer Samuel Goldwyn famously said: 'Pictures are for entertainment — messages should be delivered by Western Union.' Even so, film-makers can rarely resist an opportunity to share a little wisdom. Some of the following lines are as pithy as aphorisms, others as impenetrable as a Zen koan, but if you take their advice, choose carefully...

Front seldom tell truth. To know occupants of house, always look in backyard.
Charlie Chan in London (1934)

Never do nothing you wouldn't want printed on the front page of the *New York Times*.
Born Yesterday (1950)

Don't ever hit your mother with a shovel. It leaves a dull impression on her mind.
Butch Cassidy and the Sundance Kid (1969)

A little nonsense now and then is relished by the wisest men.
Willy Wonka & the Chocolate Factory (1971)

Two wrongs don't make a right but three rights will make a left.
Caddyshack (1980)

Named must your fear be before banish it you can.
Star Wars V: The Empire Strikes Back (1980)

It's such a fine line between stupid and clever.
This Is Spinal Tap (1984)

There are three rules that I live by: never get less than twelve hours sleep; never play cards with a guy who has the same first name as a city; and never get involved with a woman with a tattoo of a dagger on her body.
Teen Wolf (1985)

I don't make things difficult. That's the way they get, all by themselves.
Lethal Weapon (1987)

A fool and his money are lucky enough to get together in the first place.
Wall Street (1987)

Truth hurts. Maybe not as much as jumping on a bicycle with the seat missing, but it hurts.
The Naked Gun 2½: The Smell of Fear (1991)

You know what the trouble about real life is? There's no danger music.
The Cable Guy (1996)

You are not a beautiful or unique snowflake. You're the same decaying organic matter as everything else.
Fight Club (1999)

The best way to get over a man is to get under a new one.
Good Advice (2001)

Worrying is like a rocking chair. It gives you something to do but it doesn't get you anywhere.
Van Wilder (2002)

Never trust a guy who fumbles for the check.
Anything Else (2003)

Never pat a burning dog.
A Good Year (2006)

The further you run from your sins, the more exhausted you are when they catch up to you.
Inside Man (2006)

That which does not kill you only makes you...stranger.
The Dark Knight (2008)

At the end of a war you need some soldiers left, or else it looks like you've lost.
In the Loop (2009)

When you go fishing you can catch a lot of fish, or you can catch a big fish. You ever walk into a guy's den and see a picture of him standing next to fourteen trout?
The Social Network (2010)

W.R.: MYSTERIES OF THE ORGANISM (*W.R.- MISTERIJE ORGANIZMA*)

A Communist party member vents his frustration with the system.

RADMILOVIĆ

Gentlemen, in our democracy everyone is entitled to a doughnut. Some get the doughnut, others get the hole in the doughnut.

Dir: Dušan Makavejev • Scr: Dušan Makavejev • Cast: Zoran Radmilović (Zoran Radmilović)

AGUIRRE, WRATH OF GOD (*AGUIRRE, DER ZORN GOTTES*)

Insane, ambitious conquistador Aguirre leads his men in search of El Dorado.

AGUIRRE

I, the wrath of God, will marry my own daughter and with her I will found the purest dynasty the earth has ever seen.

Dir: Werner Herzog • Scr: Werner Herzog • Cast: Klaus Kinski (Don Lope de Aguirre)

Despite being shot entirely in Peru, the crew for the production consisted of only eight people. Most of the film was shot on a 35mm camera Herzog stole from his film school.

CHINATOWN

A private investigator confronts Noah Cross, an unscrupulous property developer.

NOAH

Of course I'm respectable. I'm old. Politicians, ugly buildings and whores all get respectable if they last long enough.

Dir: Roman Polanski • Scr: Robert Towne • Cast: John Huston (Noah Cross)

MICHAEL

If anything in this life is certain, if history has taught us
anything, it is that you can kill anyone.

Dir: Francis Ford Coppola • Scr: Francis Ford Coppola, Mario Puzo • Based
on a novel by Mario Puzo • Cast: Al Pacino (Michael Corleone)

1975   MONTY PYTHON AND THE HOLY GRAIL   1975

KING ARTHUR

I am your king.

WOMAN

Well, I didn't vote for you.

KING ARTHUR

You don't vote for kings.

WOMAN

Well, how did you become king then?

KING ARTHUR

The Lady of the Lake, her arm clad in the purest shimmering
samite, held aloft Excalibur from the bosom of the water,

signifying by divine providence that I, Arthur, was to carry
Excalibur. That is why I am your king.

DENNIS

Listen, strange women lying in ponds distributing swords
is no basis for a system of government. Supreme executive
power derives from a mandate from the masses, not from some
farcical aquatic ceremony.

Dir: Terry Gilliam, Terry Jones • Scr: Graham Chapman, John Cleese, Eric
Idle, Terry Gilliam, Terry Jones, Michael Palin • Cast: Graham Chapman
(King Arthur), Terry Jones (Woman), Michael Palin (Dennis)

The film's tight budget did not allow for many lavish historic locations. Another of the story's
highlights – Lancelot's running dash to Swamp Castle – was filmed on Hampstead Heath beside
one of London's busiest road junctions.

1975   NASHVILLE   1975

*Party candidate Hal hopes to woo voters with an unpretentious
speech.*

HAL

Who do you think is running Congress? Farmers? Engineers?
Teachers? Businessmen? No, my friends. Congress is run by
lawyers. A lawyer is trained for two things and two things
only. To clarify – that's one. And to confuse – that's the
other. He does whichever is to his client's advantage. Did you
ever ask a lawyer the time of day? He told you how to make
a watch, didn't he? Ever ask a lawyer how to get to Mr Jones'
house in the country? You got lost, didn't you?

Dir: Robert Altman • Scr: Joan Tewkesbury • Cast: Thomas Hal Phillips (Hal
Phillip Walker)

The film contains a huge cast of characters and the dialogue was almost entirely improvised by
them from the story outline. All the actors playing musicians wrote and performed their own
songs, and all the onscreen music was recorded live.

1976   ALL THE PRESIDENT'S MEN   1976

*The editor of the Washington Post berates two reporters who have
been uncovering the story of the Watergate break-in.*

BRADLEE

You know the results of the latest Gallup Poll? Half the
country never even heard of the word Watergate. Nobody gives
a shit. You guys are probably pretty tired, right? Well, you

should be. Go on home, get a nice hot bath. Rest up...fifteen minutes. Then get your asses back in gear. We're under a lot of pressure, you know, and you put us there. Nothing's riding on this except the, uh, First Amendment to the Constitution, freedom of the press, and maybe the future of the country. Not that any of that matters, but if you guys fuck up again, I'm going to get mad. Goodnight.

Dir: Alan J. Pakula • Scr: William Goldman • Based on a book by Carl Bernstein and Bob Woodward • Cast: Jason Robards (Ben Bradlee)

1983   MONTY PYTHON'S THE MEANING OF LIFE   1983

CHAPLAIN

Let us praise God. O Lord...

CONGREGATION

O Lord...

CHAPLAIN

...Ooh, You are so big...

CONGREGATION

...ooh, You are so big...

CHAPLAIN

...So absolutely huge.

CONGREGATION

...So absolutely huge.

CHAPLAIN

Gosh, we're all really impressed down here, I can tell You.

CONGREGATION

Gosh, we're all really impressed down here, I can tell You.

CHAPLAIN

Forgive us, O Lord, for this, our dreadful toadying, and...

CONGREGATION

And barefaced flattery.

                              CHAPLAIN
But You are so strong and, well, just so super.

                            CONGREGATION
Fantastic.

                              HUMPHREY
Amen.

                            CONGREGATION
Amen.

Dir: Terry Jones, Terry Gilliam • Scr: Graham Chapman, John Cleese, Terry
Gilliam, Eric Idle, Terry Jones, Michael Palin • Cast: Michael Palin
(Chaplain), John Cleese (Humphrey Williams)

The Python team refused to show the studio a script on the basis that 'If we couldn't work out
how to make a Monty Python film, they couldn't tell us.' Instead they submitted an outline
budget and a poem:

There's everything in this movie,
Everything that fits.
From the Meaning of Life in the universe,
To girls with great big tits.
We've got movie stars and foreign cars,
Explosions and the lot
Filmed as only we know how,
On the budget that we've got.
We spent a fortune on locations
And quite a bit on drink
And there's even the odd philosophical joke,
Just to make you buggers think.
Yet some parts are as serious
And as deep as you could wish

But largely it's all tits and ass
And quite a bit of fish.
Other bits are fairly childish
And some are frankly rude.
But at least we've got a lot of nice girls
All banging around in the nude.
So take your seats, enjoy yourselves
And let's just hope it's funny
Because it's not only done to make you laugh
But to make us lots of money.
So sit back and have a good time
With your boyfriend or your wife
Relax and just enjoy yourself
For this is the Meaning of Life.

1987   THE LAST EMPEROR   1987

*The fifteen-year-old Emperor of China quizzes his Scottish tutor
about conditions outside the palace.*

                              PU YI
Is it true, Mr Johnston, that many people out there have had
their heads cut off?

JOHNSTON

It is true, your Majesty. Many heads have been chopped off.
It does stop them thinking.

Dir: Bernardo Bertolucci • Scr: Mark Peploe, Bernardo Bertolucci • Cast:
Peter O'Toole (Reginald Johnston), John Lone (Pu Yi)

The logistics for the epic production were breathtaking. The Internet Movie Database cites the
following statistics:

19,000 extras were used over the course of the film;

Hairdresser Giancarlo De Leonardis imported 2,200 pounds of human hair to make the elaborate
wigs needed for the court. For the coronation scenes, his staff spent ten days training fifty
Chinese to pin wigs and plaits onto 2,000 extras in under two hours;

An Italian chef was brought in to cook for the international cast. He brought with him 22,000
bottles of Italian mineral water, 450 pounds of Italian coffee, 250 gallons of olive oil and 4,500
pounds of pasta;

The Buddhist lamas who appear in the film could not be touched by women, so extra male
wardrobe helpers were hired to dress them;

Security was so tight around the shoot that when, one day, Peter O'Toole forgot his pass, he was
denied entrance to the set.

1987 WALL STREET 1987

*Shareholder and corporate raider Gordon Gekko explains
his decision to buy an ailing paper company.*

GEKKO

Teldar Paper, Mr Cromwell, Teldar Paper has thirty-three
different vice presidents each earning over 200,000 dollars
a year. Now, I have spent the last two months analysing what
all these guys do, and I still can't figure it out. One thing
I do know is that our paper company lost 110 million dollars
last year, and I'll bet that half of that was spent in all
the paperwork going back and forth between all these vice
presidents. The new law of evolution in corporate America
seems to be survival of the unfittest. Well, in my book you
either do it right or you get eliminated. In the last seven
deals that I've been involved with, there were 2.5 million
stockholders who have made a pretax profit of 12 billion
dollars. Thank you. I am not a destroyer of companies. I am
a liberator of them! The point is, ladies and gentlemen, that
greed, for lack of a better word, is good. Greed is right,
greed works. Greed clarifies, cuts through, and captures the
essence of the evolutionary spirit. Greed, in all of its forms;
greed for life, for money, for love, knowledge has marked the
upward surge of mankind. And greed, you mark my words, will
not only save Teldar Paper, but that other malfunctioning
corporation called the USA.

Dir: Oliver Stone • Scr: Oliver Stone, Stanley Weiser • Cast: Michael
Douglas (Gordon Gekko)

1992 GLENGARRY GLEN ROSS 1992

*The employees in a real estate office are encouraged to be
ruthless.*

BLAKE

We're adding a little something to this month's sales contest.
As you all know, first prize is a Cadillac Eldorado... Second
prize is a set of steak knives. Third prize is you're fired.

Dir: James Foley • Scr: David Mamet, based on his play • Cast: Alec Baldwin
(Blake)

1993 PHILADELPHIA

Lawyer Joe Miller reminds a trial judge we live in an imperfect world.

JUDGE GARNETT

In this courtroom, Mr Miller, justice is blind to matters of race, creed, colour, religion, and sexual orientation.

JOE

With all due respect, your honour, we don't live in this courtroom, do we?

Dir: Jonathan Demme • Scr: Ron Nyswaner • Cast: Charles Napier (Judge Garnett), Denzel Washington (Joe Miller)

1994 COLOR OF NIGHT

A psychiatrist is questioned after one of his patients commits suicide.

DR CAPA

Do I need a lawyer?

DETECTIVE MARTINEZ

You're in LA. Everybody needs a lawyer.

Dir: Richard Rush • Scr: Matthew Chapman, Billy Ray • Cast: Bruce Willis (Dr Bill Capa), Rubén Blades (Detective Hector Martinez)

1994 DISCLOSURE

A lawyer tries to dissuade her client from taking action after he has been sexually harassed by his female boss.

CATHERINE

If you sue, you'll never get another job in the computer business; if you don't sue they'll bury you in Austin. If you sue it's news; if you don't it's gossip. If you sue nobody will believe you; if you don't, your wife won't. They will make your life into a living hell for the next three years until this case goes to trial. And for that privilege, it's going to cost you a minimum of a hundred thousand dollars. Do you not think it's a game, Mr Sanders? It's a game to them. How do you feel about losing?

Dir: Barry Levinson • Scr: Paul Attanasio • Based on a novel by Michael Crichton • Cast: Roma Maffia (Catherine Alvarez)

1995 DEAD MAN WALKING

A guard supervising an inmate on death row is surprised by the compassion shown by a visitor.

SISTER PREJEAN

I just don't see the sense of killing people to say that killing people's wrong.

PRISON GUARD

You know what the Bible says, 'An eye for an eye'.

SISTER PREJEAN

You know what else the Bible asks for death as a punishment? For adultery, prostitution, homosexuality, trespass upon sacred grounds, profaning a sabbath and contempt to parents.

PRISON GUARD

I ain't gonna get in no Bible quoting with no nun, 'cause I'm gonna lose.

Dir: Tim Robbins • Scr: Tim Robbins • Based on a book by Helen Prejean • Cast: Susan Sarandon (Sister Helen Prejean), Unknown (Prison Guard)

Director Tim Robbins cast his wife in the Oscar-winning lead role and used his parents, sons and sister in various scenes. His brother David wrote the soundtrack.

1996 SCHIZOPOLIS

In a baffling, dystopian world even the news broadcasts are surreal.

TV NEWSCASTER

A New Mexico woman was named Final Arbiter of Taste and Justice today, ending God's lengthy search for someone to straighten this country out. Eileen Harriet Palglace will have final say on every known subject, including who should be put to death, what clothes everyone should wear, what movies suck, and whether bald men who grow ponytails should still get laid.

Dir: Steven Soderbergh • Scr: Steven Soderbergh • Cast: Margaret Lawhon (TV Newscaster)

1996   SWINGERS

1996

Trent tries to persuade some girls at a nightclub that his friend is a man to be reckoned with.

TRENT
This is the guy behind the guy behind the guy.

Dir: Doug Liman • Scr: Jon Favreau • Cast: Vince Vaughn (Trent Walker)

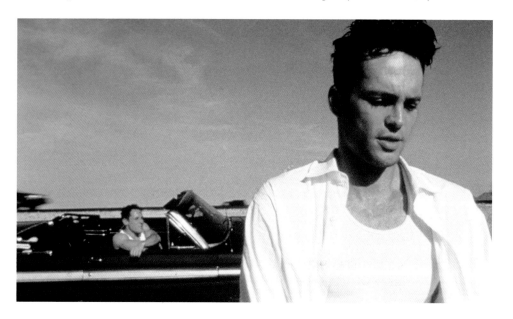

1997   DECONSTRUCTING HARRY

1997

Doris despairs of author Harry's lifestyle and preoccupations.

DORIS
You have no values. With you it's all nihilism, cynicism, sarcasm, and orgasm.

HARRY
Hey, in France I could run for office with that slogan and win.

Dir: Woody Allen • Scr: Woody Allen • Cast: Caroline Aaron (Doris), Woody Allen (Harry Block)

'IF MY FILMS DON'T SHOW A PROFIT, I KNOW I'M DOING SOMETHING RIGHT'

Enduringly known for his curmudgeonly New York Jewish wisecracks, his controversial love life and his refusal to attend award ceremonies, Woody Allen (b. 1935) has been writing, acting and directing for six decades and shows little sign of slowing. To date he has won four Oscars, two for *Annie Hall* (directing and screenplay, 1978) and one each for *Hannah and Her Sisters* (screenplay, 1987) and *Midnight in Paris* (screenplay, 2012). Although the hits have been interspersed with less successful endeavours, his inventiveness has rarely wavered and his focus on character ensures his projects attract the biggest screen stars as well as perennial collaborators.

Relying largely on regular producing partners and crew, he keeps his budgets modest and retains the right to 'final cut', ensuring his films have a unique authorial voice; even his interviews, stand-up routines and short-story collections carry the familiar Allen stamp.

From *Getting Even* (1971), a collection of short stories:

- Can we actually 'know' the universe? My God, it's hard enough finding your way around in Chinatown.

- I don't believe in an afterlife, although I am bringing a change of underwear.

- Eternal nothingness is OK if you're dressed for it.

- Not only is there no God, but try getting a plumber on weekends.

From *Without Feathers* (1975), another collection of short stories:

- As the poet said, 'Only God can make a tree' - probably because it's so hard to figure out how to get the bark on.

- Money is better than poverty, if only for financial reasons.

- What a wonderful thing, to be conscious! I wonder what the people in New Jersey do.

- Why does man kill? He kills for food. And not only food: frequently there must be a beverage.

- It's not that I'm afraid to die, I just don't want to be there when it happens.

- The lion and the calf shall lie down together but the calf won't get much sleep.

As a stand-up comic:

- I feel sex is a beautiful thing between two people. Between five, it's fantastic.

- I was involved in an extremely good example of oral contraception two weeks ago. I asked a girl to go to bed with me, she said 'no'.

- I was in analysis. I was suicidal. As a matter of fact, I would have killed myself, but I was in analysis with a strict Freudian and if you kill yourself they make you pay for the sessions you miss.

- I was thrown out of college for cheating on the metaphysics exam; I looked into the soul of the boy sitting next to me.

- When I was kidnapped, my parents snapped into action. They rented out my room.

- Interestingly, according to modern astronomers, space is finite. This is a very comforting thought – particularly for people who can never remember where they have left things.

From interviews between 1985 and 2011:

- It figures you've got to hate yourself if you've got any integrity at all.

- If my films make one more person miserable, I'll feel I have done my job.

- Life doesn't imitate art, it imitates bad television.

- My relationship with death remains the same – I'm strongly against it.

- Someone once asked me if my dream was to live on in the hearts of people, and I said I would prefer to live on in my apartment.

- I think universal harmony is a pipe dream and it may be more productive to focus on more modest goals, like a ban on yodelling.

- I do feel that [life] is a grim, painful, nightmarish, meaningless experience, and that the only way that you can be happy is if you tell yourself some lies and deceive yourself.

- The two biggest myths about me are that I'm an intellectual, because I wear these glasses, and that I'm an artist because my films lose money.

- For some reason I'm more appreciated in France than I am back home. The subtitles must be incredibly good.

- I'm not an actor. I can't play Chekhov, I can't play Shakespeare or Strindberg. I can do that thing that I do. There's a few different kinds of things I can act credibly. I can play an intellectual or a low-life.

1997   THE ICE STORM   1997

A disaffected teenager is invited to say grace at supper with her family.

WENDY

Dear Lord, thank you for this Thanksgiving holiday. And for all the material possessions we have and enjoy. And for letting us white people kill all the Indians and steal their tribal lands. And stuff ourselves like pigs, even though children in Asia are being napalmed.

Dir: Ang Lee • Scr: James Schamus • Based on a novel by Rick Moody • Cast: Christina Ricci (Wendy Hood)

1999   MAGNOLIA   1999

A police officer tries to balance compassion with justice.

JIMMY

Sometimes people need a little help. Sometimes people need to be forgiven. And sometimes they need to go to jail.

Dir: Paul Thomas Anderson • Scr: Paul Thomas Anderson • Cast: Philip Baker Hall (Jimmy Gator)

2000   TRAFFIC   2000

An Ohio judge appointed as head of the Office of National Drug Control describes his new job.

                          ROBERT

What's Washington like? Well, it's like Calcutta - surrounded by beggars. The only difference is the beggars in Washington wear 1,500-dollar suits and they don't say please or thank you.

Dir: Steven Soderbergh • Scr: Stephen Gaghan • Cast: Michael Douglas (Robert Wakefield)

On the first day of shooting *Sex, Lies, and Videotape* Soderbergh's producers sent him a joking telegram saying he 'couldn't direct traffic', let alone a feature film. Twelve years later he won an Oscar for directing *Traffic*.

As with telephone numbers in films, which are frequently composed with the structure 555-xxxx to ensure no viewer might dial and achieve a successful connection to a random subscriber, vehicle plates follow a format which means they have no actual bearing on established registrations. One of the characters' cars has the plate 2GAT123: the same California ID – on different vehicles – also appears in *Beverly Hills Cop II, L.A. Story, Go, Pay It Forward, Mulholland Drive, Crazy/Beautiful, Two and a Half Men*, and *S.W.A.T.*

2000   BOILER ROOM   2000

Ambitious stockbroker Jim addresses a new intake of recruits to his company.

                          JIM

There's an important phrase that we use here, and I think it's time that you all learned it. Act as if. You understand what that means? Act as if you are the fucking President of this firm. Act as if you got a nine-inch cock. Okay? Act as if.

Dir: Ben Younger • Scr: Ben Younger • Cast: Ben Affleck (Jim Young)

2001   THE LORD OF THE RINGS: THE FELLOWSHIP OF THE RING   2001

                          GANDALF
              One Ring to rule them all,
              One Ring to find them,
              One Ring to bring them all
              And in the darkness bind them.

Dir: Peter Jackson • Scr: Peter Jackson, Fran Walsh, Philippa Boyens • Based on a book by J. R. R. Tolkien • Cast: Ian McKellen (Gandalf)

2004   CRASH   2004

A woman crosses the street to avoid two black men in her middle-class neighbourhood.

ANTHONY

Wait, wait, wait. See what that woman just did? You see that? She got colder the minute she saw us. Man, look around you, man. You couldn't find a whiter, safer or better-lit part of the city right now. But yet this white woman sees two black guys who look like UCLA students strolling down the sidewalk, and her reaction is blind fear? I mean, look at us dawg, are we dressed like gang-bangers? Huh? No. Do we look threatening? No. Fact: If anyone should be scared around here, it's us! We're the only two black faces surrounded by a sea of over-caffeinated white people patrolled by the trigger happy LAPD. So you tell me. Why aren't we scared?

PETER

Because we have guns?

ANTHONY

You could be right.

Dir: Paul Haggis • Scr: Paul Haggis, Robert Moresco • Cast: Chris 'Ludacris' Bridges (Anthony), Larenz Tate (Peter Waters)

2005   SYRIANA   2005

An oil executive dismisses warnings that his business practices are illegal.

DANNY

Corruption is our protection. Corruption keeps us safe and warm. Corruption is why you and I are prancing around in here instead of fighting over scraps of meat out in the streets. Corruption is why we win.

Dir: Stephen Gaghan • Scr: Stephen Gaghan • Based on a book by Robert Baer • Cast: Tim Blake Nelson (Danny Dalton)

'Syriana' is a term used by US political think tanks to describe their vision of a newly structured Middle East. Writer/director Gaghan did extensive research into the global oil industry before he began work on the script, visiting Washington DC, the French Riviera, Lebanon, Syria and Dubai. He met businessmen, lobbyists, arms dealers and oil traders as well as members of Hezbollah including on one occasion – when he was blindfolded for security reasons – Sheik Mohammed Hussein Fadlallah.

Plainview explains how he no longer needs to buy Eli's land
because he has already drilled beneath it to steal his oil.

PLAINVIEW

Stop crying, you snivelling ass! Stop your nonsense. You're
just afterbirth, Eli -

ELI

No...

PLAINVIEW

slithering out of your mother's filth.

ELI

No...

PLAINVIEW

They should have put you in a glass jar on the mantlepiece.
Where were you when Paul was suckling at his mother's teat?
Where were you? Who was nursing you, poor Eli? One of Bandy's
sows? That land has been had. Nothing you can do about it.
It's gone. It's had. You lose.

ELI
If you would just take this lease, Daniel –

Plainview screams like a madman.

PLAINVIEW

Drainage! Drainage, Eli, you boy. Drained dry!

Plainview calms himself.

> I'm so sorry. Here, if you have a milkshake, and I have a
> milkshake, and I have a straw – there it is, that's a straw,
> you see? You watching? And my straw reaches *acrooooooooss* the
> room, and starts to drink your milkshake. I... drink... your...
> milkshake! I drink it up!

Dir: Paul Thomas Anderson • Scr: Paul Thomas Anderson • Based on a novel
by Upton Sinclair • Cast: Daniel Day-Lewis (Daniel Plainview), Paul Dano
(Eli Sunday)

Paul Thomas Anderson claimed he watched *The Treasure of the Sierra Madre* (1948) for
inspiration every night while shooting. That film – about gold prospectors in Mexico –
was directed by John Huston, on whom Day-Lewis based Plainview's voice and physical
manner.

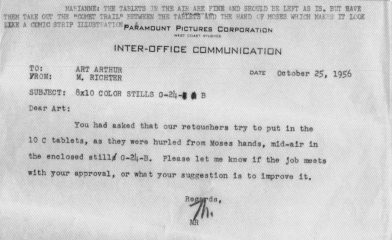

MARIANNE: THE TABLETS IN THE AIR ARE FINE AND SHOULD BE LEFT AS IS. BUT HAVE
THEM TAKE OUT THE "COMET TRAIL" BETWEEN THE TABLETS AND THE HAND OF MOSES WHICH MAKES IT LOOK
LIKE A COMIC STRIP ILLUSTRATION PARAMOUNT PICTURES CORPORATION
WEST COAST STUDIOS

INTER-OFFICE COMMUNICATION

TO: ART ARTHUR   DATE October 25, 1956
FROM: M. RICHTER

SUBJECT: 8x10 COLOR STILLS G-24-▉ ▉ B

Dear Art:

        You had asked that our retouchers try to put in the
10 C tablets, as they were hurled from Moses hands, mid-air in
the enclosed still G-24-B. Please let me know if the job meets
with your approval, or what your suggestion is to improve it.

                        Regards,

                        MR

The Ten Commandments (1956): Hollywood has always been drawn to epic tales, although today's special effects have made them easier to realize.

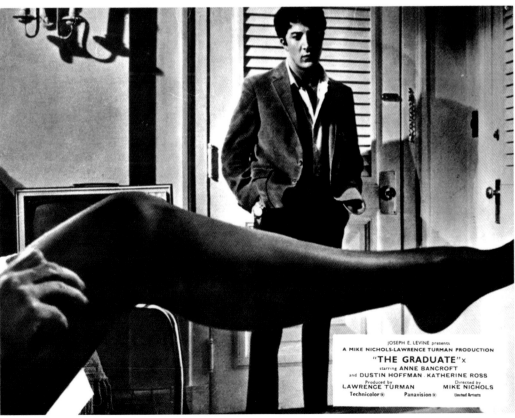

Two cinema lobby cards perfectly capture Dustin Hoffman's dilemma as his girlfriend's mother tries to seduce him in *The Graduate* (1967).

Marlon Brando and Martin Sheen face off at the climax of Francis Ford Coppola's monumental *Apocalypse Now* (1979).

War

BÄUMER

You still think it's beautiful to die for your country. The first bombardment taught us better. When it comes to dying for your country, it's better not to die at all.

Dir: Lewis Milestone • Scr: George Abbott, Maxwell Anderson, Erich Maria Remarque • Based on a book by Erich Maria Remarque • Cast: Edwin Maxwell (Herr Bäumer)

Germany was still sensitive about her defeat in the First World War and hard-core patriots tried to disrupt screenings by shouting slogans and releasing rats into theatres. When the Nazi party came to power, the film was banned and those who wanted to see it had to take special tours to neighbouring Switzerland and France where it played to full houses.

A vicar laments the parishioners his village has lost to the war.

VICAR

We, in this quiet corner of England, have suffered the loss of friends very dear to us - some close to this church: George West, choir boy; James Bellard, station master and bell ringer and a proud winner, only one hour before his death, of the Belding Cup for his beautiful Miniver rose; and our hearts go out in sympathy to the two families who share the cruel loss of a young girl who was married at this altar only two weeks ago. The homes of many of us have been destroyed, and the lives of young and old have been taken. There is scarcely a household that hasn't been struck to the heart. And why? Surely you must have asked yourself this question. Why in all conscience should these be the ones to suffer? Children, old people, a young girl at the height of her loveliness. Why these? Are these our soldiers? Are these our fighters? Why should they be sacrificed? I shall tell you why. Because this is not only a war of soldiers in uniform. It is a war of the people, of all the people, and it must be fought not only on the battlefield, but in the cities and in the villages, in the factories and on the farms, in the home, and in the heart of every man, woman and child who loves freedom. Well, we have buried our dead, but we shall not forget them. Instead they will inspire us with an unbreakable determination to free ourselves and those who come after us from the tyranny and terror that threaten to strike us down. This is the people's war! It is our war! We are the fighters! Fight it then! Fight it with all that is in us, and may God defend the right.

Dir: William Wyler • Scr: Arthur Wimperis, George Froeschel, James Hilton, Claudine West • Based on a novel by Jan Struther • Cast: Henry Wilcoxon (Vicar)

The wartime film was made at a bleak time for the Allies and director William Wyler repeatedly rewrote this speech, acutely aware of its importance for morale. President Roosevelt recognized its power and the text was the basis for much subsequent propaganda. When Greer Garson won the Oscar for Best Actress, she delivered a speech lasting five and a half minutes, prompting the Academy to impose a forty-five-second time limit thereafter.

1942 TO BE OR NOT TO BE   1942

German Colonel Ehrhardt unwittingly insults actor Josef Tura, who has disguised himself as a Nazi sympathizer.

> TURA
>
> Her husband is that great, great Polish actor Josef Tura. You've probably heard of him.

> COLONEL EHRHARDT
>
> Oh, yes. As a matter of fact I saw him on the stage when I was in Warsaw once before the war.

> TURA
>
> Really?

> COLONEL EHRHARDT
>
> What he did to Shakespeare, we are doing now to Poland.

Dir: Ernst Lubitsch • Scr: Edwin Justus Mayer • Based on a story by Melchior Lengyel • Cast: Jack Benny (Joseph Tura), Sig Ruman (Colonel Ehrhardt)

SCRIPT DOCTORS

> POLISH: to fix minor problems in an otherwise completed script.
>
> PUNCH UP: to give key scenes and dialogue extra energy.

The single most dreaded phrase in the film business is 'it died at the box office'. Nobody has yet devised a way to take out health insurance for a picture, but producers are willing to spend fortunes on script doctors. As with all specialists, their fees are steep and membership of their guild hard-won and exclusive. When a project has been given the green light — that is to say, that finances have been committed — the pressure to 'lock' the script becomes immense; once the actors are cast, the locations are fixed and the crew is on the clock, it is too late to tinker under the hood.

So where is the original writer in all this? By the time she has handed in dozens of drafts, rewrites and polishes, she may have lost her way, become burnt out or simply fallen victim to the infighting of executive factions. There may have been others involved, all of whom are vying to maintain their contractual, financial and credit positions. As the first day of principal photography approaches and directors and producers are mired in the innumerable day-to-day issues leading up to the shoot, a quick fix from a trusted expert is increasingly desirable. So, as they say in *Ghostbusters*, 'Who you gonna call?'

If you're worried about *Indiana Jones and the Last Crusade* (1989), *Sleepy Hollow* (1999) or *The Bourne Ultimatum* (2007), you need playwright Tomáš Straussler (better known as Sir Tom Stoppard, OM, CBE, FRSL). Although he has plenty of Tonys and an Oscar to his name for credited works including *Brazil* (1985), *Shakespeare in Love* (1998) and *Enigma* (2001), he is regularly hired on anonymous rewrites: 'The second reason for doing it is that you get to work with people you admire. The first reason, of course, is that it's overpaid.'

One day, while in the shower, he received a call from Steven Spielberg, an old friend. The director was shooting *Schindler's List* (1993) and was having trouble getting a scene written by Steven Zaillian to work on camera. Still dripping wet, Stoppard improvised a solution on the spot while the crew waited on location in Poland. Like most in his trade, Stoppard has huge respect for the writers whose work he is summoned to 'fix', but accepts it as an unavoidable part of the way the business works. 'I [urged] him just to film Zaillian's script. But Steven, like a lot of other people in movies, tends to think one more opinion can't hurt.'

Zaillian was almost certainly untroubled by contributions from others as he retained sole credit when the film won the Best Adapted Screenplay Oscar. The Screenwriters Guild of America has strict rules about how much of a filmed work must have been written by any individual to qualify for a shared credit: for original work 50 per cent, and for adapted material 33 per cent. Without a credit, there will be no residuals (royalties) or any chance of nomination for awards, so script doctors accept anonymity in return for a fee that may run to $300,000 a week.

As far back as the 1930s Ben Hecht (*Scarface*, *Notorious*, *Wuthering Heights*) was in demand for his uncredited assistance on such hits as *Gone with the Wind*, *Foreign Correspondent* and *Mutiny on the Bounty*. Today the hottest names include David Koepp (*Jurassic Park*), Scott Frank (*Minority Report*), Aaron Sorkin (*The Social Network*) and Susannah Grant (*Erin Brockovich*). Most studios have their favourite writers on speed-dial for last-minute fixes, even as late as post-production when the editing process sometimes reveals weaknesses in the story line and re-shoots are hurriedly ordered. Even actors have their preferred saviours: Vince Vaughn uses Dana Fox (*Couples Retreat*), Will Smith asks for Akiva Goldsman (*The Da Vinci Code*) and Matt Damon counts on George Nolfi (*The Bourne Ultimatum*).

Despite the hefty cheques they write, studio executives remain reluctant to discuss the prevalence of these last-minute fixes — and are ambivalent about their benefits. Two anonymous LA sources highlight the dilemma: 'Once a movie is green-lit, you're no longer spending development dollars, so it's not speculative spending. You're now making an investment on making this the best movie it can be. And at that point in the process, that last 10 per cent of the script is the most important.' Even so, 'Sometimes you have to spend even more money to fix the problem created by the script doctor you just hired. It's a crapshoot.'

1944 HAIL THE CONQUERING HERO 1944

LIBBY'S AUNT

Well, that's the war for you. It's always hard on women. Either they take your men away and never send them back at all, or they send them back unexpectedly just to embarrass you. No consideration at all.

Dir: Preston Sturges • Scr: Preston Sturges • Cast: Elizabeth Patterson (Martha, Libby's Aunt)

1947 CROSSFIRE 1947

CAPTAIN FINLAY

My grandfather was killed just because he was an Irish Catholic. Hating is always the same, always senseless. One day it kills Irish Catholics, the next day Jews, the next day Protestants, the next day Quakers. It's hard to stop. It can end up killing people who wear striped neckties.

Dir: Edward Dmytryk • Scr: John Paxton • Based on a novel by Richard Brooks • Cast: Robert Young (Captain Finlay)

The Japanese commander of a POW camp discusses with the commander of his Allied prisoners the importance of the railway bridge they have been forced to build.

COLONEL SAITO

Do you know what will happen to me if the bridge is not built on time?

LIEUTENANT COLONEL NICHOLSON

I haven't the foggiest.

COLONEL SAITO

I'll have to kill myself. What would you do if you were me?

LIEUTENANT COLONEL NICHOLSON

I suppose if I were you... I'd have to kill myself.

Dir: David Lean • Scr: Carl Foreman, Michael Wilson • Based on a novel by Pierre Boulle • Cast: Sessue Hayakawa (Colonel Saito), Alec Guinness (Lieutenant Colonel Nicholson)

Pierre Boulle's novel was a bestseller and producer Sam Spiegel bought a copy to read on his flight from Paris to London. By the time he arrived in England he was so determined to make a film of it that he got on the next flight back and demanded a meeting with the author, who promptly agreed to sell him the rights.

1960   THE MAGNIFICENT SEVEN

VIN

We deal in lead, friend.

Dir: John Sturges • Scr: William Roberts • Based on a film by Akira
Kurosawa • Cast: Steve McQueen (Vin Tanner)

1964   DR STRANGELOVE

*Faced with a nuclear crisis, the President tries to quell uproar
among his military staff.*

PRESIDENT MUFFLEY

Gentlemen, you can't fight in here! This is the War Room.

Dir: Stanley Kubrick • Scr: Stanley Kubrick, Terry Southern, Peter
George • Based on a novel by Peter George • Cast: Peter Sellers (President
Muffley)

Peter Sellers was paid $1 million [$7.5 million], over half the film's budget, for playing the parts of President Merkin Muffley, Group Captain Lionel Mandrake and Dr Strangelove; Stanley Kubrick famously quipped: 'I got three for the price of six.' International paranoia about nuclear war was running so high at the time the film was made that a camera crew shooting aerial footage near a US base in Greenland was forced down and accused of being Soviet spies.

1964   ZULU

*Outnumbered British soldiers do battle with Zulu warriors at
Rorke's Drift, 1879.*

SERGEANT BOURNE

It's a miracle.

LIEUTENANT CHARD

If it's a miracle, Colour Sergeant, it's a short-chamber Boxer
Henry .45 calibre miracle.

SERGEANT BOURNE

And a bayonet, sir, with some guts behind.

Dir: Cy Endfield • Scr: John Prebble, Cy Endfield • Cast: Nigel Green
(Colour Sergeant Frank Bourne), Stanley Baker (Lieutenant John Chard)

Racial tensions had not eased in the century that passed between the historical events and their portrayal on film. Cast and crew on location in South Africa were warned not to fraternize with the topless tribal dancers as the penalty for inter-racial sex at the time was seven years' hard labour.

THE BATTLE OF ALGIERS (*LA BATTAGLIA DI ALGERI*)

JOURNALIST

M. Ben M'Hidi, don't you think it's a bit cowardly to use women's baskets and handbags to carry explosive devices that kill so many innocent people?

BEN M'HIDI

And doesn't it seem to you even more cowardly to drop napalm bombs on defenceless villages, so that there are a thousand times more innocent victims? Of course, if we had your airplanes it would be a lot easier for us. Give us your bombers, and you can have our baskets.

Dir: Gillo Pontecorvo • Scr: Gillo Pontecorvo, Franco Solinas • Based on a book by Saadi Yacef • Cast: Uncredited

The film was commissioned by the Algerian government to portray the 1954 revolution in an even-handed way. In 2003 the *New York Times* reported that the Pentagon screened the film for senior troops involved in the Iraq conflict. The invitation read: 'How to win a battle against terrorism and lose the war of ideas.'

1969 BATTLE OF BRITAIN 1969

A German pilot shocks the commander of the Luftwaffe by speaking the truth.

GÖRING

I'm here to help. Is there anything I can do for you?

AIRMAN

Yes, Reichsmarschall. Give me a squadron of Spitfires.

Dir: Guy Hamilton • Scr: James Kennaway, Wilfred Greatorex • Based on a novel by Derek Dempster, Derek Wood • Cast: Hein Riess (Reichsmarschall Hermann Göring), Unknown (Airman)

1970 PATTON 1970

General Patton addresses his troops.

GENERAL PATTON

Be seated. Now I want you to remember that no bastard ever won a war by dying for his country. He won it by making the other poor dumb bastard die for *his* country.

Dir: Franklin J. Schaffner • Scr: Francis Ford Coppola, Edmund H. North •
Based on a book by Ladislas Farago, Omar Bradley • Cast: George C. Scott
(General Patton)

The quote above comes from a long speech by Patton at the very start of the film and has
become so well known that it is now frequently cited as an actual remark by the general.
Scott won an Oscar for his performance but refused to accept it because he disapproved of
competitive awards for acting.

1970 CROMWELL 1970

> CROMWELL
>
> Every man who wages war believes God is on his side. I'll
> warrant God should often wonder who is on His.

Dir: Ken Hughes • Scr: Ken Hughes • Cast: Richard Harris (Oliver Cromwell)

1979 APOCALYPSE NOW 1979

*An air cavalry commander relishes the destruction his regiment
has wrought.*

> LIEUTENANT COLONEL KILGORE
>
> Smell that? You smell that?
>
> LANCE
>
> What?
>
> LIEUTENANT COLONEL KILGORE
>
> Napalm, son. Nothing else in the world smells like that.

He kneels, savouring it.

> I love the smell of napalm in the morning. You know, one time
> we had a hill bombed for twelve hours. When it was all over,
> I walked up. We didn't find one of 'em, not one stinkin' dink
> body. The smell, you know that gasoline smell, the whole hill.
> Smelled like...

He scents the air.

> ...victory.

Dir: Francis Ford Coppola • Scr: John Milius, Francis Ford Coppola,
Michael Herr • Based on a novella by Joseph Conrad • Cast: Robert Duvall
(Lieutenant Colonel Bill Kilgore), Sam Bottoms (Lance B. Johnson)

'IT'S NOT ABOUT VIETNAM. IT *IS* VIETNAM'

The making of Francis Ford Coppola's magisterial *Apocalypse Now* mirrors the end result as an epic, barely credible adventure; the schedule on location in the Philippines went from five to seventeen months, the budget from $12 million to $31 million [$38 million to $98 million], the director himself contemplated suicide on several occasions and by the end of the shoot he had lost nearly 50kg.

Based on Conrad's short novel *Heart of Darkness* (1899), the film moves the story from colonial Congo to Vietnam where Willard, a US captain, is sent to kill Kurtz, a Green Beret general driven mad by the wilderness and by his own power. The war and the jungle itself become characters in an exploration of morality and civilization; Coppola identified increasingly closely with Kurtz and introduced the film at its Cannes début by saying:

> My film is not a movie; it is not about Vietnam. It *is* Vietnam.
> It's what it was really like; it was crazy. And the way we
> made it was very much like the way the Americans were in
> Vietnam. We were in the jungle, there were too many of us, we
> had access to too much money, too much equipment, and little
> by little we went insane.

The original adaptation was by John Milius but later drafts grew to incorporate much documentary material about the war from Michael Herr's Vietnam war memoir *Dispatches* (1977). As a result of the diverse inspirations, wayward actors and extraordinary upheavals

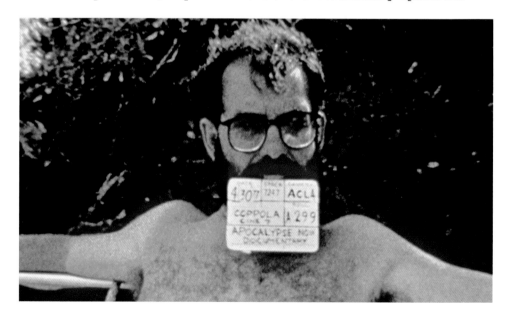

during production, Coppola ended up rewriting a huge amount as he went along. Several weeks into shooting he replaced Harvey Keitel (as Willard) with Martin Sheen and was forced to begin the movie again.

When Sheen filmed the opening scenes, he was so drunk he punched his reflection in a mirror, slicing his hand open; Coppola just told the camera to keep rolling and filmed the ensuing mayhem as he yelled improvised directions at the actor. During hugely expensive battle sequences, the helicopters the production had borrowed from President Marcos were recalled to fight a real war. Tropical storms destroyed several large sets, causing a hiatus of eight weeks. Despite full-time security guards, the crew's payroll was stolen.

By this stage Coppola had mortgaged everything he owned to cover the budget overages; when filming resumed, Sheen (aged thirty-six) had a heart attack. Although Coppola's prime concern was the actor's safety, he was terrified the studios would shut him down if they discovered the truth, saying: '[Even] if Marty dies I want to hear that everything's okay until I say Marty is dead.' While Sheen recovered, his brother Joe Estevez was used to double him in wide shots.

When Marlon Brando, the film's principal star, arrived for a month's work, he was grotesquely overweight and extremely sensitive about how he would be filmed; Coppola sidestepped the issue by shooting him largely in half-lit close-ups. Despite being paid $3.5 million [$11 million] for a month's work, Brando also declared he had not read the script — and when he did so, refused to play it.

Realizing he could not force his star to perform, Coppola decided to 'just shoot for the next three weeks irrationally'. After Brando ended one crucial scene by saying 'I can't think of any more dialogue today', Coppola bared his heart to his wife's documentary camera:

> [I'm] feeling like an idiot for having set in motion stuff that doesn't make any sense, that doesn't match [other scenes], and yet I'm doing it and the reason that I'm doing it is out of desperation because I have no rational way to do it. What I have to do is to admit that I don't know what I'm doing.

Both Captain Willard and Colonel Kurtz deliver speeches which reflect Coppola's mindset:

> CAPTAIN WILLARD: How many people had I already killed? There were those six that I knew about for sure. Close enough to blow their last breath in my face. But this time, it was an American and an officer. That wasn't supposed to make any

difference to me, but it did. Shit...charging a man with murder in this place was like handing out speeding tickets in the Indy 500.

COLONEL KURTZ: I remember when I was with Special Forces. Seems a thousand centuries ago. We went into a camp to inoculate some children. We'd left the camp after we had inoculated the children for polio. And this old man came running after us, and he was crying. He couldn't see. We went back there, and they had come and hacked off every inoculated arm. There they were, in a pile - a pile of little arms. And I remember, I... I... I cried. I wept like some grandmother. I wanted to tear my teeth out. I didn't know what I wanted to do. And I want to remember it. I never want to forget it. I never want to forget. And then I realized - like I was shot, like I was shot with a diamond, a diamond bullet right through my forehead. And I thought, 'My God, the genius of that. The genius.' The will to do that. Perfect, genuine, complete, crystalline, pure! And then I realized, they were stronger than me because they could stand it. These were not monsters. These were men - trained cadres. These men who fought with their hearts who have families, who have children, who are filled with love - that they had the strength, the strength to do that. If I had ten divisions of those men, then our troubles here would be over very quickly.

Shooting was eventually completed in May 1977, but the editing took a further two years. Initially released to mixed reviews, it was recut on several occasions and quickly recouped its costs; today it stands close to the top of every significant poll for the greatest film of the past one hundred years.

1979   THE GREAT SANTINI   1979

LIEUTENANT COLONEL 'BULL' MEECHUM

Now, I don't want you to consider me as just your commanding officer. I want you to look on me like I was, well - God. If I say something, you pretend it's coming from the burning bush. Now, we're members of the proudest, most elite group of fighting men in the history of the world. We are Marines! Marines Corps fighter pilots! We have no other function. That is our mission and you are either gonna hack it or pack it. Do you read me? Within thirty days, I am gonna lead

the toughest, flyingest sons-of-bitches in the world. The 312
Werewolf Squadron will make history, or it will die trying.
Now, you're flying with Bull Meecham now and I kid you not,
this is the eye of the storm. Welcome aboard.

Dir: • Lewis John Carlino • Scr: Lewis John Carlino, Herman Raucher • Based
on a novel by Pat Conroy • Cast: Robert Duvall (Lieutenant Colonel Wilbur
'Bull' Meechum)

1980 THE BIG RED ONE 1980

*During the Second World War, an American platoon in Europe
passes a war memorial.*

PRIVATE JOHNSON

Would you look at how fast they put the names of all our
guys who got killed?

SERGEANT

That's a World War One memorial.

PRIVATE JOHNSON

But the names are the same.

SERGEANT

They always are.

Dir: Samuel Fuller • Scr: Samuel Fuller • Cast: Kelly Ward (Private
Johnson), Lee Marvin (The Sergeant)

1986 PLATOON 1986

*Bunny has made his peace with his tour of Vietnam in a way that
unsettles his platoon mate Junior.*

BUNNY

You know, Junior, some of the things we done, man... I don't
feel like we done something wrong. But sometimes, man, I get
this bad feeling. I told the Padre the truth, man. I like it
here. You get to do what you want. Nobody fucks with you. The
only worry you got is dying. And if that happens, you won't
know about it anyway. So, what the fuck, man.

JUNIOR

JUNIOR

Shit, I got to be in this hole with you, man? I just know I shouldn't have come.

Dir: Oliver Stone • Scr: Oliver Stone • Cast: Kevin Dillon (Bunny), Reggie Johnson (Junior)

1987 FULL METAL JACKET   1987

A drill sergeant welcomes a batch of new recruits to the US Marines.

GUNNERY SERGEANT HARTMAN

Today... is Christmas! There will be a magic show at zero-nine-thirty! Chaplain Charlie will tell you about how the free world will conquer Communism with the aid of God and a few Marines! God has a hard-on for Marines because we kill everything we see! He plays His games, we play ours! To show our appreciation for so much power, we keep heaven packed with fresh souls! God was here before the Marine Corps! So you can give your heart to Jesus, but your ass belongs to the Corps! Do you ladies understand?

Dir: Stanley Kubrick • Scr: Stanley Kubrick, Michael Herr, Gustav Hasford • Based on a novel by Gustav Hasford • Cast: R. Lee Ermey (Gunnery Sergeant Hartman)

R. Lee Ermey had been a Marine instructor during the Vietnam War; Kubrick hired him as a technical adviser but Ermey wanted to play the role written for Hartman, the drill sergeant. To persuade the director he was right for the part, Ermey filmed an audition in which he improvised a torrent of expletives and insults while being bombarded by tennis balls. After he won the part, Ermey gave Kubrick 150 pages of suggested dialogue and was eventually permitted to improvise most of his own lines.

1992 A FEW GOOD MEN 1992

US Marine Colonel Jessep challenges a liberal lawyer to weigh the value of one life against many. 'Code Red' is a military term for punishment by one's peers.

LIEUTENANT KAFFEE

Colonel Jessep, did you order the Code Red?

JUDGE RANDOLPH

You don't have to answer that question!

COLONEL JESSEP

I'll answer the question! You want answers?

LIEUTENANT KAFFEE

I think I'm entitled to.

COLONEL JESSEP

You want answers?

LIEUTENANT KAFFEE

I want the truth!

COLONEL JESSEP

You can't handle the truth! Son, we live in a world that has walls, and those walls have to be guarded by men with guns. Who's gonna do it? You? You, Lt. Weinburg? I have a greater responsibility than you could possibly fathom. You weep for Santiago, and you curse the Marines. You have that luxury. You have the luxury of not knowing what I know. That Santiago's death, while tragic, probably saved lives. And my existence, while grotesque and incomprehensible to you, saves lives. You don't want the truth because deep down in places you don't talk about at parties, you want me on that wall, you need me on that wall. We use words like honour, code, loyalty. We use these words as the backbone of a life spent defending something. You use them as a punchline. I have neither the time nor the inclination to explain myself to a man who rises and sleeps under the blanket of the very freedom that I provide, and then questions the manner in which I provide it. I would rather you just said thank you, and went on your way. Otherwise, I suggest you pick up a weapon, and stand a post. Either way, I don't give a damn what you think you are entitled to.

LIEUTENANT KAFFEE

Did you order the Code Red?

COLONEL JESSEP

I did the job I...

LIEUTENANT KAFFEE

Did you order the Code Red?

COLONEL JESSEP

You're goddamn right I did!

Dir: Rob Reiner • Scr: Aaron Sorkin • Cast: Tom Cruise (Lieutenant Daniel Kaffee), J. A. Preston (Judge Randolph), Jack Nicholson (Colonel Nathan Jessep)

1997   JACKIE BROWN   1997

Arms dealer Ordell has perfected his own particular sales patter.

ORDELL

AK-47. The very best there is. When you absolutely, positively got to kill every motherfucker in the room, accept no substitutes.

Dir: Quentin Tarantino • Scr: Quentin Tarantino • Based on a novel by Elmore Leonard • Cast: Samuel L. Jackson (Ordell Robbie)

Despite the fact that Samuel L. Jackson's character sells guns for a living the film contains the least violence and the lowest body count of any of Tarantino's films; nine shots are fired, and only four deaths result.

FADE IN...

> 'If I really considered myself a writer, I wouldn't be writing screenplays. I'd be writing novels.'
> Quentin Tarantino

Why is a screenplay not just a book with lazy punctuation and a clunky typeface? A good novel is an artefact as well as an inspiration, lying comfortably in the hand and stored carefully on a shelf among other favourites waiting to be revisited. It unlocks a different world for each reader, provoking and enlarging their imagination. It is a perpetual beginning, and an end in itself. A screenplay, really just a handbook detailing action and dialogue, is as likely to be used as a wedge for an unsteady video monitor as a notepad for taking orders for the make-up department's lunch requests. Pages are torn out as sequences are completed and scenes are annotated with timings, continuity requirements and lens data. At the end of the shoot most will be thrown away.

A script, for all the love and attention the screenwriter has given it, is a tool. It will never be seen by its intended audience; what lies within exists to be shaped by directors, spoken by actors and visualized by cinematographers. Computer graphics departments may provide mountains, space ships, explosions and tears, and each will have a reality the audience is not invited to imagine for themselves. The editor will tell us when to look at our hero — and when to look away — and the composer will let us know whether we should laugh or cry.

Although the crew hope to do justice to the power and vision of the script, their primary task is to deliver around ninety minutes of material to a precise set of technical standards while dealing with changeable weather, cold-ridden actors, dogs barking nearby and tricky props. The writer may have spent whole days perfecting the closing dialogue but at the moment it will be spoken aloud the camera department is likely be more concerned with reframing a shot to exclude a traffic light in the distance or laying sandbags on the pavement to ensure the actor can stop at the correct point for the focus-puller.

Generally, writers find life on set either disappointingly slow or maddeningly complex. Although some have a close relationship with directors, it is usually because they are familiar with these realities and willing to view writing as a wider process which accommodates egos, rainstorms and tea breaks. Those who fight for the honour of every last word on the page are usually given a brief introduction to the cast and then hastily driven home.

Stories abound of writers being banished from the sets of 'their' movies; with production costs running into hundreds of thousands of dollars a day, a disagreement with the director about the kind of car the actor would drive can cost as much as the car itself. Since everyone on the set is keen to avoid expense and delay, the typical writer's contract will read as follows:

> OWNERSHIP OF THE WORK: Writer hereby assigns to Producer the sole and exclusive ownership throughout the world and in perpetuity of all rights, title and interest of every kind and nature (including without limitation copyright and the right to create derivative works based on the Work) in the Work, and waives his or her moral rights in and to the Work.

1998   SAVING PRIVATE RYAN   1998

A team of US soldiers is sent behind enemy lines to rescue a paratrooper whose four brothers have been lost in combat.

CAPTAIN MILLER

He better be worth it. He better go home and cure a disease, or invent a longer-lasting light bulb.

Dir: Steven Spielberg • Scr: Robert Rodat • Cast: Tom Hanks (Captain John Miller)

All the lead actors were made to undergo exhaustive military training with the exception of Matt Damon, playing Private Ryan, since director Spielberg wanted the other soldiers to feel a genuine resentment towards him.

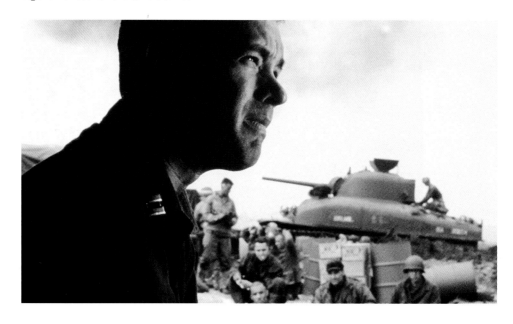

MAXIMUS

Five thousand of my men are out there in the freezing
mud. Three thousand of them are bloodied and cleaved. Two
thousand will never leave this place. I will not believe that
they fought and died for nothing.

MARCUS AURELIUS

And what would you believe?

MAXIMUS

They fought for you and for Rome.

MARCUS AURELIUS

And what is Rome, Maximus?

MAXIMUS

I've seen much of the rest of the world. It is brutal and cruel
and dark. Rome is the light.

MARCUS AURELIUS

Yet you have never been there. You have not seen what it
has become. I am dying, Maximus. When a man sees his end, he
wants to know there was some purpose to his life. How will
the world speak my name in years to come? Will I be known as
the philosopher? The warrior? The tyrant? Or will I be the
emperor who gave Rome back her true self? There was once a
dream that was Rome. You could only whisper it. Anything more
than a whisper and it would vanish, it was so fragile. And I
fear that it will not survive the winter.

Dir: Ridley Scott • Scr: David Franzoni, John Logan, William
Nicholson • Cast: Russell Crowe (Maximus Decimus Meridius), Richard
Harris (Marcus Aurelius)

The two horses depicted on Maximus's breastplate are named Argento and Scarto – Silver and
Trigger (literally, Lever).

2000 **RULES OF ENGAGEMENT** 2000

*Hodges – now a lawyer – tries to convey what life was really like
as a young marine.*

COLONEL HODGES

I'll make you a deal. If you can tell me right now what the
life expectancy was for a second lieutenant dropped into a
hot landing zone in Vietnam in 1968, I'll tell you everything
I remember about Ca Lu.

MAJOR BIGGS

One week.

COLONEL HODGES

Negative. Sixteen minutes. Sixteen fucking minutes. That's all
I remember about Ca Lu.

Dir: William Friedkin • Scr: Stephen Gaghan, James Webb • Cast: Tommy Lee
Jones (Colonel Hayes 'Hodge' Hodges), Guy Pearce (Major Mark Biggs)

2001   BLACK HAWK DOWN   2001

*A Special Forces sergeant explains the fierce camaraderie of
combat.*

HOOT

When I get home people will ask me, 'Hey Hoot, why do you do
it, man? Why? You some war junkie?' You know what I'll say? I
won't say a goddamn word. Why? They won't understand. They
won't understand why we do it. They won't understand that it's
about the men next to you, and that's it. That's all it is.

Dir: Ridley Scott • Scr: Ken Nolan • Based on a book by Mark Bowden • Cast:
Eric Bana (Special Forces Sergeant Norm 'Hoot' Gibson)

The film was scrupulous in its attention to detail and factual accuracy, even including some
authentic satellite imagery and radio transmissions from the battle. Director Ridley Scott only
betrayed the realism by insisting that soldiers had their names painted on their helmets as he
worried that audiences would be unable to distinguish between actors in otherwise identical
uniforms.

2004   TROY   2004

*Odysseus, King of Ithaca, is under no illusion how the Greek
battle for Troy will unfold.*

ODYSSEUS

War is young men dying and old men talking.

Dir: Wolfgang Petersen • Scr: David Benioff • Cast: Sean Bean (Odysseus)

An SS Colonel suspects a French farmer of sheltering a Jewish family.

COLONEL LANDA

So, Monsieur LaPadite, let me purpose a question. In this time of war, what is your number one duty? Is it to fight the Germans in the name of France to your last breath? Or is it to harass the occupying army to the best of your ability? Or is it to protect the poor unfortunate victims of warfare who cannot protect themselves? Or is your number one duty in this time of bloodshed to protect those very beautiful women who constitute your family?

The Colonel waits.

That was a question, Monsieur LaPadite. In this time of war, what do you consider your number one duty?

LAPADITE

To protect my family.

COLONEL LANDA

Now, my job dictates that I must have my men enter your home and conduct a thorough search before I can officially cross your family's name off my list. And if there are any irregularities to be found, rest assured, they will be.

He pauses.

That is, unless you have something to tell me that will make the conducting of a search unnecessary. I might add also that any information that makes the performing of my duty easier will not be met with punishment. Actually, quite the contrary; it will be met with reward. And that reward will be that your family will cease to be harassed in any way by the German military during the rest of our occupation of your country.

The farmer stares across the table at his German opponent.

You are sheltering enemies of the state, are you not?

Ashamed, the farmer knows he is beaten.

LAPADITE

Yes.

COLONEL LANDA

You're sheltering them underneath your floorboards, aren't you?

LaPadite is crying silently now.

LAPADITE

Yes.

COLONEL LANDA

Point out to me the areas where they're hiding.

Slowly, the farmer stands and indicates.

Since I haven't heard any disturbance, I assume that while they're listening they don't speak English?

LAPADITE

Yes.

COLONEL LANDA

I'm going to switch back to French now, and I want you to follow my masquerade. Is that clear?

LAPADITE

Yes.

Colonel Landa stands up from the table. He speaks in French now:

COLONEL LANDA

Monsieur LaPadite, I thank you for milk and your hospitality.
I do believe our business here is done.

He opens the front door and waves for his troops to approach the house.

Mademoiselle LaPadite, I thank you for your time. We shan't be
bothering your family any longer.

The LaPadite women watch the Nazi soldiers, machine guns at the ready, enter the house. Colonel Landa silently points out the area of the floor the farmer showed him.

So, Monsieur and Madame LaPadite, I bid you adieu.

He motions to the soldiers with his index finger. They tear up the wood floor with machine-gun fire.

Dir: Quentin Tarantino • Scr: Quentin Tarantino • Cast: Christoph Waltz
(Colonel Hans Landa), Denis Ménochet (M. LaPadite)

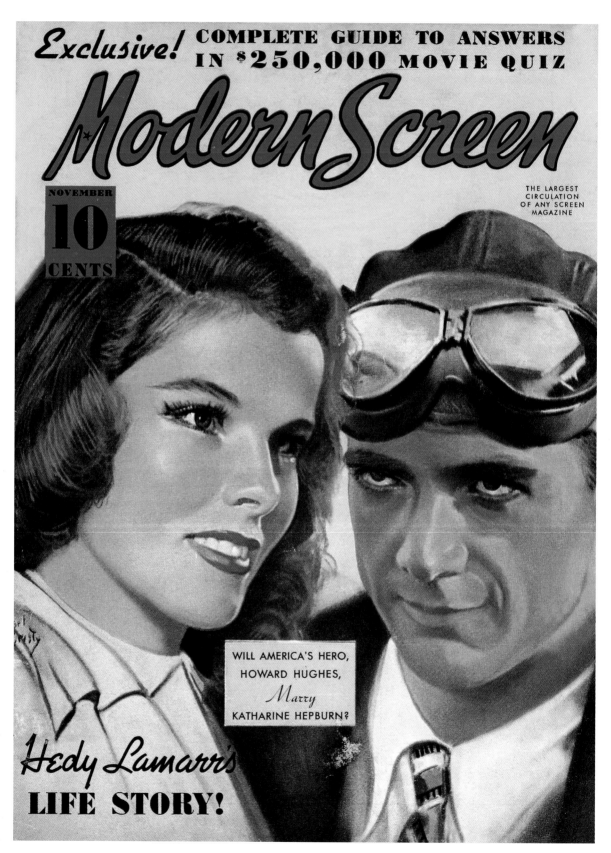

Modern Screen

NOVEMBER
10 CENTS

THE LARGEST
CIRCULATION
OF ANY SCREEN
MAGAZINE

WILL AMERICA'S HERO,
HOWARD HUGHES,
Marry
KATHARINE HEPBURN?

Hedy Lamarr's
LIFE STORY!

Millionaire recluse Howard Hughes, a successful film producer in his early career, was romantically linked to many of his stars.

Cabaret (1972): nobody could have played Sally Bowles more perfectly than Liza Minnelli, daughter of Hollywood royalty Vincente Minnelli and Judy Garland.

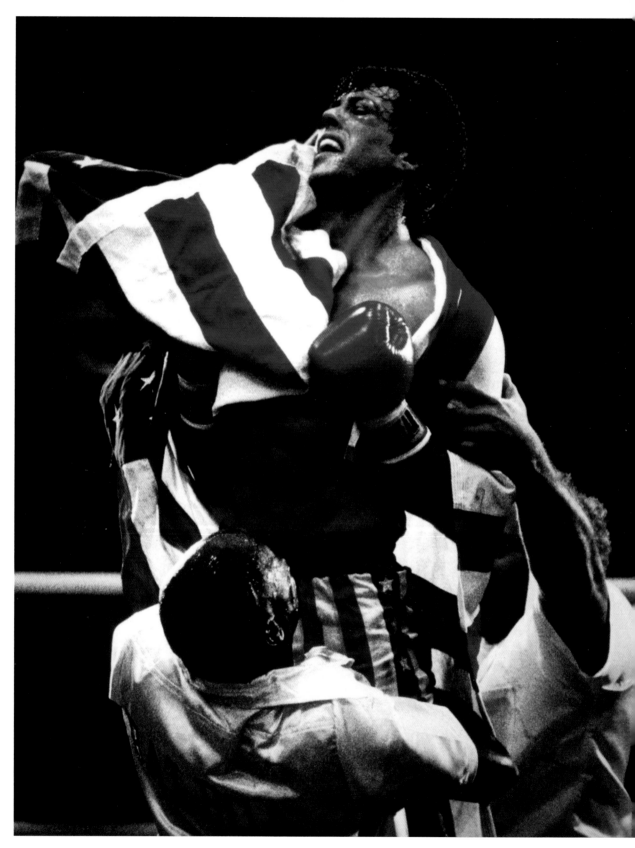

Rocky (1976): a heroic image for a heroic film. Written by Sylvester Stallone and shot in twenty-eight days, its success was as unexpected as that of its protagonist.

Heroes

THE THIN MAN

Nick and Nora have successfully solved a murder mystery.

NICK

I'm a hero. I was shot twice in the *Tribune*.

NORA

I read you were shot five times in the tabloids.

NICK

It's not true. He didn't come anywhere near my tabloids.

Dir: W. S. Van Dyke • Scr: Albert Hackett, Frances Goodrich • Based on a
novel by Dashiell Hammett • Cast: William Powell (Nick Charles), Myrna
Loy (Nora Charles)

MR DEEDS GOES TO TOWN

*Longfellow Deeds hopes to use his fortune to protect those less
fortunate than himself.*

DEEDS

From what I can see, no matter what system of government we
have, there will always be leaders and always be followers.
It's like the road out in front of my house. It's on a steep
hill. Every day I watch the cars climbing up. Some go lickety-
split up that hill on high, some have to shift into second,
and some sputter and shake and slip back to the bottom
again. Same cars, same gasoline, yet some make it and some
don't. And I say the fellas who can make the hill on high
should stop once in a while and help those who can't. That's
all I'm trying to do with this money. Help the fellas who
can't make the hill on high.

Dir: Frank Capra • Scr: Robert Riskin, Clarence Budington Kelland • Cast:
Gary Cooper (Longfellow Deeds)

Capra, famous for his warm-hearted but intelligent films during the 1930s and 1940s, said in
an interview towards the end of his life: 'I made mistakes in drama. I thought drama was when
actors cried. But drama is when the audience cries.'

Harry Cohn, who produced the film, always kept a keen eye on costs and insisted his directors
only be allowed to print one shot per set-up. Capra circumvented the rule by keeping the
cameras rolling at the end of each take; instead of calling 'cut', he would just tell the actors and
crew to 'do it again'.

MR SMITH GOES TO WASHINGTON

Junior senator Jefferson Smith may be new to politics but he is determined to uphold his beliefs.

SMITH

Liberty's too precious a thing to be buried in books, Miss Saunders. Men should hold it up in front of them every single day of their lives and say: I'm free to think and to speak. My ancestors couldn't, I can, and my children will. Boys ought to grow up remembering that.

Dir: Frank Capra • Scr: Sidney Buchman, Myles Connolly • Cast: James Stewart (Jefferson Smith)

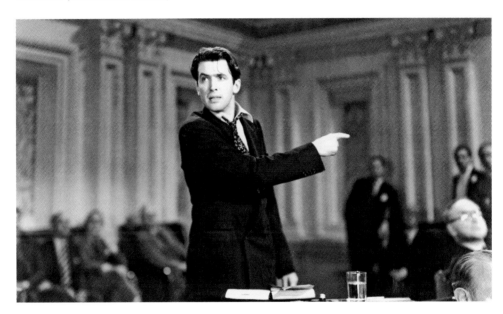

THE GRAPES OF WRATH

Tom Joad promises to be a tireless champion of the oppressed.

TOM

I'll be all around in the dark - I'll be everywhere. Wherever you can look - wherever there's a fight, so hungry people can eat, I'll be there. Wherever there's a cop beatin' up a guy, I'll be there. I'll be in the way guys yell when they're mad. I'll be in the way kids laugh when they're hungry and they know supper's ready, and when the people are eatin' the stuff they raise and livin' in the houses they build - I'll be there, too.

Dir: John Ford • Scr: Nunnally Johnson • Based on a novel by John Steinbeck • Cast: Henry Fonda (Tom Joad)

Darryl F. Zanuck paid $100,000 [$1.6 million] for the rights to John Steinbeck's novel, a huge amount of money for the time. Steinbeck insisted the film-makers treat the book – and its subject, the plight of the working man during the Great Depression – with due respect; when he saw the result he was delighted and said Henry Fonda's performance as Tom Joad made him 'believe my own words'. Before production started, Zanuck sent undercover investigators to the migrant camps to see if Steinbeck had exaggerated the appalling conditions, but discovered the reality was even more shocking than the book had suggested.

1946 IT'S A WONDERFUL LIFE 1946

An angel shows a suicidal man what the world would be like without him.

> CLARENCE
>
> Strange, isn't it? Each man's life touches so many other lives. When he isn't around he leaves an awful hole, doesn't he?

Dir: Frank Capra • Scr: Frances Goodrich, Albert Hackett, Frank Capra • Based on a short story by Philip Van Doren Stern • Cast: Henry Travers (Clarence)

1946 THE BIG SLEEP 1946

The wayward Carmen resents private investigator Marlowe's intrusion into her family's life.

> CARMEN
> You're not very tall, are you?

> MARLOWE
> Well, I, uh, I try to be.

Dir: Howard Hawks • Scr: William Faulkner, Leigh Brackett, Jules Furthman • Based on a novel by Raymond Chandler • Cast: Martha Vickers (Carmen Sternwood), Humphrey Bogart (Philip Marlowe)

'MY GOD, THE HERO IS A BEE!'

Hollywood has always enjoyed the lustre of a famous name, so when the talkies took off and screenplays began to require dialogue as well as spectacle, producers sought the best talent money could buy. So many contemporary novelists were happy to work for the inflated fees offered that when the *Film Daily* Product Guide published a 'List of Available Writers' in 1937, the names for hire included three Nobel prize nominees (Theodore Dreiser, Upton Sinclair and Thornton Wilder) and one future winner, William Faulkner (he received the award in 1950).

The rest of the bunch included such literary luminaries as James M. Cain, F. Scott Fitzgerald, Anita Loos, Mary McCarthy, Ogden Nash, Dorothy Parker, S. J. Perelman, J. B. Priestley, Ayn Rand, Damon Runyon, James Thurber, Evelyn Waugh, Rebecca West, P. G. Wodehouse, Thomas Wolfe, Alexander Woollcott, Stefan Zweig and, astonishingly, the experimental writer and poet Gertrude Stein.

Perhaps unsurprisingly, producers entranced by literary fame were not always fully aware of their protégés' oeuvre. Belgian author Maurice Maeterlinck had won the Nobel prize in 1911 largely for a play about fairies, *The Blue Bird*, and in 1919 Samuel Goldwyn lured him to Los Angeles with a contract worth $100,000 [$1.3 million]. He installed the great man in a hilltop villa and left him alone to adapt some of his earlier works. Each day a translator would take away the scant pages and translate them; after three months a script took shape. Goldwyn read it at once in his office but is said to have burst out immediately, waving the papers in astonishment: 'My God, the hero is a bee!'

Not all producers were so lavish in their inducements: after signing Faulkner to work for him, Jack Warner once crowed to another screenwriter that 'I've got America's best writer for $300 [$4,000] a week.'

Noted authors hired to adapt their own work for the screen or to contribute to other films include:

- Arnold Bennett (*Piccadilly*, 1929)

- John Steinbeck (*The Red Pony*, 1949)

- Somerset Maugham (*Trio*, 1955)

- Vladimir Nabokov (*Lolita*, 1962)

- Roald Dahl (*You Only Live Twice*, 1967)

- Anthony Burgess (*A Clockwork Orange*, 1971)

- Mario Puzo (*The Godfather*, 1972)

- Martin Amis (*Saturn 3*, 1980)

- William Boyd (*Chaplin*, 1992)

- Gabriel Garcia Márquez (*Love in the Time of Cholera*, 1997)

- Harold Pinter (*Sleuth*, 1997)

- John Irving (*The Cider House Rules*, 1999)

- Frederic Raphael (*Eyes Wide Shut*, 1999)

- Bret Easton Ellis (*American Psycho*, 2000)

- Ian McEwan (*Atonement*, 2007)

- Dave Eggers (*Where the Wild Things Are*, 2009)

- Robert Harris (*The Ghost*, 2010)

One of the most bizarre encounters between the highbrow and the lowbrow occurred in 1957 when United Pictures of America approached Aldous Huxley, author of *Brave New World*, to devise a screenplay for a full-length Mr Magoo cartoon. The story was to have been based on Cervantes' *Don Quixote* but the project was abandoned after the studio encountered a small hitch: Mr Magoo is comically short-sighted, and none of the executives had had the courage to tell Huxley (who was virtually blind himself) this key fact.

1952   HIGH NOON   **1952**

Retired sheriff Martin Howe explains why he refuses to help the new lawman in town.

MARTIN

It's a great life. You risk your skin catchin' killers and the
juries turn 'em loose so they can come back and shoot at ya
again. If you're honest, you're poor your whole life, and in
the end you wind up dyin' all alone on some dirty street. For
what? For nothin'. For a tin star.

Dir: Fred Zinnemann • Scr: Carl Foreman • Based on a story by John W.
Cunningham • Cast: Lon Chaney Jr (Martin Howe)

High Noon was directly responsible for the existence of *Rio Bravo*, itself a classic Western. John 'Duke' Wayne, the genre's most enduring star, hated it and teamed up with Howard Hawks to fashion a personal response. Hawks explained: 'I made *Rio Bravo* because I didn't like *High Noon*. Neither did Duke. I didn't think a good town marshal was going to run around town like a chicken with his head cut off, asking everyone to help. And who saves him? His Quaker wife. That isn't my idea of a good Western.'

1954   JOHNNY GUITAR   1954

A mysterious gunslinger enters town.

OLD TOM

That's a lot of man you're carrying in those boots, stranger.

Dir: Nicholas Ray • Scr: Philip Yordan • Based on a novel by Roy
Chanslor • Cast: John Carradine (Old Tom)

1962   LAWRENCE OF ARABIA   1962

Lawrence puts out a lit match between his thumb and forefinger.
Corporal Potter watches and tries to copy him.

POTTER

It damn well hurts!

LAWRENCE

Certainly it hurts.

POTTER

What's the trick then?

LAWRENCE

The trick, William Potter, is not minding that it hurts.

Dir: David Lean • Scr: Robert Bolt, Michael Wilson • Cast: Harry Fowler
(William Potter), Peter O'Toole (T. E. Lawrence)

The film was based on T. E. Lawrence's military memoirs *Seven Pillars of Wisdom* (1926); he turned down several offers to film the story during his lifetime. In 1960 Michael Wilson wrote a screen version explicitly to persuade Lawrence's literary executors that a worthy adaptation could be made, and the rights were granted to producer Sam Spiegel. Robert Bolt received sole credit for the final script until the Writers Guild of America reinstated Wilson's name in 1995.

David Lean shot the entire film favouring movement from left to right across the screen to emphasize the sense of a journey. When Technicolor released a subsequent master print, they inadvertently flipped one of the reels and the error persisted through the film's release on video. Lean had to wait until the material was restored and reissued in 1989 to correct the mistake. Although the original version is over three and a half hours long, it contains not a single line spoken by a woman.

1964   A FISTFUL OF DOLLARS   1964

A Wild West drifter risks his life to free a family from their violent captors.

MARISOL

Why do you do it for us?

JOE

Why? I knew someone like you once. There was no one there to help. Now, get moving.

Dir: Sergio Leone • Scr: Victor Andrés Catena, Jaime Comas Gil, Sergio Leone • Cast: Marianne Koch (Marisol), Clint Eastwood (Joe)

1965   LORD JIM   1965

Lord Jim, a sailor ashamed of having abandoned his ship with passengers still aboard, tries to come to terms with his past.

LORD JIM

I've been a so-called coward and a so-called hero and there's not the thickness of a sheet of paper between them. Maybe cowards and heroes are just ordinary men who, for a split second, do something out of the ordinary. That's all.

Dir: Richard Brooks • Scr: Richard Brooks • Based on a novel by Joseph Conrad • Cast: Peter O'Toole (Lord Jim)

Joseph Conrad (1857–1924) – originally Józef Teodor Konrad Korzeniowski – was a Polish author who wrote in English after becoming a British subject in 1886. Although his most famous story is almost certainly *Heart of Darkness*, films have also been made of his other works including *Lord Jim*, *Almayer's Folly*, *An Outcast of the Islands*, *Nostromo*, *The Secret Agent*, *The Duel*, *Victory*, *The Shadow Line* and *The Boxer*.

DIRTY HARRY

Policeman Harry Callahan is forced to adopt the tactics of the criminal he is pursuing.

HARRY

I know what you're thinking. 'Did he fire six shots or only five?' Well, to tell you the truth, in all this excitement I kind of lost track myself. But being as this is a .44 Magnum, the most powerful handgun in the world, and would blow your head clean off, you've got to ask yourself one question: Do I feel lucky? Well, do ya, punk?

Dir: Don Siegel • Scr: Harry Julian Fink, Rita M. Fink, Dean Riesner • Cast: Clint Eastwood (Harry Callahan)

Andrew Robinson, who plays the 'Scorpio' killer, is a sworn pacifist and deeply uncomfortable around guns. He would visibly flinch whenever he pulled a trigger, so director Don Siegel had to shut down the production while he was sent to a training range to gain confidence. In some shots in the finished film he can still be seen to blink as he fires.

JAWS

Police chief Brody warns bounty hunters they have underestimated the size of the shark that threatens their beaches.

BRODY

You're gonna need a bigger boat.

Dir: Steven Spielberg • Scr: Carl Gottlieb • Based on a novel by Peter Benchley • Cast: Roy Scheider (Martin Brody)

According to principal writer Carl Gottlieb, this line was not scripted but improvised by Roy Scheider.

I SHALL NOT RETURN

Based on Peter Benchley's bestselling book, *Jaws* was the first film to gross $100 million [$430 million] in its theatrical release: over the summer of 1975, sixty-seven million Americans bought a ticket to see it and it recouped its production costs within two weeks. Although it is still hailed as one of the young Spielberg's finest films, many have lamented that it paved the way for the dominance of the blockbuster, encouraging the industry to focus on the massive marketing campaigns and merchandising tie-ins still favoured today.

The making of the film, however, gave little reassurance that its release would be such a hit. The producers paid Benchley $175,000 [$750,000] for the rights before the book had even been published, but rejected his first three attempts at a script. When Spielberg — after some hesitation — was hired to direct, he wrote his own version before turning to Howard Sackler, whom he credited with the structural changes necessary for a screen version.

Spielberg then asked Carl Gottlieb, better known as a sitcom writer, to come on board for a week to 'polish' the script and prevent it from feeling too dark. Gottlieb stayed on, only completing the task after the production had already been underway for nine weeks; scenes were often delivered the night before they were scheduled to be shot. Just as Roy Scheider had come up with the much-quoted line 'You're gonna need a bigger boat', Robert Shaw (Quint) rewrote the famous scene about his survival after the torpedoing of the USS *Indianapolis* by the Japanese in July 1945.

QUINT: Japanese submarine slammed two torpedoes into our side, Chief. We was comin' back from the island of Tinian to Leyte... just delivered the bomb. The Hiroshima bomb. Eleven hundred men went into the water. Vessel went down in twelve minutes. Didn't see the first shark for about a half an hour. Tiger. Thirteen-footer. You know how you know that when you're in the water, Chief? You tell by looking from the dorsal to the tail fin. What we didn't know, was our bomb mission had been so secret, no distress signal had been sent. They didn't even list us overdue for a week. Very first light, Chief, sharks come cruisin', so we formed ourselves into tight groups. You know, it was kinda like old squares in the battle like you see in the calendar named 'The Battle of Waterloo', and the idea was: shark comes to the nearest man, that man he starts poundin' and hollerin' and screamin' and sometimes the shark will go away...but sometimes he wouldn't go away. Sometimes that shark he looks right into ya. Right into your eyes. And, you know, the thing about a shark...he's got lifeless eyes. Black eyes. Like a doll's eyes. When he comes at ya, doesn't seem to be living...until he bites ya, and those black eyes roll over white and then...ah, then you hear that terrible high-pitched screamin'. The ocean turns red, and despite all the poundin' and the hollerin', they all come in and they...rip you to pieces. You know by the end of that first dawn, lost a hundred men. I don't know how many sharks, maybe a thousand. I know how many men, they averaged six an hour. On Thursday morning, Chief, I bumped into a friend of mine, Herbie Robinson from Cleveland. Baseball player. Boatswain's mate. I thought he was asleep. I reached over to wake him up. He bobbed up, down in the water just like a kinda top. Upended. Well, he'd been bitten in half below the waist. Noon, the fifth day, Mr Hooper, a Lockheed Ventura saw us. He swung in low and he saw us...he was a young pilot, a lot younger than Mr Hooper. Anyway, he saw us and he come in low and three hours later a big fat PBY comes down and starts to pick us up. You know that was the time I was most frightened...waitin' for my turn. I'll never put on a lifejacket again. So, 1,100 men went in the water; 316 men come out and the sharks took the rest, June the 29th, 1945. Anyway, we delivered the bomb.

Principal photography was originally estimated at fifty-two days but lasted nearly six months as a result of technical delays, bad weather and the inevitable complications of staging complex drama and special effects with real boats as camera platforms. The mechanical shark — nicknamed Bruce, after Spielberg's lawyer — suffered repeated mechanical failures, trapping George Lucas's head in its mouth during testing and sinking to the ocean floor on its first outing. Desperate to keep to the schedule during Bruce's frequent trips to the repair shop, Spielberg resorted to filming several sequences with a moving underwater camera suggesting the predator's point-of-view. This stop-gap measure eventually contributed hugely to the film's atmosphere.

On dry land, things were just as fraught. Robert Shaw, cast only days before shooting started, was in trouble with the US tax authorities and had to be flown to Canada on his days off. Shaw and

Richard Dreyfuss (playing Matt Hooper) had frequent disagreements on set — and occasional actual fights — although their animosity benefited the story. Peter Benchley disliked the ending Spielberg had devised and objected so vehemently he was barred from the set.

By the end of the gruelling production period, the crew were at the end of their tether. Carl Gottlieb recalls how on the last day Spielberg, sensing he would be the focus of their wrath, wore his most expensive clothes in the hope he might avoid being thrown overboard. When the final shot was approved, he leaped into a waiting speedboat and raced away, shouting: 'I shall not return!'

When composer John Williams first played the ominous opening theme for the director, Spielberg is reported to have thought it was a joke. The score went on to win an Oscar, although the film suffered one final setback: Williams was conducting the orchestra for the ceremony when the result was announced, and had to run up on stage to collect his statuette before returning to his duties in the pit.

1976 NETWORK   1976

On live TV, a news presenter controversially encourages his viewers to become more involved in the world around them.

HOWARD

We know things are bad - worse than bad. They're crazy. It's like everything everywhere is going crazy, so we don't go out any more. We sit in the house, and slowly the world we're living in is getting smaller, and all we say is: 'Please, at least leave us alone in our living rooms. Let me have my toaster and my TV and my steel-belted radials and I won't say anything. Just leave us alone.' Well, I'm not gonna leave you alone. I want you to get MAD! I don't want you to protest. I don't want you to riot - I don't want you to write to your congressman, because I wouldn't know what to tell you to write. I don't know what to do about the depression and the inflation and the Russians and the crime in the street. All I know is that first you've got to get mad.

He begins to shout at the camera:

You've got to say: 'I'm a human being, goddammit! My life has value!' So, I want you to get up now. I want all of you to get up out of your chairs. I want you to get up right now and go to the window. Open it, and stick your head out, and yell: 'I'm as mad as hell, and I'm not gonna take this any more!'

Dir: Sidney Lumet • Scr: Paddy Chayefsky • Cast: Peter Finch (Howard Beale)

1976 ROCKY   1976

Two friends wonder whether underdog boxer Rocky has what it takes to win.

                              ADRIAN

Einstein flunked out of school, twice.

                              PAULIE

Is that so?

                              ADRIAN

Yeah. Beethoven was deaf. Helen Keller was blind. I think Rocky's got a good chance.

Dir: John G. Avildsen • Scr: Sylvester Stallone • Cast: Talia Shire (Adrian Pennino), Burt Young (Paulie Pennino)

1976 THE SHOOTIST   1976

An ageing gunfighter tries to live his last days with the dignity and integrity of his youth.

                              BOOKS

I won't be wronged. I won't be insulted. I won't be laid a hand on. I don't do these things to other people, and I require the same from them.

Dir: Don Siegel • Scr: Miles Hood Swarthout, Scott Hale • Based on a novel by Glendon Swarthout • Cast: John Wayne (J. B. Books)

Sequences in the story showing Books as a young man were taken directly from Wayne's earlier films, including *Red River*, *Rio Bravo* and *El Dorado*.

1977 STAR WARS   1977

                              HAN SOLO

Hokey religions and ancient weapons are no match for a good blaster by your side, kid.

Dir: George Lucas • Scr: George Lucas • Cast: Harrison Ford (Han Solo)

Director George Lucas based the character of Han Solo on his friend Francis Ford Coppola, modestly admitting: 'Before I met [Francis] I couldn't write a word, and now I'm the King of Wooden Dialogue.' Lucas himself was surprised by the film's extraordinary success, saying afterwards: 'I thought [*Star Wars*] was too wacky for the general public.'

1978 SUPERMAN 1978

Superman carries Lois Lane to safety high above Metropolis.

SUPERMAN

Easy, Miss, I've got you.

LOIS LANE

You've got me? Who's got you?

Dir: Richard Donner • Scr: Mario Puzo, David Newman, Leslie Newman,
Robert Benton • Based on characters created by Jerry Siegel, Joe
Shuster • Cast: Christopher Reeve (Superman/Clark Kent), Margot Kidder
(Lois Lane)

1979 LIFE OF BRIAN 1979

*Brian of Nazareth is tired of being mistaken for his neighbour
Jesus.*

BRIAN

I'm not the Messiah! Will you please listen? I am not the
Messiah, do you understand? Honestly!

GIRL

Only the true Messiah denies His divinity.

BRIAN

What? Well, what sort of chance does that give me? All right! I am the Messiah!

FOLLOWERS

He is! He is the Messiah!

BRIAN

Now fuck off!

Silence.

ARTHUR

How shall we fuck off, O Lord?

Dir: Terry Jones • Scr: Terry Jones, John Cleese, Graham Chapman, Terry Gilliam, Eric Idle, Michael Palin • Cast: Graham Chapman (Brian Cohen), John Cleese (Arthur)

The film also contains the memorable put-down from Brian's mother: 'He's not the Messiah, he's a very naughty boy.' After the team finished *Monty Python and the Holy Grail,* they grew tired of journalists endlessly asking what their next project would be – until Eric Idle answered as a joke: 'Jesus Christ: The Lust For Glory.' The first scene they dreamed up was to show Jesus, a professional carpenter, complaining about the shoddy construction of the cross used to crucify him.

1983   THE RIGHT STUFF   1983

Pancho's Bar is the only place local Air Force test pilots can drink, and it attracts plenty of groupies.

GIRL

I just noticed that a fancy pilot like Slick over there doesn't have his picture on your wall. What do you have to do to get your picture up there anyway?

PANCHO BARNES

You have to die, sweetie.

Dir: Philip Kaufman • Scr: Philip Kaufman • Based on a book by Tom Wolfe • Cast: O-Lan Shepard (Girl), Kim Stanley (Pancho Barnes)

1987   THE UNTOUCHABLES 1987

Federal Agent Eliot Ness has finally arrested Chicago's most
notorious mobster. A journalist pursues him.

> SCOOP

Mr Ness! Any comment for the record? 'The man who put Al
Capone on the spot.'

> NESS

I just happened to be there when the wheel went round.

> SCOOP

Word is they're going to repeal Prohibition. What'll you do
then?

> NESS

I think I'll have a drink.

Dir: Brian De Palma • Scr: David Mamet • Based on the book by Oscar Fraley,
Eliot Ness • Cast: Steven Goldstein (Scoop), Kevin Costner (Eliot Ness)

1988   DIE HARD 1988

A terrorist talks to his unknown adversary on a walkie-talkie.

> GRUBER

Mr Mystery Guest? Are you still there?

> MCCLANE

Yeah, I'm still here. Unless you wanna open the front door for
me.

> GRUBER

No, I'm afraid not. But you have me at a loss. You know my
name, but who are you? Just another American who saw too
many movies as a child? Another orphan of a bankrupt
culture who thinks he's John Wayne? Rambo? Marshal Dillon?

> MCCLANE

I was always kinda partial to Roy Rogers, actually. I really
like those sequined shirts.

GRUBER

Do you really think you have a chance against us, Mr Cowboy?

MCCLANE

Yippee-ki-yay, motherfucker.

Dir: John McTiernan • Scr: Steven E. de Souza, Jeb Stuart • Based on a
novel by Roderick Thorp • Cast: Alan Rickman (Hans Gruber), Bruce Willis
(John McClane)

'SLUG IN A DITCH!'

As with many movies, *Die Hard* was considered too rollicking for
younger audiences watching the film on television. In order to
create an acceptable family viewing experience, the frequent swear-
words were overdubbed — with varying degrees of success. As the
story unfolded, the results became increasingly surreal:

Yippee-ki-yay, my friend!

Yippee-ki-yay, melon farmer!

Yippee-ki-yay, Mr Falcon!

This last is especially intriguing since nobody in the film is
actually called Falcon.

These days Hollywood favours 'fricking' to cover the most popular
expletive, and a direct version of the insult can be softened by re-
recording it as 'thank you'. Not content to play that game, the Coen
brothers enjoy a dig at TV prudishness by replacing the offensive
word with 'froozing'.

Here are a few more mealy-mouthed examples. In most cases the
original dialogue is clear enough, but translations follow the more
truly inventive:

Your mother sews socks that smell, Karras, you faithless
slime. (Your mother sucks cocks in Hell, Karras, you faithless
slime.)
The Exorcist (1973)

Scum buzzard. (Sonofabitch.)
Smokey and the Bandit (1977)

Man, who do I look like, Christopher Columbo? (Fuck yo mama!)
National Lampoon's Vacation (1983)

This town is like a great big chicken just waiting to get plucked. (This town is like a great big pussy just waiting to get fucked.)
Scarface (1983)

Slug in a ditch!
Repo Man (1984)

Did you slip her the hot wild affection? (Did you slip her the hot beef injection?)
The Breakfast Club (1985)

Pardon my French, but you're an aardvark.
Ferris Bueller's Day Off (1986)

We bury the funsters!
Lethal Weapon (1987)

You're gonna be a bad mothercrusher!
Robocop (1987)

Mickey Fickey!
Do the Right Thing (1989)

We were going to ask Ty Cobb to play, but none of us could stand that son of a squid.
Field of Dreams (1989)

Go feel your mother!
Goodfellas (1990)

Come back here, you steroid!
Total Recall (1990)

I popped your wife, and later I'm gonna pop her again.
The Last Boy Scout (1991)

Hand me the keys, you fuzzy sock-sucker.
The Usual Suspects (1994)

Give me the keys, you fairy godmother!
The Usual Suspects (1994)

Forget me? Forget you, you mother forgetter!
Casino (1995)

Jesus, how much did you smoke? All it took was a phat karate punch. (All it took was a phat chronic blunt.)
Mallrats (1995)

Get out of my freshly vacuumed house.
Fargo (1996)

I gave simple fruitful instructions.
Fargo (1996)

This is what happens when you find a stranger in the Alps! (This is what happens when you fuck a stranger in the ass!)
The Big Lebowski (1998)

I've had it with these monkey-fightin' snakes on this Monday-to-Friday plane.
Snakes on a Plane (2006)

1993 NAKED 1993

A disturbed young man rails against the unthinking culture that surrounds us.

JOHNNY

Was I bored? No, I wasn't fuckin' bored. I'm never bored. That's the trouble with everybody - you're all so bored. You've had nature explained to you and you're bored with it, you've had the living body explained to you and you're bored with it, you've had the universe explained to you and you're bored with it, so now you want cheap thrills and, like, plenty of them, and it doesn't matter how tawdry or vacuous they are as long as it's new... as long as it's new as long as it flashes and fuckin' bleeps in forty fuckin' different colours. So whatever else you can say about me, I'm not fuckin' bored.

Dir: Mike Leigh • Scr: Mike Leigh • Cast: David Thewlis (Johnny)

Mike Leigh's technique for shaping a story is the opposite of the traditional process. On this project the cast rehearsed for three months to refine their improvisations and the actual shooting 'script' was only two dozen pages long.

1996 FARGO   1996

*An imperturbable small-town police officer arrests a murderer at
the scene of the crime.*

> MARGE
>
> So that was Mrs Lundegaard on the floor in there. And I guess
> that was your accomplice in the wood chipper. And those three
> people in Brainerd. And for what? For a little bit of money.
> There's more to life than a little money, you know. Don'tcha
> know that? And here ya are, and it's a beautiful day. Well, I
> just don't understand it.

Dir: Joel Coen, Ethan Coen • Scr: Ethan Coen, Joel Coen • Cast: Frances
McDormand (Marge Gunderson)

The film states that its events are based on a true story but the Coen brothers later admitted
they only added the disclaimer to make the unusual narrative seem more plausible. The wood
chipper used in the movie is now on display at the Fargo-Moorhead Visitors Center.

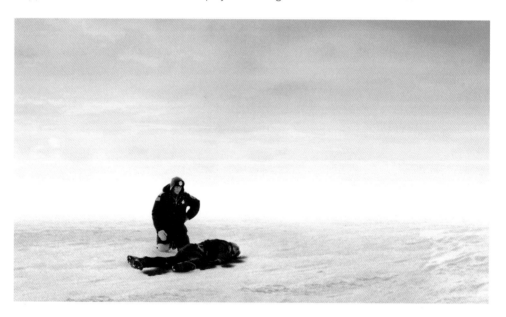

1996 THE PEOPLE VS. LARRY FLYNT   1996

*A pornography tycoon asks the court to consider society's
hypocrisy.*

> FLYNT
>
> I think the real obscenity comes from raising our youth to
> believe that sex is bad and ugly and dirty, and yet it is

heroic to go spill guts and blood in the most ghastly manner in the name of humanity. With all the taboos attached to sex, it's no wonder we have the problems we have. It's no wonder we're angry and violent and genocidal. But ask yourself the question: what is more obscene? Sex or war?

Dir: Miloš Forman • Scr: Scott Alexander, Larry Karaszewski • Cast: Woody Harrelson (Larry Flynt)

1996   THE ROCK   1996

A veteran agent mistrusts his young accomplice.

MASON

Are you sure you're ready for this?

GOODSPEED

I'll do my best.

MASON

Your best! Losers always whine about their best. Winners go home and fuck the prom queen.

GOODSPEED

Carla *was* the prom queen.

Dir: Michael Bay • Scr: Douglas S. Cook, David Weisberg, Mark Rosner Cast: Sean Connery (John Mason), Nicolas Cage (Stanley Goodspeed)

1998   THE BIG LEBOWSKI   1998

Jeff Lebowski may be laid back but he has strong views about how he should be addressed.

THE DUDE

Let me explain something to you. Um, I am not 'Mr Lebowski'. You're Mr Lebowski. I'm the Dude. So that's what you call me. You know, that or, uh, His Dudeness, or uh, Duder, or El Duderino if you're not into the whole brevity thing.

Dir: Joel Coen, Ethan Coen • Scr: Joel Coen, Ethan Coen • Cast: Jeff Bridges (The Dude)

Several key scenes are set in a bowling alley. The film-makers might be delighted to know that in Norway posters and VHS covers carried the endorsement *'anbefales av norsk bowling forbund'* ('recommended by the Norwegian Bowling Association').

2000 ERIN BROCKOVICH 2000

Erin Brockovich represents the people of Hinkley, California, in a class-action suit against a company accused of poisoning the town's water.

ERIN

These people don't dream about being rich. They dream about being able to watch their kids swim in a pool without worrying that they'll have to have a hysterectomy at the age of twenty. Like Rosa Diaz, a client of ours. Or have their spine deteriorate, like Stan Blume, another client of ours. So before you come back here with another lame-ass offer, I want you to think real hard about what your spine is worth, Mr Walker. Or what you might expect someone to pay you for your uterus, Ms Sanchez? Then you take out your calculator and you multiply that number by a hundred. Anything less than that is a waste of our time. By the way, we had that water brought in special for you folks. It came from a well in Hinkley.

Dir: Steven Soderbergh • Scr: Susannah Grant • Cast: Julia Roberts (Erin Brockovich)

2000 GLADIATOR 2000

MAXIMUS

My name is Maximus Decimus Meridius, commander of the Armies of the North, General of the Felix Legions, loyal servant to the true emperor Marcus Aurelius. Father to a murdered son, husband to a murdered wife. And I will have my vengeance, in this life or the next.

Dir: Ridley Scott • Scr: David Franzoni, John Logan, William Nicholson • Cast: Russell Crowe (Maximus)

THUMBS DOWN

The making of *Gladiator* was almost as huge an undertaking as the events it portrayed. The wardrobe department was required to provide more than 10,000 costumes, the props department built twenty-four full-size functional chariots and most of the larger animals in the Rabat zoo were borrowed for the sequences shot in Morocco. The Germania battle scenes took twenty days to complete; they were shot in Surrey where an area had already been earmarked for deforestation, so the local council were delighted when the production designer told them they wanted to burn the woodland to the ground.

Any script which deals with historic events must tread a careful line between what is factually accurate and what is dramatically desirable and credible. For *Gladiator*, the production team carried out plenty of research but found that not everything they discovered could be used in the final film. The documented fact that gladiators endorsed commercial products in the arena was dropped because they felt the audience would believe it a crass anachronism. When Ridley Scott and his production designer visited the Colosseum, they deemed it too small for cinematic spectacle and built a partial, expanded version in Malta. It was so large and detailed that when the shoot was over the producers offered it to the local authorities as the basis for a theme park.

Scott originally came on board after two producers showed him a painting, *Pollice Verso* (*Thumbs Down*), of a gladiator turning to the crowd for their verdict on whether or not he should kill the man he has just defeated. Scott said: 'That image spoke to me of the Roman Empire in all its glory and wickedness. I knew right then and there I was hooked.' Many scholars now doubt this was standard procedure in the arena but the film-makers decided not to deny their audience such a familiar visual gesture. The most egregious bending of the truth is the story itself, which portrays Commodus (Joaquin Phoenix) as a vain, insecure tyrant who kills his father Marcus Aurelius (Richard Harris) in desperation to secure his appointment as emperor. In reality, father and son ruled together for several years and many historians now suspect Marcus Aurelius died of the plague.

Commodus was the only emperor known to have fought as a gladiator and there is some evidence his opponents would have been disabled with stiletto wounds before the fights in order to ensure his victory. In reality this underhand practice was kept from Commodus in order to flatter him, although the screenwriters portray him stabbing Maximus (Russell Crowe) in the back before they confront each other in the arena. Historically Maximus (an entirely fictional creation) did not kill Commodus; the emperor was strangled in his dressing room by his wrestling partner Narcissus.

The film had several writers. The first, David Franzoni, had been inspired by a book about gladiatorial combat (*Those About To Die*) although one source suggests the early script is 'different in almost every detail from the finished movie'. John Logan was then brought on board, followed by William Nicholson who subsequently reinstated many of the scenes Logan had cut from Franzoni's drafts. Eventually Franzoni was brought back as a co-producer to supervise the rewrites, and thanks to his new role shared that year's Best Picture Oscar.

According to Nicholson, Russell Crowe was never fully satisfied with the script and frequently refused to appear if changes he demanded were not made. He disliked the crucial speech 'in this life or the next, I will have my vengeance', telling the writer: 'Your lines are garbage, but I'm the greatest actor in the world and I can make even garbage sound good.' Even so, Crowe's commitment to realism was impressive — many of the cuts and stitches in the battle sequences were real, and in filming the gladiatorial fights he broke bones in his foot and hip.

As if Crowe's behaviour were not trying enough for the writers, Richard Harris disliked learning new lines when changes were made and would frequently just speak the dialogue he had already memorized. Oliver Reed, a famously wayward performer, accepted the role of Proximo because he liked the idea of a 'free trip to London to see a couple of shows'; his only demand was that he never work past five in the evening. Supporting the film's narrative, if not the film-makers themselves, Crowe and Harris became friends on set but Reed disliked Crowe and on one occasion challenged him to a fight.

Reed suffered a fatal heart attack in Malta with much of his key material still to be shot. As his role was vital, the insurance company faced a claim estimated at $25 million [$33 million] to reshoot a large proportion of the footage with a new actor. After nearly six months of shooting, Scott and his crew were already exhausted so the director decided to complete Reed's scenes using a mix of body doubles and CGI (computer-generated imagery); the decision saved the insurers $22 million [$29 million].

The film, dedicated to Oliver Reed's memory, recouped its costs within weeks of its release and went on to win five Oscars.

2002   24 HOUR PARTY PEOPLE   2002

Real-life music legend Tony Wilson tries to justify a disastrous turnout for the opening night of his new Hacienda club.

> TONY
>
> The smaller the attendance the bigger the history. There were twelve people at the Last Supper. Half a dozen at Kitty Hawk. Archimedes was on his own in the bath.

Dir: Michael Winterbottom • Scr: Frank Cottrell Boyce • Cast: Steve Coogan (Tony Wilson)

Not everyone represented in the story appreciated the way they were portrayed. Peter Hook, New Order's bassist, described the result as 'a film about the biggest cunt in Manchester, played by the second biggest'.

2008   TAKEN   2008

A retired CIA agent speaks with the man who has kidnapped his daughter.

> BRYAN
>
> I don't know who you are. I don't know what you want. If you are looking for ransom, I can tell you I don't have money. But what I do have are a very particular set of skills; skills I have acquired over a very long career. Skills that make me a nightmare for people like you. If you let my daughter go now, that'll be the end of it. I will not look for you, I will not pursue you. But if you don't, I will look for you, I will find you, and I will kill you.

Dir: Pierre Morel • Scr: Luc Besson, Robert Mark Kamen • Cast: Liam Neeson (Bryan Mills)

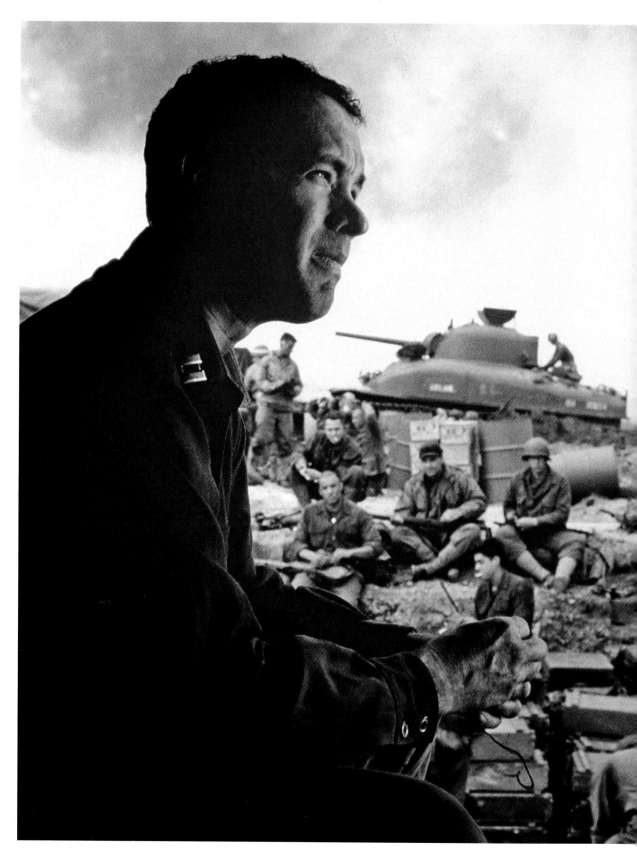

Steven Spielberg's *Saving Private Ryan* kept a strong human focus despite its unsparing depiction of combat.

Though many of her most memorable roles came later in her career, Joan Crawford's youthful beauty remains iconic.

Woody Allen's characteristic bemused expression remains as familiar as his sardonic humour and neurotic characters.

Zeroes

1937   LA GRANDE ILLUSION 1937

Lieutenant Maréchal is a man of simple pleasures.

LIEUTENANT MARÉCHAL

The theatre is too deep for me. I prefer bicycling.

Dir: Jean Renoir • Scr: Jean Renoir, Charles Spaak • Cast: Jean Gabin (Lieutenant Maréchal)

1941   SULLIVAN'S TRAVELS 1941

LeBrand and Hadrian discuss Sullivan's previous film – a flop.

LEBRAND

It died in Pittsburgh.

HADRIAN

Like a dog!

SULLIVAN

Aw, what do they know in Pittsburgh.

HADRIAN

They know what they like.

SULLIVAN

If they knew what they liked, they wouldn't live in Pittsburgh!

Dir: Preston Sturges • Scr: Preston Sturges • Cast: Robert Warwick (Mr LeBrand), Porter Hall (Mr Hadrian), Joel McCrea (John Lloyd Sullivan)

Sturges got the idea for the movie from John Garfield's account of his travels as a hobo during the 1930s. Apparently without irony, the secretary of the National Association for the Advancement of Colored People wrote a letter to the director congratulating him on his 'dignified and decent treatment of Negroes' in the film.

1947   THE LADY FROM SHANGHAI 1947

A lawyer is caught up in an increasingly complex plot to fake a man's death.

MICHAEL

Some people can smell danger. Not me.

Dir: Orson Welles • Scr: Orson Welles • Based on a novel by Sherwood King • Cast: Orson Welles (Michael O'Hara)

1949 KIND HEARTS AND CORONETS 1949

Murderer Louis Mazzini tracks a D'Ascoyne family member.

SIBELLA

He says he wants to go to Europe to expand his mind.

LOUIS

He certainly has room to do so.

Dir: Robert Hamer • Scr: Robert Hamer, John Dighton • Based on a novel
by Roy Horniman • Cast: Joan Greenwood (Sibella Holland), Dennis Price
(Louis Mazzini)

1951 ACE IN THE HOLE 1951

A newsman always gets his story - even if he has to make it up.

CHUCK

I can handle big news and little news. And if there's no news,
I'll go out and bite a dog.

Dir: Billy Wilder • Scr: Billy Wilder, Lesser Samuels, Walter Newman •
Cast: Kirk Douglas (Chuck Tatum)

1957 A FACE IN THE CROWD 1957

Mel disparages the brash television star he and Marcia work for.

MARCIA

Got his introduction ready?

MEL

Home town boy, not only making good, but making everybody.

MARCIA

For a mild man, you sound vicious.

MEL

Didn't you know? All mild men are vicious. They hate
themselves for being mild, and they hate the windy extroverts
whose violence seems to have a strange attraction for nice
girls... who should know better.

Dir: Elia Kazan • Scr: Budd Schulberg • Cast: Patricia Neal (Marcia
Jeffries), Walter Matthau (Mel Miller)

An innocent businessman is pursued by a gang who believe he is a government spy; the authorities try to persuade him he is not in danger.

ROGER

Now you listen to me, I'm an advertising man, not a red herring. I've got a job, a secretary, a mother, two ex-wives and several bartenders that depend upon me, and I don't intend to disappoint them all by getting myself 'slightly' killed.

Dir: Alfred Hitchcock • Scr: Ernest Lehman • Cast: Cary Grant (Roger O. Thornhill)

The famously dapper Grant was profiled in *Esquire* magazine in 1960: 'Although Grant, who is fifty-six, favours such abominations as large tie knots and claims to have originated the square-style breast-pocket handkerchief, he is so extraordinarily attractive that he looks good in practically anything. He insists upon tight armholes in his suit jackets [and] finds the most comfortable of all underwear to be women's nylon panties.'

THE MAN WHO SNEEZED IN LINCOLN'S NOSE

The creation of *North by Northwest* (1959) is a fine example of the collaboration between writer and director on a wholly original screenplay. Alfred Hitchcock was planning to adapt Hammond Innes's novel *The Wreck of the Mary Deare* and his composer friend Bernard Hermann suggested he hire Ernest Lehman (*Sabrina*, *Sweet Smell of Success*, *West Side Story*) to write it. After several weeks, Lehman claimed he couldn't find a way to make the book play on screen, but the two men enjoyed each other's company so much they resolved to put their energies into a different project. When Hermann said he wanted to write 'the Hitchcock picture to end all Hitchcock pictures', the director confessed he had always wanted to shoot a chase on Mount Rushmore, a vast carving in the Black Hills of South Dakota featuring the faces of four American presidents.

The way they developed the plot was almost the exact opposite of the traditional process for a narrative work. Starting only with this brief visual sequence, they devised several other scenarios as building blocks: a murder at the United Nations, a dead body in a car on an automobile production line, a tornado and a grand finale in Alaska. Hitchcock suggested a narrative focusing on a protagonist mistaken for a spy by a criminal gang and the result did indeed deliver one of the director's most perfect creations: Lehman was nominated for an Oscar, and the film remains as popular with critics as it was with the public.

Not all the initial scenarios made it into the final draft: Alaska was abandoned in favour of the Mount Rushmore chase, and Hitchcock was eventually persuaded that a scene where Thornhill hid in one of Lincoln's nostrils only to suffer a sneezing fit was undignified. The sequence where Thornhill finds himself alone on the vast Indiana plains pursued by a tornado was rejected by Lehman on the basis that the cyclone is certainly dangerous but could hardly be blamed on the criminals. Hitchcock capitulated, and the famous biplane sequence ('That's funny, that plane's dustin' crops where there ain't no crops') was devised.

The result is seamlessly crafted and contains many outstanding cinematic moments; screenwriter William Goldman suggests the ending is one of the greatest ever examples of filmic storytelling. In his memoir *Adventures in the Screen Trade* (1983), he writes:

> Near the conclusion of *North by Northwest*, Cary Grant finds himself in something of a pickle.

> His true love, Eva Marie Saint, is dangling helplessly in space on the face of Mount Rushmore. If she falls, splat. The reason she has not fallen is that Grant is holding her with

one hand while with the other he grabs a rock ledge. Not easy. Watching all this is Martin Landau, the sub-villain, who stands a few feet away, holding the precious statuette that contains valuable microfilm inside, said microfilm being of great danger to America should it fall into enemy hands. Grant, desperate, looks up at Landau and asks for help.

Landau walks over to Grant and, instead of bending down and aiding him, puts his foot on Grant's fingers and begins pressing down. He grinds his shoe down as hard as he can.

That's the pickle.

Now, between that moment and the end of this superb Ernest Lehman-Alfred Hitchcock collaboration, the following occurs.

(a)   Landau is made to cease and desist.

(b)   Grant saves himself.

(c)   Grant also saves Eva Marie Saint.

(d)   The two of them get married.

(e)   The microfilm is saved for America.

(f)   James Mason, the chief villain, is captured and handed over to the authorities.

(g)   Grant and Saint take a train ride back east.

That's a lot of narrative to be successfully tied up. And I would like you to guess how long it takes in terms of screentime for it to be accomplished. Got your guess? Here's the answer - forty-three seconds.

Here's how they do it, from the moment where Landau is crunching Grant's hand. The camera's in close-up on the shoe and the fingers. A shot rings out. The shoe begins to slide away from the fingers. Next, a cut of the statuette falling safely to the ground and cracking, revealing the microfilm inside. Now Landau falls to his death off Mount Rushmore. Now another part of Mount Rushmore, where Leo G. Carroll, a good guy, thanks a police officer who is holding a rifle. Behind Carroll is Mason, flanked by more officers. Now back to Grant and Eva Marie, him saying you can do it, her saying I can't, back and forth, quick cuts between them, and then a really brilliant shot of Grant pulling her up, only now he's not on Mount Rushmore, he's in the upper berth of a train, and he brings her to him, calls her 'Mrs Thornhill' - Thornhill being his last name, so we know they're married now - and as they embrace, a final shot of the train roaring into a tunnel as 'The End' flashes on the screen.

I don't know a more adroit ending to a film.

1960   THE APARTMENT   1960

Mild-mannered Baxter has a keen eye for detail.

C. C. BAXTER

On November 1st, 1959, the population of New York City was 8,042,783. If you laid all these people end to end, figuring an average height of five feet six and a half inches, they would reach from Times Square to the outskirts of Karachi, Pakistan. I know facts like this because I work for an insurance company - Consolidated Life of New York. We're one of the top five companies in the country. Our home office has 31,259 employees, which is more than the entire population of uhh... Natchez, Mississippi. I work on the 19th floor. Ordinary Policy Department, Premium Accounting Division, Section W, desk number 861.

Dir: Billy Wilder • Scr: Billy Wilder, I. A. L. Diamond • Cast: Jack Lemmon (C.C. 'Bud' Baxter)

1965   THE SOUND OF MUSIC   1965

As Germany threatens to annex Austria, the cowardly Max reluctantly agrees to help the von Trapp family escape.

MAX

I hope you appreciate the sacrifice I'm making.

CAPTAIN VON TRAPP

You have no choice.

MAX

I know... That's why I'm making it.

Dir: Robert Wise • Scr: Ernest Lehman • Cast: Richard Haydn (Max Detweiler), Christopher Plummer (Captain Von Trapp)

Christopher Plummer hated his role in the hugely successful film, referring to it in subsequent interviews as 'The Sound of Mucus'. He also said of Julie Andrews (a rising star after the release of *Mary Poppins* the previous year) that 'working with her is like being hit over the head by a Valentine's Day card'.

1965   **THE SPY WHO CAME IN FROM THE COLD**   1965

British secret agent Leamas finds himself disgusted by the hypocrisy of his trade.

LEAMAS

What the hell do you think spies are? Moral philosophers measuring everything they do against the word of God or Karl Marx? They're not! They're just a bunch of seedy, squalid bastards like me: little men, drunkards, queers, hen-pecked husbands, civil servants playing cowboys and Indians to brighten their rotten little lives. Do you think they sit like monks in a cell, balancing right against wrong?

Dir: Martin Ritt • Scr: Paul Dehn, Guy Trosper • Based on a novel by John le Carré • Cast: Richard Burton (Alec Leamas)

1968   **ONCE UPON A TIME IN THE WEST**   1968

A brutal gunslinger puts a member of his gang in his place.

FRANK

How can you trust a man who wears both a belt and suspenders? The man can't even trust his own pants.

Dir: Sergio Leone • Scr: Sergio Leone, Sergio Donati • Cast: Henry Fonda (Frank)

A desperate producer tries to impress his new partner.

BIALYSTOCK

You know who I used to be?

Dir: Mel Brooks • Scr: Mel Brooks • Cast: Zero Mostel (Max Bialystock)

A PRODUCER'S HEART

While directors turn their attention to the physical creation of a film, producers are more interested in the waiting public. Without tickets sold there can be no movie at all — or, to be more accurate, no next movie. For an artist, acclaim is success. For a financier, success is success.

Once a producer has decided what kind of story he wants to see and hired a team to deliver it, he has to imagine an audience and take an educated guess as to how many of them will actually make the journey to the cinema. His job title may sound glamorous but its nature is complex: from raising finance to securing distribution, shepherding wayward talent and finessing promises into contracts, every step of the journey is fraught. As the old saying goes, 'you're not making a movie until the camera is rolling'. Where many of the cast and crew breathe a sigh of relief that the process is finally under way and they now have a chance to do what they love best, a producer begins to sweat: this is the point where the money is going out — and it may never come back in.

With this level of risk as well as the huge investment of time involved, it is no wonder that financiers keep their eye on the bottom line while they wield a firm hand in the running of the show. But with so many egos under their command, we should not be surprised either that rivalries appear:

> You can take all the sincerity in Hollywood, place it in the navel of a firefly and still have room enough for three caraway seeds and a producer's heart.
> Fred Allen

> Producers are men who will keep their heads in the noisy presence of writers and directors and not be carried away by art in any of its subversive guises. Their task is to guard against the unusual. They are the trusted loyalists of cliché.
> Ben Hecht

If producers suffer such familiar complaints, it is largely because those who may have reason to gripe about them — the actors, writers and directors — have easy access to the press. The challenges of getting a project off the ground can seem a thankless task, although when a project is a hit gratitude is rarely needed; prizes and profit points are perfectly sufficient. When the golden envelopes are opened and *Variety* publishes the weekly takings, producers leap into the limelight claiming, often rightly, that the movie was their personal dream and that it could never have seen the light of day without their persistence.

> If no producer, no movie.
> Dino De Laurentiis

The Oscar for Best Picture is always awarded to the producer, even though in the eyes of the public the film's kudos is associated with the director; in 1972 Albert Ruddy took home a statuette for *The Godfather* while Francis Ford Coppola lost out to Bob Fosse with *Cabaret*. After that, Coppola made sure he also took a producer's role on *The Godfather: Part II*.

In the heyday of the studio system — from the dawn of the talkies to the 1950s — the heads of MGM, Universal or Fox could green-light their favourite projects with a simple memo, choosing among their tightly controlled empire of stars, directors and writers to create an instant team. Many of their contracted artists resented this control:

> I discovered early in my movie work that a movie is never any better than the stupidest man connected with it. There are times when this distinction may be given to the writer or director. Most often it belongs to the producer... Ninety per cent of the producers I have known were not bright. They were as slow-witted and unprofessional toward making up a story as stockbrokers might be, or bus drivers.
> Ben Hecht

By 1950, two changes had begun to be felt: the Supreme Court had ended the studios' monopoly over cinema distribution, and television had given artists greater freedom to work on their own terms. Even so, working outside the framework of Hollywood's fiefdoms, film-makers still needed financiers and ambassadors for their projects. Thus began the rise of the independent producer. Sam Spiegel (*Lawrence of Arabia*, 1962), Robert Evans (*Chinatown*, 1974) and Joseph E. Levine (*A Bridge Too Far*, 1977) were some of the first in the industry to gain a reputation for power, integrity and intelligence. Not surprisingly, such men took care to protect themselves when they hired the rest of the talent:

> Hollywood has always been full of bartenders and waiters
> who want to be directors. Trouble is, most of them have
> achieved their ambition.
> Sam Spiegel

> When a director hires a producer, you're in deep shit.
> A director needs a boss, not a yes man.
> Robert Evans

The ultimate sign of success for a producer is when his own name helps sell the film to the public, or when he can be associated with a distinct style of production. Familiar names today include:

- Jerry Bruckheimer (*Pirates of the Caribbean*, *Armageddon*)

- Kathleen Kennedy (*Schindler's List*, *The Sixth Sense*)

- Ron Howard (*The Da Vinci Code*, *A Beautiful Mind*)

- Brian Grazer (*Apollo 13*, *Frost/Nixon*)

- Scott Rudin (*The Social Network*, *No Country for Old Men*).

1969   THE ITALIAN JOB   1969

Charlie's henchmen use too much explosive when breaking into a car.

CHARLIE

You're only supposed to blow the bloody doors off!

Dir: Peter Collinson • Scr: Troy Kennedy Martin • Cast: Michael Caine (Charlie Croker)

Director Peter Collinson was raised by his grandparents before attending the Actors' Orphanage in Surrey. Noël Coward was President there and became Collinson's godfather, helping him find his way into the world of entertainment. When Collinson got his first big break on the film, he repaid the favour by casting Coward as Mr Bridger, the pampered criminal mastermind.

1973   BADLANDS   1973

Two lovers flee after killing the girl's father.

HOLLY

I didn't feel shame or fear but just kind of...blah. Like when you're sitting there and all the water's run out of the bathtub.

Dir: Terrence Malick • Scr: Terrence Malick • Cast: Sissy Spacek (Holly Sargis)

A bumbling detective discovers that assumption is not the same as deduction.

> CLOUSEAU

Does your dog bite?

> HOTEL CLERK

No.

Clouseau pets the dog.

> CLOUSEAU

Nice doggie.

The dog barks and bites Clouseau.

I thought you said your dog did not bite!

> HOTEL CLERK

That is not my dog.

Dir: Blake Edwards • Scr: Frank Waldman • Cast: Peter Sellers (Chief Inspector Clouseau), Harold Berens (Hotel Clerk)

Clouseau is painfully aware of his mistakes. In the same film he tries to suggest his frequent clumsiness is just part of a detective's technique: 'I see you are familiar with the falling-down-on-the-floor ploy.'

1980 **CADDYSHACK**   1980

A golf caddy consoles himself over the lost opportunity of a tip.

> CARL

So I jump ship in Hong Kong and I make my way over to Tibet, and I get on as a looper at a course over in the Himalayas.

> MAGGIE

A looper?

> CARL

A looper, you know, a caddy, a looper, a jock. So, I tell them I'm a pro jock, and who do you think they give me? The Dalai Lama, himself. Twelfth son of the Lama. The flowing robes, the grace, bald...striking. So, I'm on the first tee with him. I give him the driver. He hauls off and whacks one - big hitter, the

Lama - long, into a ten-thousand-foot crevasse, right at the base of this glacier. Do you know what the Lama says? Gunga galunga...gunga, gunga-lagunga. So we finish the eighteenth and he's gonna stiff me. And I say, 'Hey, Lama, hey, how about a little something, you know, for the effort, you know?' And he says, 'Oh...there won't be any money, but when you die, on your deathbed, you will receive total consciousness.' So I got that going for me, which is nice.

Dir: Harold Ramis • Scr: Harold Ramis, Douglas Kenney, Brian Doyle-Murray • Cast: Bill Murray (Carl Spackler), Sarah Holcomb (Maggie O'Hoolihan)

1982 TOOTSIE 1982

An actor complains to his agent that he is not getting enough work.

MICHAEL

Are you saying that nobody in New York will work with me?

GEORGE

No, no, that's too limited... nobody in Hollywood wants to work with you either. I can't even set you up for a commercial. You played a tomato for 30 seconds - they went a half a day over schedule because you wouldn't sit down.

MICHAEL

Of course. It was illogical.

GEORGE

You were a tomato. A tomato doesn't have logic. A tomato can't move.

MICHAEL

That's what I said. So if he can't move, how's he gonna sit down, George? I was a stand-up tomato: a juicy, sexy, beefsteak tomato. Nobody does vegetables like me. I did an evening of vegetables off-Broadway. I did the best tomato, the best cucumber. I did an endive salad that knocked the critics on their ass.

Dir: Sydney Pollack • Scr: Larry Gelbart, Murray Schisgal, Don McGuire • Cast: Dustin Hoffman (Michael Dorsey/Dorothy Michaels), Sydney Pollack (George Fields)

1983 KING OF COMEDY   1983

An embittered stand-up comedian forces a TV talk show host to put him on his programme.

                          SECRETARY

Is Mr Langford expecting you?

                         RUPERT PUPKIN

Yes, I don't think he is.

Dir: Martin Scorsese • Scr: Paul D. Zimmerman • Cast: Marta Heflin (Secretary), Robert De Niro (Rupert Pupkin)

1984 THIS IS SPINAL TAP   1984

Marty, a documentary film-maker, interviews rock star Nigel as he improvises at the piano.

                            MARTY

It's very pretty.

                            NIGEL

Yeah, I've been fooling around with it for a few months.

                            MARTY

It's a bit of a departure from what you normally play.

                            NIGEL

It's part of a trilogy, a musical trilogy I'm working on in D minor which is the saddest of all keys, I find. People weep instantly when they hear it, and I don't know why.

                            MARTY

It's very nice.

                            NIGEL

You know, just simple lines intertwining, very much like - I'm really influenced by Mozart and Bach, and it's sort of in between those, really. It's like a 'Mach' piece, really. It's sort of...

                            MARTY

What do you call this?

NIGEL

Well, this piece is called 'Lick My Love Pump'.

Dir: Rob Reiner • Scr: Christopher Guest, Michael McKean, Harry Shearer,
Rob Reiner • Cast: Rob Reiner (Marty DiBergi), Christopher Guest (Nigel
Tufnel)

The film was improvised by all the performers, so lead actors Rob Reiner, Christopher Guest,
Michael McKean and Harry Shearer went to the Writers' Guild hoping to give proper credit to
everyone. The Board of Directors voted fifteen to none that the credits should stay as they were,
listing only the four of them.

1984 **AMADEUS**   1984

Though a fierce rival, Salieri recognizes Mozart's genius.

SALIERI

I heard the music of true forgiveness filling the theatre,
conferring on all who sat there perfect absolution. God was
singing through this little man to all the world, unstoppable,
making my defeat more bitter with every passing bar.

Dir: Miloš Forman • Scr: Peter Shaffer • Cast: F. Murray Abraham (Antonio
Salieri)

Prague, where the film was shot, still contained so much of its original architecture that only four
sets needed to be built. Sir Neville Marriner agreed to conduct the Academy of St Martin in the
Fields for the soundtrack on condition that not a single note of Mozart's music be changed.

FERRIS BUELLER'S DAY OFF

A freewheeling high school student fears his best friend is too timid.

FERRIS

Cameron is so tight that if you stuck a lump of coal up his ass, in two weeks you'd have a diamond.

Dir: John Hughes • Scr: John Hughes • Cast: Matthew Broderick (Ferris Bueller)

WITHNAIL AND I

Marwood and Withnail are startled by Danny's politics - and his narcotics.

MARWOOD

Give me a Valium, I'm getting the fear!

DANNY

You have done something to your brain. You have made it high. If I lay 10 mils of diazepam on you, it will do something else to your brain. You will make it low. Why trust one drug and not the other? That's politics, innit?

MARWOOD

I'm gonna eat some sugar.

He goes to the kitchen.

DANNY

I recommend you smoke some more grass.

MARWOOD

No way, no fucking way.

DANNY

That is an unfortunate political decision. Reflecting these times.

WITHNAIL

What are you talking about, Danny?

DANNY

Politics, man. If you're hanging onto a rising balloon, you're presented with a difficult decision - let go before it's too late - or hang on and keep getting higher, posing the question: how long can you keep a grip on the rope? They're selling hippie wigs in Woolworth's, man. The greatest decade in the history of mankind is over. And as Presuming Ed here has so consistently pointed out, we have failed to paint it black.

Dir: Bruce Robinson • Scr: Bruce Robinson • Cast: Paul McGann (Marwood, 'I'), Ralph Brown (Danny), Richard E. Grant (Withnail)

1987 WHITE MISCHIEF 1987

A jaded British expatriate opens her curtains to reveal the gorgeous hills of Kenya.

ALICE

Oh God - not another fucking beautiful day.

Dir: Michael Radford • Scr: Michael Radford, Jonathan Gems • Based on a novel by James Fox • Cast: Sarah Miles (Alice de Janzé)

1988 A FISH CALLED WANDA 1988

A con artist finds her plans undermined by her idiotic partner-in-crime.

WANDA

Aristotle was not Belgian. The central message of Buddhism is not 'Every man for himself'. And the London Underground is not a political movement. Those are all mistakes, Otto. I looked them up.

Dir: Charles Crichton, John Cleese (uncredited) • Scr: John Cleese, Charles Crichton • Cast: Jamie Lee Curtis (Wanda Gershwitz)

The scenes in which Otto seduces Wanda in clumsy Italian had to be dubbed into Spanish for the Italian market. During the scene where a poodle is buried, the choirboys sing 'Miserere Dominus, canis mortuus est' ('Have mercy, Lord, the dog is dead').

John Cleese insisted the film was really directed by Crichton alone, and that Cleese had agreed to share the role solely because Crichton was seventy-seven and the financiers were nervous he might have lost his touch. Crichton was responsible for the Ealing comedies *The Lavender Hill Mob* (1951) and *The Titfield Thunderbolt* (1953).

1995 COPYCAT 1995

A serial killer taunts one of his targets.

PETER

Don't you ever get tired... Of being a day late and a dollar short?

Dir: Jon Amiel • Scr: Ann Biderman, David Madsen • Cast: William McNamara (Peter Foley)

1995 CASINO 1995

Ferocious mobster Nicky Santoro does not suffer fools gladly.

NICKY

This guy could fuck up a cup of coffee.

Dir: Martin Scorsese • Scr: Nicholas Pileggi, Martin Scorsese • Based on a book by Nicholas Pileggi • Cast: Joe Pesci (Nicky Santoro)

The owners of the Riviera casino where the film was shot did not want the production to deter their real gambling clients, so scenes were scheduled in the brief slot between 1 a.m. and 4 a.m. Somewhat disingenuously, the casino owners boosted business by posting a large sign outside saying 'Robert De Niro, Sharon Stone, and Joe Pesci Filming the New Movie "Casino" Inside!'

'YOUR MOTHER WAS A HAMSTER'

An insult can be a finely honed stiletto or a sledgehammer, each effective according to adversary and circumstance. Screenwriters in the earlier part of the twentieth century were hamstrung by censors and public sensitivities but these constraints only served to focus their barbs. The following quotes, in chronological order, show how changing times can sharpen — or not — cinema's rapier wit.

> You clinking clanking clattering collection of caliginous junk!
> *The Wizard of Oz* (1939)

> There's a name for you ladies, but it isn't used in high society... outside of a kennel.
> *The Women* (1939)

> UGARTE: You despise me, don't you?
> RICK: If I gave you any thought, I probably would.
> *Casablanca* (1942)

> I know you like a book, you little tramp. You'd sell your own mother for a piece of fudge. But you're smart with it. Smart enough to know when to sell and when to sit tight. You've got a great big dollar sign there where most women have a heart.
> *The Killing* (1956)

> You're the son of a thousand fathers, all bastards like you.
> *The Good, the Bad and the Ugly* (1966)

> Take your stinking paws off me, you damn dirty ape.
> *Planet of the Apes* (1968)

> I call that bold talk for a one-eyed fat man.
> *True Grit* (1969)

> Well, if it isn't fat stinking billy goat Billy Boy in poison! How art thou, thou globby bottle of cheap, stinking chip oil? Come and get one in the yarbles, if you have any yarbles, you eunuch jelly thou!
> *A Clockwork Orange* (1971)

> You know, I'd almost forgotten what your eyes looked like. Still the same. Pissholes in the snow.
> *Get Carter* (1971)

I don't wanna talk to you no more, you empty headed, animal food trough wiper. I fart in your general direction. Your mother was a hamster and your father smelled of elderberries.
Monty Python and the Holy Grail (1975)

The day they lay you away, what I do on your grave won't pass for flowers.
The Shootist (1976)

You punch like you take it up the ass!
Raging Bull (1980)

You're not too smart, are you? I like that in a man.
Body Heat (1981)

You're a neo maxi zoom dweebie.
The Breakfast Club (1985)

Did your parents have any children that lived?
Full Metal Jacket (1987)

You're in more dire need of a blow job than any white man in history.
Good Morning Vietnam (1987)

You're one ugly motherfucker.
Predator (1987)

I'll use small words so that you'll be sure to understand, you warthog faced buffoon.
The Princess Bride (1987)

[Soldier], you'd need three promotions to get to be an asshole.
Biloxi Blues (1988)

She's got a heart like a twelve-minute egg.
Bright Lights, Big City (1988)

To call you stupid would be an insult to stupid people. I've known sheep who could outwit you. I've worn dresses with higher IQs.
A Fish Called Wanda (1988)

If my dog had a face like yours, I'd shave his ass and teach him to walk backwards.
Gleaming the Cube (1989)

I wouldn't live with you if the world were flooded with piss and you lived in a tree.
Parenthood (1989)

He was so crooked, he could eat soup with a corkscrew.
The Grifters (1990)

You lewd, crude, rude, bag of pre-chewed food dude.
Hook (1991)

Sit your five-dollar ass down before I make change.
New Jack City (1991)

Mr Madison, what you've just said is one of the most insanely idiotic things I have ever heard. At no point in your rambling, incoherent response were you even close to anything that could be considered a rational thought. Everyone in this room is now dumber for having listened to it. I award you no points, and may God have mercy on your soul.
Billy Madison (1995)

Were you always this stupid, or did you take lessons?
The Long Kiss Goodnight (1996)

I don't give a tuppeny fuck about your moral conundrum, you meat-headed shit sack.
Gangs of New York (2002)

You cock-juggling thunder-cunt!
Blade: Trinity (2004)

Harry, let's face it. And I'm not being funny. I mean no disrespect, but you're a cunt. You're a cunt now, and you've always been a cunt. And the only thing that's going to change is that you're going to be an even bigger cunt.
In Bruges (2008)

Stop crying, you snivelling ass! Stop your nonsense. You're just an afterbirth, Eli. You slithered out of your mother's filth. They should have put you in a glass jar on the mantelpiece.
There Will Be Blood (2008)

1997 GOOD WILL HUNTING   1997

A talented but wayward college student criticizes a friend for being too conventional.

> **WILL**
>
> You dropped a hundred and fifty grand on a fucking education you coulda got for a dollar fifty in late charges at the public library.

Dir: Gus Van Sant • Scr: Matt Damon, Ben Affleck • Cast: Matt Damon (Will Hunting)

1997 JACKIE BROWN   1997

> **ORDELL**
>
> You know you smoke too much of that shit, that shit gonna rob you of your own ambition.

> **MELANIE**
>
> Not if your ambition is to get high and watch TV.

Dir: Quentin Tarantino • Scr: Quentin Tarantino • Based on a novel by Elmore Leonard • Cast: Samuel L. Jackson (Ordell Robbie), Bridget Fonda (Melanie Ralston)

1999 AMERICAN BEAUTY   1999

> **CAROLYN**
>
> Your father and I were just discussing his day at work. Why don't you tell our daughter about it, honey?

> **LESTER**
>
> Janie, today I quit my job. And then I told my boss to go fuck himself, and then I blackmailed him for almost $60,000. Pass the asparagus.

> **CAROLYN**
>
> Your father seems to think this kind of behaviour is something to be proud of.

> **LESTER**
>
> And your mother seems to prefer that I go through life like a fucking prisoner while she keeps my dick in a mason jar under the sink.

CAROLYN

How dare you speak to me that way in front of her. And I
marvel that you can be so contemptuous of me, on the same day
that you LOSE your job.

LESTER

Lose it? I didn't lose it. It's not like, 'Whoops! Where'd my job
go?' I *quit*. Someone pass the asparagus, please.

Dir: Sam Mendes • Scr: Alan Ball • Cast: Annette Bening (Carolyn Burnham),
Kevin Spacey (Lester Burnham)

Earlier versions of the script contained one scene in which Lester does actually sleep with the
underage Angela, and another where Ricky and Jane are arrested for Lester's murder.

2000   O BROTHER, WHERE ART THOU?   2000

Three escaped convicts meet a travelling musician.

MCGILL

What'd the devil give you for your soul, Tommy?

JOHNSON

Well, he taught me to play this here guitar real good.

O'DONNELL

Oh son, for that you sold your everlasting soul?

JOHNSON

Well, I wasn't usin' it.

Dir: Joel Coen, Ethan Coen (uncredited) • Scr: Ethan Coen, Joel Coen • Based on *The Odyssey* by Homer • Cast: George Clooney (Ulysses Everett McGill), Chris Thomas King (Tommy Johnson), Tim Blake Nelson (Delmar O'Donnell)

Although set in 1930s Mississippi, the film is a loose adaptation of *The Odyssey*, an epic poem written during the eighth century BC. The picture contains dozens of detailed references and the screenplay credits include Homer himself, although directors Joel and Ethan Coen have admitted that they never read the original work.

2001   WAKING LIFE   2001

Celine is sceptical about past life experiences.

CELINE

Everybody says they've been the reincarnation of Cleopatra or Alexander the Great. I always want to tell them they were probably some dumb fuck like everybody else.

Dir: Richard Linklater • Scr: Richard Linklater • Cast: Julie Delpy (Celine)

2001   ZOOLANDER   2001

Male supermodel Derek Zoolander pays tribute to his late associates.

ZOOLANDER

Rufus, Brint and Meekus were like brothers to me. And when I say brother, I don't mean, like, an actual brother, but I mean it like the way black people use it. Which is more meaningful, I think.

He pauses to reflect.

If there is anything that this horrible tragedy can teach us, it's that a male model's life is a precious, precious commodity. Just because we have chiselled abs and stunning features, it doesn't mean that we too can't die in a freak gasoline-fight accident.

Dir: Ben Stiller • Scr: Ben Stiller, Drake Sather, John Hamburg • Cast: Ben Stiller (Derek Zoolander)

Bret Easton Ellis wrote *Glamorama*, a novel about a moronic male supermodel who gets caught up in a fashion-related terrorist conspiracy, three years before *Zoolander* was released. He sued Ben Stiller for copyright infringement but the case was settled out of court. Although the story is a highly exaggerated satire on the modelling world, many of the industry's most successful faces admitted the details of the lifestyle were remarkably accurate.

The film was banned in Malaysia because it depicts the assassination of its (fictional) prime minister.

2004 SIDEWAYS 2004

Two middle-aged friends on a road trip contemplate their achievements.

>   MILES
> Half my life is over and I have nothing to show for it.
> Nothing. I'm a thumbprint on the window of a skyscraper. I'm
> a smudge of excrement on a tissue surging out to sea with a
> million tons of raw sewage.

>   JACK
> See? Right there   you just said. That is beautiful. 'A
> smudge of   out to sea.'

Bukowski.

Dir   Taylor • Based on a novel
by R   nd), Thomas Haden Church
(Jack

Miles is   .es his preferred grape variety as Pinot Noir.
Following   ...es of this wine type rose by 20 per cent. The screenplay was
the first eve   .major American film industry ceremonies: National Board of Review,
New York Fi   s Circle, Los Angeles Film Critics Association, Golden Globes, WGA and
Academy Awards.

Kate despairs of her under-achieving boyfriend.

> KATE
>
> I'm curious - is it strictly apathy, or do you really not have a goal in life?

> PETER
>
> I found that if you have a goal you might not reach it. But if you don't have one, then you are never disappointed. And I gotta tell you... it feels phenomenal.

Dir: Rawson Marshall Thurber • Scr: Rawson Marshall Thurber • Cast: Christine Taylor (Kate Veatch), Vince Vaughn (Peter La Fleur)

2007 EAGLE VS SHARK   2007

Jarrod attempts to place a threatening phone call to someone who - in the distant past - humiliated him at school. Jarrod's intended victim, however, is not at home.

> MAN ON PHONE
>
> Do you want to leave a message?

> JARROD
>
> Tell him that justice is waiting for him.

> MAN ON PHONE
>
> OK, Justin. Thank you. Bye bye.

He hangs up.

> JARROD
>
> No! Justice. Justice!

Dir: Taika Waititi • Scr: Taika Waititi • Cast: Uncredited (Man on Phone), Jemaine Clement (Jarrod)

2007 SUPERBAD   2007

Two high school nerds decide to throw a party in the hope of boosting their love lives.

You know when you hear girls say 'Ah man, I was so shit-faced last night, I shouldn't have fucked that guy'? We could be that mistake!

Dir: Greg Mottola • Scr: Seth Rogen, Evan Goldberg • Cast: Jonah Hill (Seth)

2011 BAD TEACHER   2011

A red-hot high school teacher offers some dating advice.

ELIZABETH

I tell you what I know. A kid who wears the same gymnastics sweatshirt three days a week isn't getting laid until he's twenty-nine. That's what I know.

Dir: Jake Kasdan • Scr: Gene Stupnitsky, Lee Eisenberg • Cast: Cameron Diaz (Elizabeth Halsey)

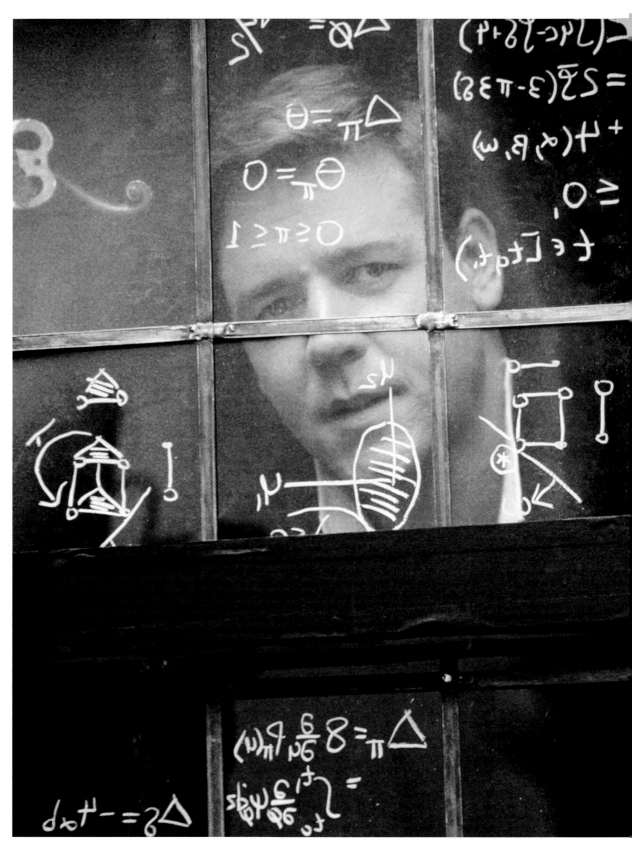

Russell Crowe as mathematician John Nash ponders the mystery of his work in *A Beautiful Mind*.

Audrey Hepburn combines her reputations as fashion icon and screen legend in this shot from *Breakfast at Tiffany's* (1961).

Marlene Dietrich shows her smouldering screen presence remained undimmed to the end of her career.

Memories

CITIZEN KANE

BERNSTEIN

```
A fellow will remember a lot of things you wouldn't think
he'd remember. You take me. One day, back in 1896, I was
crossing over to Jersey on the ferry, and as we pulled out
there was another ferry pulling in, and on it there was a
girl waiting to get off. A white dress she had on. She was
carrying a white parasol. I only saw her for one second. She
didn't see me at all, but I'll bet a month hasn't gone by since
that I haven't thought of that girl.
```

Dir: Orson Welles • Scr: Orson Welles, Herman J. Mankiewicz • Cast: Everett Sloane (Mr Bernstein)

This monologue was surely the inspiration for John Gage's speech in *Indecent Proposal* (1993):

I remember once when I was young, and I was coming back from some place, a movie or something. I was on the subway. And there was a girl sitting across from me, and she was wearing this dress that was buttoned clear right up to here. She was the most beautiful thing I'd ever seen. And I was shy then, so when she would look at me, I would look away. Then afterwards, when I would look back, she would look away. Then I got to where I was gonna get off, and got off. The doors closed. And as the train was pulling away, she looked right at me and gave me the most incredible smile. It was awful. I wanted to tear the doors open. I went back every night, same time for two weeks but she never showed up. That was thirty years ago, and I don't think that there's a day that goes by that I don't think about her. I don't want that to happen again.

NEVER GIVE A SUCKER AN EVEN BREAK

THE GREAT MAN

```
I was in love with a beautiful blonde once, dear. She drove me
to drink. 'Tis the one thing I'm indebted to her for.
```

Dir: Edward F. Cline • Scr: John T. Neville, Prescott Chaplin • Cast: W. C. Fields (The Great Man)

OLD ACQUAINTANCE

KIT

```
There comes a time in every woman's life when the only thing
that helps is a glass of champagne.
```

Dir: Vincent Sherman • Scr: John Van Druten, Lenore J. Coffee • Cast: Bette Davis (Kit Marlowe)

A group of thieves kill time as they wait for their passage to Africa.

                              O'HARA

What is time? Swiss manufacture it. French hoard it. Italians
squander it. Americans say it's money. Hindus say it doesn't
exist. Do you know what I say? I say time is a crook.

Dir: John Huston • Scr: Truman Capote, John Huston • Based on a novel by
James Helvick (aka Claud Cockburn) • Cast: Peter Lorre (Julius O'Hara)

Humphrey Bogart was involved in a car accident during the shoot and lost several teeth,
compromising his recorded dialogue. Peter Sellers, known at that time only as a capable
mimic, overdubbed the lines.

BY THE WAY, THE PRODUCER THINKS IT'S A GREAT IDEA

A screenwriter rarely creates a character with a particular actor
in mind unless she knows her director or producer has good access to
them. If she fills her script with enticingly tailored description
('his chiselled features and silver hair lend gravitas to his
steely gaze as he surveys the dry plains before him, a cheroot in
one hand and a Colt revolver in the other') then she will have a
good deal of revision to do if Clint Eastwood passes on the project
and the next available name is Daniel Radcliffe.

Canny writers prefer to paint an attractive one-size-fits-all
portrait: 'sexy in an understated way, her elegant presence exudes
a powerful wordless confidence'. If Anne Hathaway is not available
but Julia Roberts likes it, the story still makes sense.

Once the lottery of casting is complete the writer can only hope
that the actors will connect with her story and realize their roles
sympathetically. If a big name is cast, she may dream of a smash hit
but faces the possibility that the star will be powerful enough to
demand fresh drafts.

Sometimes this is because they have a keen insight into her story's
unseen potential; sometimes it is because they have always wanted
to drive a Lamborghini, and feel a chase sequence will show that the
college professor they have been hired to play is not just a two-
dimensional, desk-bound, middle-aged academic. Oh, and also — the
star's girlfriend has just graduated from drama school and feels
that although the role of the history lecturer was written for a
fifty-year-old whose grandparents died in the Holocaust, with a
little tinkering it could be perfect for her.

By the way, the producer thinks it's a great idea.

1968 THE SWIMMER 1968

Ned reminisces ruefully with a former lover.

NED

My mother gave me 25 cents for mowing the lawn around our house. Seems only a minute ago I could smell the grass... It's so fast. People grow up, and then they... We're all gonna die, Shirley. That doesn't make much sense, does it?

SHIRLEY

Sometimes it does... Sometimes at three o'clock in the morning.

Dir: Frank Perry • Scr: Eleanor Perry • Based on a story by John Cheever • Cast: Burt Lancaster (Ned Merrill), Janice Rule (Shirley Abbott)

1976 MURDER BY DEATH 1976

A group of detectives summoned to solve a crime remain suspicious of one another.

SAM

The last time I trusted a dame was in Paris in 1940. She said she was going out to get a bottle of wine. Two hours later, the Germans marched into France.

Dir: Robert Moore • Scr: Neil Simon • Cast: Peter Falk (Sam Diamond)

1980 HEAVEN'S GATE 1980

Rancher Billy Irvine and Marshal James Averill find their friendship tested as homesteaders settle in Wyoming.

BILLY

James, do you remember the good gone days?

JAMES

Clearer and better, every day I get older.

Dir: Michael Cimino • Scr: Michael Cimino • Cast: John Hurt (Billy Irvine), Kris Kristofferson (James Averill)

Director Michael Cimino leveraged his success with *The Deer Hunter* (1978) to make *Heaven's Gate* entirely on his own terms, leaving no aspect of the production untouched by his perfectionism. By the end of the fifth day's filming the crew were already four days behind schedule; one scene for which the stage direction says simply an actor 'walks past a cock-fight' took over two weeks to complete, and the main shoot lasted over a year. The budget was expanded from $7.5 million [$21 million] to $44 million [$122 million] but the US box office only recouped $3.5 million [$10 million] and the loss nearly bankrupted United Artists.

Critical reception at the time was almost universally negative. Vincent Canby of the *New York Times* wrote: ' it fails so completely that you might suspect Mr Cimino sold his soul to obtain the success of *The Deer Hunter* and the Devil has just come around to collect'.

1981   **MAD MAX II**   1981

NARRATOR

My life fades, my vision dims. All that remains are memories.
I remember a time of chaos, ruined dreams, this wasted land.
Most of all, I remember the man we called Max, the road
warrior. To understand who he was we have to go back to the
other time. When the world was powered by the black fuel, and
the desert sprung great cities of pipe and steel. Gone now,
swept away. For reasons long forgotten, two mighty warrior
tribes went to war and touched off a blaze which engulfed
them all. Without fuel they were nothing. They'd built a house
of straw. Suddenly their machines sputtered and stopped.
Their leaders talked and talked and talked, but nothing
could stem the avalanche. Their world crumbled. Cities
exploded. A whirlwind of looting and a firestorm of fear.
Men began to feed on men.

Dir: George Miller • Scr: Terry Hayes, George Miller, Brian
Hannant • Cast: Harold Baigent (Narrator)

1990 THE TWO JAKES 1990

Private investigator Jake Gittes reminisces about Los Angeles, his life and his work.

> **JAKE**
> Time changes things, like the fruit stand that turns into a filling station. But the footprints and signs from the past are everywhere. They've been fighting over this land since the first Spanish missionaries showed the Indians the benefits of religion, horses and a few years of forced labour. The Indians had it right all along. They respected ghosts. You can't forget the past any more than you can change it. Hearing Katherine Mulwray's name started me thinking about old secrets, family, property, and a guy doin' his partner dirt. Memories are like that - as unpredictable as nitro, and you never know what's gonna set one off. Like the clues that keep you on the right track are never where you look for them. They fall out of the pocket of somebody else's suit you pick up at the cleaners. They're in the tune you can't stop humming, that you never heard in your life. They're at the other end of the wrong number you dial in the middle of the night. The signs are in those old familiar places you only think you've never been before. But you get used to seeing them out of the corner of your eye, and you end up tripping over the ones that are right in front of you.

Dir: Jack Nicholson • Scr: Robert Towne • Cast: Jack Nicholson (J. J. 'Jake' Gittes)

1993 GROUNDHOG DAY 1993

Phil is trapped in a time loop, reliving one single day forever - but nobody believes him.

> **RITA**
> What about me, Phil? Do you know me too?

> **PHIL**
> I know all about you. You like producing, but you hope for more than Channel 9 Pittsburgh.

> **RITA**
> Well, everyone knows that!

                              PHIL

You like boats, but not the ocean. You go to a lake in the
summer with your family up in the mountains. There's a long
wooden dock and a boathouse with boards missing from the
roof, and a place you used to crawl underneath to be alone.
You're a sucker for French poetry and rhinestones. You're very
generous. You're kind to strangers and children, and when you
stand in the snow you look like an angel.

Rita is amazed.

                              RITA

How are you doing this?

                              PHIL

I told you. I wake up every day, right here, right in
Punxsutawney, and it's always February 2nd, and there's
nothing I can do about it.

Dir: Harold Ramis • Scr: Danny Rubin, Harold Ramis • Cast: Andie MacDowell
(Rita), Bill Murray (Phil Connors)

No reason is given why Phil should find himself trapped in time, although earlier drafts
suggested a disaffected ex-lover had cast a spell on him.

1993 **SHADOWLANDS**   1993

A spirited poet inspires a passionless professor.

                              JOY

We can't have the happiness of yesterday without the pain of
today. That's the deal.

Dir: Richard Attenborough • Scr: William Nicholson • Cast: Debra Winger
(Joy Gresham)

1997 **AUSTIN POWERS: INTERNATIONAL MAN OF MYSTERY**   1997

                              DR EVIL

The details of my life are quite inconsequential... Very well,
where do I begin? My father was a relentlessly self-improving
boulangerie owner from Belgium with low grade narcolepsy
and a penchant for buggery. My mother was a fifteen-year-old
French prostitute named Chloe with webbed feet. My father would
womanize, he would drink. He would make outrageous claims like he

invented the question mark. Sometimes, he would accuse chestnuts of being lazy. The sort of general malaise that only the genius possess and the insane lament. My childhood was typical. Summers in Rangoon, luge lessons. In the spring, we'd make meat helmets. When I was insolent, I was placed in a burlap bag and beaten with reeds - pretty standard, really. At the age of twelve, I received my first scribe. At the age of fourteen, a Zoroastrian named Vilma ritualistically shaved my testicles. There really is nothing like a shorn scrotum... it's breathtaking - I suggest you try it.

Dir: Jay Roach • Scr: Mike Myers • Cast: Mike Myers (Dr Evil)

2000   MEMENTO   2000

Leonard has lost his short-term memory and can only manage his life by leaving himself written prompts.

LEONARD

So you have information for me?

NATALIE

Is that what your little note says?

LEONARD

Yes.

NATALIE

NATALIE

It must be hard living your life off a couple of scraps of paper. You mix your laundry list with your grocery list, you'll end up eating your underwear for breakfast.

Dir: Christopher Nolan • Scr: Christopher Nolan • Based on a story by Jonathan Nolan • Cast: Guy Pearce (Leonard Shelby), Carrie-Anne Moss (Natalie)

The entire opening scene is shown backwards but the sound effects were too disorienting in reverse so they were re-edited to match the altered cues.

2001 AMÉLIE (*LE FABULEUX DESTIN D'AMÉLIE POULAIN*) 2001

NARRATOR

On September 3rd 1973, at 6:28pm and 32 seconds, a bluebottle fly capable of 14,670 wing beats a minute landed on Rue St Vincent, Montmartre. At the same moment, on a restaurant terrace nearby, the wind magically made two glasses dance unseen on a tablecloth. Meanwhile, in a fifth floor flat, 28 Avenue Trudaine, Paris 9, returning from his best friend's funeral, Eugène Colère erased his name from his address book. At the same moment, a sperm with one X chromosome, belonging to Raphaël Poulain, made a dash for an egg in his wife Amandine. Nine months later, Amélie Poulain was born.

Dir: Jean-Pierre Jeunet • Scr: Guillaume Laurant, Jean-Pierre Jeunet • Cast: André Dussollier (Narrator)

2002 ONE HOUR PHOTO 2002

A photo technician becomes obsessed by a family whose prints he processes.

SY

No one ever takes a photograph of something they want to forget.

Dir: Mark Romanek • Scr: Mark Romanek • Cast: Robin Williams (Seymour 'Sy' Parrish)

THE GREATEST STORY EVER SOLD

While the writers of Hollywood's golden age were peppering their screenplays with sparkling one-liners, their counterparts in the marketing departments seemed to be having a tougher time. The earliest attempts at poster captions are surprisingly flat-footed, relying almost without exception on lively punctuation to bolster sagging imaginations. Gradually, decade by decade, their techniques grew more sophisticated.

In the 1940s they seemed to feel audiences needed a talking point:

The World's Greatest Dancers in the World's Greatest Musical Show!
Broadway Melody of 1940 (1940)

Walt Disney's Technicolor FEATURE triumph!
Fantasia (1940)

EVERYBODY'S TALKING ABOUT IT! It's Terrific!
Citizen Kane (1941)

Millions Have Read This Great Novel... Millions more will see an even greater picture!
How Green Was My Valley (1941)

The Screen Dares To Open The Strange And Savage Pages Of A Shocking Best-Seller!
The Lost Weekend (1945)

In the 1950s they seemed keen to make sure nobody missed the point of the film:

It's all about women... and their men!
All About Eve (1950)

The Bride gets the THRILLS! Father gets the BILLS!
Father of the Bride (1950)

The story of a blonde who wanted to go places, and a brute who got her there - the hard way!
The Bad and the Beautiful (1952)

The story of a family's ugly secret and the stark moment that thrust their private lives into public view!
Written on the Wind (1956)

A Man's Life in Their Hands...
12 Angry Men (1957)

Unspeakable Horrors From Outer Space Paralyse the Living
and Resurrect The Dead!
Plan 9 From Outer Space (1959)

In the 1960s they assumed audiences were smarter, and favoured a
more conversational tone:

Check in. Relax. Take a shower.
Psycho (1960)

How did they ever make a movie of Lolita?
Lolita (1962)

Remember, the next scream you hear may be your own!
The Birds (1963)

You are cordially invited to George and Martha's for an
evening of fun and games.
Who's Afraid of Virginia Woolf? (1966)

This is Benjamin. He's a little worried about his future.
The Graduate (1967)

Pray for Rosemary's Baby.
Rosemary's Baby (1968)

In the 1970s they realized that rhetoric and exclamation marks were for squares, and gave us laconic catchphrases instead:

M∗A∗S∗H Gives a D∗A∗M∗N.
M∗A∗S∗H (1970)

Name Your Poison.
McCabe & Mrs Miller (1971)

Shaft's his name. Shaft's his game.
Shaft (1971)

Life is a Cabaret.
Cabaret (1972)

Don't go in the water.
Jaws (1975)

By the end of the 1970s, the decade in which the idea of the block-buster and its associated saturation marketing was born, the discipline had finally come of age. A recent survey of advertising and branding professionals declared the following the greatest ever taglines:

We are not alone.
Close Encounters of the Third Kind (1977)

A long time ago in a galaxy far, far away...
Star Wars (1977)

Just when you thought it was safe to go back in the water.
Jaws 2 (1978)

In space no one can hear you scream.
Alien (1979)

Who ya gonna call?
Ghostbusters (1984)

Be afraid. Be very afraid.
The Fly (1986)

They're back.
Poltergeist II (1986)

The list is life.
Schindler's List (1993)

Houston, we have a problem.
Apollo 13 (1995)

Earth. It was fun while it lasted.
Armageddon (1998)

Proving that those who do not study the history of this arcane discipline are condemned to repeat it, the *Huffington Post* recently resurrected these ham-fisted examples:

Today the pond. Tomorrow the world.
Frogs (1972)

Unwittingly, he trained a dolphin to kill the President of the United States.
The Day of the Dolphin (1973)

Not to be confused with King Kong.
Ape (1976)

The Only Thing More Terrifying Than the Last 12 Minutes of This Film are the First 92.
Suspiria (1977)

Science Created Him. Now Chuck Norris Must Destroy Him.
Silent Rage (1982)

They came to Space Camp with the dream of becoming astronauts. Suddenly... Without warning... Before they were ready... They were launched into space.
SpaceCamp (1986)

Laugh. Cry. Share The Pants.
The Sisterhood of the Traveling Pants (2005)

He Was Dead... But He Got Better.
Crank (2006)

Titans Will Clash.
Clash of the Titans (2010)

THE BOURNE IDENTITY

A secret agent saved from death has no memory of who – or what – he is.

> BOURNE
>
> I can tell you the license plate numbers of all six cars outside. I can tell you that our waitress is left-handed and the guy sitting up at the counter weighs 215 pounds and knows how to handle himself. I know the best place to look for a gun is the cab of the grey truck outside, and at this altitude I can run flat out for a half mile before my hands start shaking. Now, why would I know that? How can I know that and not know who I am?

Dir: Doug Liman • Scr: Tony Gilroy, William Blake Herron • Based on a novel by Robert Ludlum • Cast: Matt Damon (Jason Bourne)

Director Doug Liman asked screenwriter Tony Gilroy not to read the original novel but simply to work from an outline he had prepared.

MINORITY REPORT

A detective worries that his chief is getting out of his depth.

> GIDEON
>
> Careful, Chief. Dig up the past, all you get is dirty.

Dir: Steven Spielberg • Scr: Scott Frank, Jon Cohen • Based on a story by Philip K. Dick • Cast: Tim Blake Nelson (Gideon)

Three years before production began, Spielberg assembled sixteen 'future experts' to sketch out how the year 2054 might look. The team included Neil Gershenfeld, professor at MIT's Media Lab; Shaun Jones, director of biomedical research at DARPA (Defense Advanced Research Projects Agency); William Mitchell, dean of the school of architecture at MIT; and Jaron Lanier, one of the inventors of virtual reality technology.

2004 GARDEN STATE 2004

Andrew and Sam look back on their New Jersey childhoods.

ANDREW

There's a handful of normal kid things I kinda missed.

SAM

There's a handful of normal kid things I kinda wish I had missed.

Dir: Zach Braff • Scr: Zach Braff • Cast: Zach Braff (Andrew Largeman), Natalie Portman (Sam)

2004 50 FIRST DATES 2004

Lucy suffers from short-term memory loss, so her lover Henry is forced to remind her every day that they are together.

LUCY

Can I have one last first kiss?

Dir: Peter Segal • Scr: George Wing • Cast: Drew Barrymore (Lucy Whitmore)

2008 LET THE RIGHT ONE IN (*LÅT DEN RÄTTE KOMMA IN*) 2008

Schoolboy Oskar befriends his reclusive young neighbour.

OSKAR

Are you a vampire?

ELI

I live off blood... Yes.

OSKAR

Are you... dead?

                         ELI

No. Can't you tell?

                         OSKAR

But... Are you old?

                         ELI

I'm twelve. But I've been twelve for a long time.

Dir: Tomas Alfredson • Scr: John Ajvide Lindqvist, based on his
novel • Cast: Kåre Hedebrant (Oskar), Lina Leandersson (Eli)

The film contains several innovative sound effects. Puncturing a sausage was used to emulate biting into flesh, while drinking yogurt was used to sound like sucking blood. Blinking eyelids were dubbed with a recording of grape skins being pressed together.

2009 CRAZY HEART   2009

A country and western singer finally manages to quit drinking.

                      'BAD' BLAKE

   Ain't rememberin' wonderful?

Dir: Scott Cooper • Scr: Scott Cooper • Based on a novel by Thomas
Cobb • Cast: Jeff Bridges (Otis 'Bad' Blake)

2010 INCEPTION   2010

*Cobb teaches his pupils how to create dreamscapes other people
can enter. Here, he experiences Ariadne's first attempt.*

                         COBB

I know this bridge - this place is real. You didn't imagine it,
you remembered it...

                       ARIADNE

I cross it every day on my way to the college.

                         COBB

Never recreate places from memory. Always imagine new places.

                       ARIADNE

You have to draw from what you know.

Cobb shakes his head.

> COBB

Use pieces – a streetlamp, phone booths, a type of brick – not whole areas.

> ARIADNE

Why not?

> COBB

Because building dreams out of your own memories is the surest way to lose your grip on what's real and what's a dream.

Dir: Christopher Nolan • Scr: Christopher Nolan • Cast: Leonardo DiCaprio (Cobb), Ellen Page (Ariadne)

Four set stills from *Last Tango in Paris* (1972) capture the shadowy intimacy of the lovers' story.

The camera adored Marilyn Monroe just as her public did, capturing her every mood from the demure
to the exuberant.

The chiaroscuro photography and swelling Rachmaninov score of *Brief Encounter* set the scene for a heartbreakingly British love story.

Tears

Paul warns Betsy that life on the tropical island holds hidden terrors.

PAUL

It's easy enough to read the thoughts of a newcomer. Everything seems beautiful because you don't understand. Those flying fish, they're not leaping for joy, they're jumping in terror. Bigger fish want to eat them. That luminous water, it takes its gleam from millions of tiny dead bodies. The glitter of putrescence. There is no beauty here, only death and decay.

BETSY

You can't really believe that.

PAUL

Everything good dies here. Even the stars.

Dir: Jacques Tourneur • Scr: Curt Siodmak, Ardel Wray • Based on an article by Inez Wallace and on *Jane Eyre* by Charlotte Brontë • Cast: Tom Conway (Paul Holland), Frances Dee (Betsy Connell)

Perhaps missing the point of Tourneur's zombie metaphor, a *New York Times* reviewer dismissed the film as 'a dull, disgusting exaggeration of an unhealthy, abnormal concept of life'.

1944   **LIFEBOAT**   1944

Adrift at sea, German U-boat captain Willi and American citizen Connie await rescue. To pass the time, Willi fixes Connie's diamond bracelet.

WILLI

Looks like bits of ice.

CONNIE

I wish they were.

WILLI

They're really nothing but a few pieces of carbon crystallized under high pressure at great heat.

CONNIE

Quite so, if you want to be scientific about it.

                              WILLI

I'm a great believer in science.

                              CONNIE

    Like tears, for instance. They're nothing but H2O with a trace
    of sodium chloride.

Dir: Alfred Hitchcock • Scr: Jo Swerling • Based on a story by John
Steinbeck • Cast: Walter Slezak (Willi), Tallulah Bankhead (Connie Porter)

Even though most of the film was shot in a studio water tank, the entire cast suffered from
seasickness at some point. When someone mentioned to Hitchcock that Tallulah Bankhead
was not wearing underwear during one take, he replied: 'I don't know if this is a matter for the
costume department, make-up, or hairdressing.'

WHERE'S ALFRED?

A 'cameo' role (named after a type of brooch which bears a bust
or portrait) was originally a brief appearance by a real-life
figure instantly recognizable to the audience. This usually meant
that the person in question was playing themselves as opposed to
a character in the story. *In The Lodger* (1927), Alfred Hitchcock
(1899—1980) cast himself in the insignificant role of a newsman on
the telephone — facing away from the camera — and the term has now
come to mean a member of the crew who has a part, however small, in
the film itself.

Hitchcock amused himself — and us, once his mischievous appearances
had become established as part of his house style — by taking
cameos in thirty-nine of his fifty-two films. To begin with, the
moments were innocuous enough: posting a letter, travelling on a
bus, reading a newspaper. Before long, the appearances were more
obvious: walking a horse across the screen or standing in front of
a sign promoting 'Cut Rate Drugs'. In *Lifeboat* (1944), he is seen
in the 'before' and 'after' pictures of a newspaper advertisement
for 'Reduco Obesity Slayer', a fictitious weight-loss product
(Hitchcock was almost comically portly).

The subtlest can be found in *Rope* (1948), where, apart from the
opening credits, in which Hitchcock is glimpsed far away entering
an apartment building, the entire story takes place in a single
room with a cast of only nine. Fifty-five minutes into the film, in
the skyline of New York seen through the windows, a distant red neon
sign flashes: an image of the director's head appears once again
above the logo for 'Reduco'.

Hitchcock briefly pursued a musical theme, appearing in various
films carrying a violin, a cello, a trumpet, and in *Strangers on a*

Train (1951) — magnificently — a double bass. The most unsettling sequence is surely in *Topaz* (1969), where the director is pushed through an airport terminal in a wheelchair, only to stand up, shake hands with a fellow traveller and walk out of the picture; the most brazen is the shot where Cary Grant travels on a bus and Hitchcock sits stony-faced and unmissable right beside him (*To Catch a Thief*, 1955).

1944   NONE BUT THE LONELY HEART   1944

A young ne'er-do-well tries to reform his life.

ERNIE

They say money talks... all it's ever said to me is goodbye.

Dir: Clifford Odets • Scr: Clifford Odets • Based on a novel by Richard Llewellyn • Cast: Cary Grant (Ernie Mott)

1945   BRIEF ENCOUNTER   1945

Married Laura feels guilty about the affair she is having.

LAURA

It's awfully easy to lie when you know that you're trusted implicitly. So very easy, and so very degrading.

Dir: David Lean • Scr: David Lean • Based on a play by Noël Coward • Cast: Celia Johnson (Laura Jesson)

1947   OUT OF THE PAST

Gangster Whit Sterling realizes he is still in love with a woman from his past.

WHIT

My feelings? About ten years ago, I hid them somewhere and haven't been able to find them.

Dir: Jacques Tourneur • Scr: Daniel Mainwaring, based on his novel (writing as Geoffrey Homes) • Cast: Kirk Douglas (Whit Sterling)

1950   SUNSET BOULEVARD

A proud but ageing film star implores her favourite director to cast her just one more time.

NORMA

And I promise you I'll never desert you again because after *Salome* we'll make another picture and another picture. You see, this is my life! It always will be! Nothing else! Just us, the cameras, and those wonderful people out there in the dark. All right, Mr DeMille, I'm ready for my close-up.

Dir: Billy Wilder • Scr: Charles Brackett, Billy Wilder, D. M. Marshman Jr • Cast: Gloria Swanson (Norma Desmond)

Legendary studio head Louis B. Mayer felt the film painted an unfairly bleak portrait of the film business and told Wilder: 'You bastard! You have disgraced the industry that made and fed you. You should be tarred and feathered and run out of Hollywood.' Wilder, never usually lost for an elegant riposte, could only muster, 'Fuck you.'

1951   THE LAVENDER HILL MOB

PENDLEBURY

Of all sad words of tongue or pen, the saddest are these – 'it might have been'.

Dir: Charles Crichton • Scr: T. E. B. Clarke • Cast: Stanley Holloway (Alfred 'Al' Pendlebury)

The poignant words spoken by the crooked Pendlebury are from the poem Maud Muller by John Greenleaf Whittier (1807–92).

The Bank of England was consulted to find a plausible way to steal a million pounds, and their plan formed the basis for the plot. The only reason the robbers fail in their mission at the end is that the British producers were aware US censorship rules regarding criminal behaviour would have meant the film could not be released in America.

Boxer Terry Malloy is furious with his brother Charley for persuading him to participate in fixed bouts.

TERRY

It wasn't him, Charley, it was you. Remember that night in the Garden you came down to my dressing room and you said, 'Kid, this ain't your night. We're going for the price on Wilson.' You remember that? 'This ain't your night'! My night! I coulda taken Wilson apart! So what happens? He gets the title shot outdoors on the ballpark and what do I get? A one-way ticket to Palookaville! You was my brother, Charley, you shoulda looked out for me a little bit. You shoulda taken care of me just a little bit so I wouldn't have to take them dives for the short-end money.

CHARLEY

Oh, I had some bets down for you. You saw some money.

TERRY

You don't understand. I coulda had class. I coulda been a contender. I coulda been somebody, instead of a bum - which is what I am, let's face it. It was you, Charley.

Dir: Elia Kazan • Scr: Budd Schulberg • Cast: Marlon Brando (Terry Malloy), Rod Steiger (Charley Malloy)

Before sending the screenplay to Marlon Brando, producer Sam Spiegel slipped small pieces of paper between its pages so he could check in due course whether it had ever been opened. Brando turned the project down and the scraps were still in place when he returned the script; only after Spiegel approached Frank Sinatra for the role did Brando change his mind and ask to 're'-read it.

Baxter discovers Fran's private life is less glamorous than he has imagined.

BAXTER

The mirror... it's broken.

FRAN

Yes, I know. I like it that way. Makes me look the way I feel.

Dir: Billy Wilder • Scr: Billy Wilder, I. A. L. Diamond • Cast: Jack Lemmon (C. C. Baxter), Shirley MacLaine (Fran Kubelik)

'SHUT UP AND DEAL'

Billy Wilder (1906–2002) had been impressed by Noël Coward and David Lean's *Brief Encounter* (1945), in which a character who never appears in the film lends the adulterous couple a key to his home so they can meet in secret. With *The Apartment* (1960), Wilder wanted to tell a story in which the owner of this vital venue takes centre-stage, but because the topic of marital infidelity was still controversial he had to wait several years until the Hays Production Code (see p.190) was relaxed.

When the film finally went ahead, Wilder set much of the action in the offices of a dull insurance company as a comic counterpoint to the sexual shenanigans the story describes. Marilyn Monroe (whom Wilder disliked after her difficult behaviour on *Some Like It Hot*) attended an early screening, but the risqué subject matter seems to have passed her by as she declared the picture 'a wonderful examination of the corporate world'.

Wilder and long-term collaborator I. A. L. Diamond (1920–88) wrote the script specifically with Jack Lemmon in mind as the hapless C. C. Baxter. When the director approached Shirley MacLaine for the part of Miss Kubelik, the elevator operator, he removed the last pages because he wanted her to play the lovelorn character with no idea she might eventually win Baxter's affections; MacLaine simply assumed Wilder had not yet figured out a suitable ending. She also claimed much of the film was written as the shoot progressed, and that the recurring gin rummy game came about because she was learning to play it with Frank Sinatra and Dean Martin during her lunch breaks.

The film contains plenty of classic Wilder and Diamond dialogue:

FRAN: I was jinxed from the word go. The first time I was ever kissed was in a cemetery.

BAXTER: Mrs MacDougall, I think it is only fair to warn you that you are now alone with a notorious sexpot.
MARGIE: No kidding.

BAXTER: That's the way it crumbles, cookie-wise.
KIRKEBY: Premium-wise and billing-wise, we are 18 per cent ahead of last year, October-wise.

SHELDRAKE: Ya know, you see a girl a couple of times a week, just for laughs, and right away they think you're gonna divorce your wife. Now I ask you, is that fair?

BAXTER: No, sir, it's very unfair... Especially to your wife.

FRAN: What's a tennis racket doing in the kitchen?

BAXTER: Tennis racket? Oh, I remember, I was cooking myself an Italian dinner.

Even the closing lines were apparently written as the final scene was being shot:

BAXTER: You hear what I said, Miss Kubelik? I absolutely adore you.

FRAN: Shut up and deal.

1968 FUNNY GIRL 1968

A comedienne laments her plain looks.

FANNY

That's my problem – I'm a bagel on a plate full of onion rolls.

Dir: William Wyler • Scr: Isobel Lennart, based on her Broadway musical • Cast: Barbra Streisand (Fanny Brice)

Cinematographer Vilmos Zsigmond – who would go on to win an Oscar for *Close Encounters of the Third Kind* (1977) – was fired by Streisand after three days because he ignored her stipulation that her face should only ever be filmed from her preferred (left) side.

1972   PLAY IT AGAIN, SAM

Allan approaches a pretty girl in an art gallery.

> ALLAN

That's quite a lovely Jackson Pollock, isn't it?

> MUSEUM GIRL

Yes, it is.

> ALLAN

What does it say to you?

> MUSEUM GIRL

It restates the negativeness of the universe. The hideous lonely emptiness of existence. Nothingness. The predicament of Man forced to live in a barren, Godless eternity like a tiny flame flickering in an immense void with nothing but waste, horror and degradation, forming a useless bleak straitjacket in a black absurd cosmos.

> ALLAN

What are you doing Saturday night?

> MUSEUM GIRL

Committing suicide.

> ALLAN

What about Friday night?

Dir: Herbert Ross • Scr: Woody Allen, based on his play • Cast: Woody Allen (Allan Felix), Diana Davila (Museum Girl)

1976   TAXI DRIVER

> TRAVIS

Loneliness has followed me my whole life. Everywhere. In bars, in cars, sidewalks, stores, everywhere. There's no escape. I'm God's lonely man.

Dir: Martin Scorsese • Scr: Paul Schrader • Cast: Robert De Niro (Travis Bickle)

1977 ANNIE HALL

1977

> ALVY
>
> A relationship, I think, is like a shark. You know? It has to
> constantly move forward or it dies. And I think what we've got
> on our hands is a dead shark.

Dir: Woody Allen • Scr: Woody Allen, Marshall Brickman • Cast: Woody Allen
(Alvy Singer)

1980 THE ELEPHANT MAN

1980

*Two doctors assume a patient with a grotesquely disfigured face
and body is also mentally subnormal.*

> DR FOX
>
> Have you ever mentioned his mental state?
>
> DR FREDERICK TREVES
>
> Oh, he's an imbecile, probably from birth. Man's a complete
> idiot. Pray to God he's an idiot.

Dir: David Lynch • Scr: Christopher De Vore, Eric Bergren, David
Lynch • Based on books by Sir Frederick Treves and Ashley Montagu • Cast:
John Standing (Dr Fox), Anthony Hopkins (Dr Frederick Treves)

John Hurt's prosthetics took eight hours to apply each day and two hours to remove, so to
prevent the actor from becoming exhausted he was only scheduled to work alternate days.

1987 THE WHALES OF AUGUST

1987

*On the anniversary of her wedding, Sarah holds an imaginary
conversation with the husband she lost in the Second World War.*

> SARAH
>
> Forty-six years, Phillip. Forty-six red roses; forty-six white.
> White for truth, red for passion. That's what you always
> said: 'Passion and truth; that's all we need'... Oh, if only you
> were here, Phillip. Oh, Phillip, my corset has so many stays
> and so many ties. You said, 'Too many, my love. The moon will
> set before I have you completely undone.' But I said, 'Never,
> my love. I won't be entirely undone – even by you. For what
> mystery would keep you with me if you unwrap them all?'

Dir: Lindsay Anderson • Scr: David Berry, based on his play • Cast:
Lillian Gish (Sarah Webber)

1989   STEEL MAGNOLIAS   1989

Truvy chats with friends in her beauty salon.

TRUVY

Honey, time marches on and eventually you realize it's marching across your face.

Dir: Herbert Ross • Scr: Robert Harling, based on his play • Cast: Dolly Parton (Truvy Jones)

Disappointed by a poor take, director Herbert Ross unchivalrously asked singer Dolly Parton if she could actually act. Undeterred, she replied: 'No, but it's your job to make me look like I can.'

1996   SECRETS & LIES   1996

Maurice does his best to support and placate his fractious family.

MAURICE

Secrets and lies! We're all in pain! Why can't we share our pain? I've spent my entire life trying to make people happy, and the three people I love the most in the world hate each other's guts and I'm in the middle! I can't take it any more!

Dir: Mike Leigh • Scr: Mike Leigh • Cast: Timothy Spall (Maurice Purley)

As with all Mike Leigh films, the script was improvised around a simple outline devised by the director. Leigh told each actor only as much as they would need to know at the beginning of the story and let them develop their own character from there; that way, the secrets revealed along the way would come as a genuine surprise as each scene was shot.

1999   NOTTING HILL   1999

Among friends, a film star laments the pressures of her career.

ANNA

I've been on a diet every day since I was nineteen, which basically means I've been hungry for a decade. I've had a series of not nice boyfriends, one of whom hit me, and every time I get my heart broken the newspapers splash it about as though it's entertainment. And it's taken two rather painful operations to get me looking like this...Really. And, one day not long from now, my looks will go, they'll discover I can't act and I'll become some sad middle-aged woman who looks a bit like someone who was famous for a while.

Dir: Roger Michell • Scr: Richard Curtis • Cast: Julia Roberts (Anna Scott)

THE VIRGIN SUICIDES

Cecilia is taken to hospital after cutting her wrists.

> DOCTOR
>
> What are you doing here, honey? You're not even old enough to know how bad life gets.

> CECILIA
>
> Obviously, Doctor, you've never been a thirteen-year-old girl.

Dir: Sofia Coppola • Scr: Sofia Coppola • Based on a novel by Jeffrey Eugenides • Cast: François Klanfer (Doctor), Hanna R. Hall (Cecilia Lisbon)

LOST IN TRANSLATION

A lonely wife and a famous actor fall to talking in a Tokyo bar.

> CHARLOTTE
>
> So, what are you doing here?

> BOB
>
> Uh, a couple of things. Taking a break from my wife, forgetting my son's birthday. And getting paid $2 million to endorse a whiskey when I could be doing a play somewhere.

> CHARLOTTE
>
> Oh.

> BOB
>
> But the good news is, the whiskey works.

Dir: Sofia Coppola • Scr: Sofia Coppola • Cast: Scarlett Johansson (Charlotte), Bill Murray (Bob Harris)

MILLION DOLLAR BABY

A local priest wonders what is troubling one of his regular parishioners.

> FATHER HORVAK
>
> Frankie, I've seen you at Mass almost every day for twenty-three years. The only person comes to church that much is the kind who can't forgive himself for something.

Dir: Clint Eastwood • Scr: Paul Haggis • Based on short stories by F. X. Toole • Cast: Brian F. O'Byrne (Father Horvak)

2004   THE CONSEQUENCES OF LOVE (*LE CONSEGUENZE DELL'AMORE*)   2004

A middle-aged mafia courier refuses to believe in fate.

> TITTA
>
> Bad luck doesn't exist. It is just an invention of losers and poor people.

Dir: Paolo Sorrentino • Scr: Paolo Sorrentino • Cast: Toni Servillo (Titta di Girolamo)

2005   BROKEBACK MOUNTAIN   2005

Two cowboys have been forced to hide their homosexual relationship from their families and community for too long.

> JACK
>
> Tell you what, we coulda had a good life together! Fuckin' real good life! Had us a place of our own. But you didn't want it, Ennis! So what we got now is Brokeback Mountain! Everything's built on that! That's all we got, boy, fuckin' all. So I hope you know that, even if you don't never know the rest! You count the damn few times we have been together in nearly twenty years and you measure the short fucking leash you keep me on - and then you ask me about Mexico and tell

me you'll kill me for needing somethin' I don't hardly never get. You have no idea how bad it gets! I'm not you... I can't make it on a coupla high-altitude fucks once or twice a year! You are too much for me Ennis, you sonofawhoreson bitch! I wish I knew how to quit you.

Ennis is crying now.

ENNIS

Well, why don't you? Why don't you just let me be? It's because of you Jack, that I'm like this! I'm nothin'... I'm nowhere... Get the fuck off me! I can't stand being like this no more, Jack.

Dir: Ang Lee • Scr: Larry McMurtry and Diana Ossana • Based on a novel by Annie Proulx • Cast: Jake Gyllenhaal (Jack), Heath Ledger (Ennis)

2006 LITTLE MISS SUNSHINE 2006

Unhappy teenager Dwayne receives some unlikely encouragement from his uncle.

DWAYNE

I wish I could just sleep until I was eighteen and skip all this crap - high school and everything - just skip it.

FRANK

Do you know who Marcel Proust is?

DWAYNE

He's the guy you teach.

FRANK

Yeah. French writer. Total loser. Never had a real job. Unrequited love affairs. Gay. Spent twenty years writing a book almost no one reads. But he's also probably the greatest writer since Shakespeare. Anyway, he uh... he gets down to the end of his life, and he looks back and decides that all those years he suffered, those were the best years of his life 'cause they made him who he was. All those years he was happy? You know, total waste. Didn't learn a thing. So, if you sleep until you're eighteen... Ah, think of the suffering you're gonna miss. I mean high school? High school - those are your prime suffering years. You don't get better suffering than that.

Dir: Jonathan Dayton, Valerie Faris • Scr: Michael Arndt • Cast: Paul Dano (Dwayne), Steve Carell (Frank Ginsberg)

A grieving mother rejects the bland consolations of her priest.

FATHER HAYNES

He's in God's hands now.

MRS O'BRIEN

He was in God's hands the whole time, wasn't he?

Dir: Terrence Malick • Scr: Terrence Malick • Cast: Kelly Koonce (Father Haynes), Jessica Chastain (Mrs O'Brien)

Terrence Malick has never been noted for his conventional narrative style. Even so, viewers in one Italian cinema may have thought the director had surpassed himself when *Tree of Life* was shown for an entire week with the first two reels reversed. Until the projectionist spotted the error, nobody else noticed.

INCITING INCIDENTS AND PINCH POINTS

'Screenplays are structure.'
William Goldman

Some time around 335 BC the Greek philosopher Aristotle wrote his *Poetics*, a treatise on dramatic theory. Identifying six key elements — plot, character, theme, diction, music and spectacle — he attributed the greatest importance to plot (mythos). He also suggested that 'a whole is what has a beginning and middle and end', and this maxim has endured among playwrights down the centuries through the idea that narrative action should be divided into three parts.

Since then many others have attempted to anatomize the ingredients of a coherent and resonant story. The British writer and scholar Arthur Quiller-Couch (1863–1944) suggested seven fundamental scenarios:

- Man against Man

- Man against Nature

- Man against God

- Man against Society

- Man in the Middle

- Man and Woman

- Man against Himself.

In 1916 the French writer George Polti (1867–1946) proposed a mathematically pleasing thirty-six situations ranging from 'vengeance' and 'deliverance' to 'necessity of sacrificing loved ones' and 'fatal imprudence'. In 1946 Lajos Egri (1888–1967), widely recognized as 'the father of modern screenwriting gurus', published *The Art of Dramatic Writing*. Developing many of Aristotle's ideas, he established a logical method for setting out narrative structure. Within a matter of decades, the world of screenwriting was flooded with similar books analysing successful films, showing how their episodes conformed to such theories and thus seeming to prove that any script is fundamentally a set of rules for shepherding its characters from opening titles to credits.

Although today's largest productions have budgets upward of $200 million, studio executives — and their development staff — frequently test their investment with 'screenwriters' bibles' readily available from any good bookshop. 'Creative meetings' echo with reassuring buzz-phrases such as character arc, the call to adventure and threshold guardians.

Contemporary analysts have distilled their theories into a clear prescriptive outline. Joseph Campbell (1904–87), borrowing the term 'monomyth' from James Joyce's *Finnegans Wake*, proposes seventeen heroic stages:

Departure

1.1 The Call to Adventure

1.2 Refusal of the Call

1.3 Supernatural Aid

1.4 The Crossing of the First Threshold

1.5 Belly of the Whale

Initiation

2.1 The Road of Trials

2.2 The Meeting with the Goddess

2.3 Woman as Temptress

2.4 Atonement with the Father

2.5 Apotheosis

2.6 The Ultimate Boon

Return

3.1 Refusal of the Return

3.2 The Magic Flight

3.3 Rescue from Without

3.4 The Crossing of the Return Threshold

3.5 Master of Two Worlds

3.6 Freedom to Live

Other well-known gurus today include Christopher Vogler, Syd Field and Robert McKee. McKee's former students include thirty-six Oscar winners and he has advised companies as diverse as Disney, MTV, Microsoft and NASA, although his own writing credits run to a modest five TV movies. Syd Field's last screenplay was for a documentary in 1967 but the *Hollywood Reporter* calls him 'the most sought-after screenwriting teacher in the world'. His books have been translated into nineteen languages and he has even recently released an iPhone app, *Script Launcher*.

Julia Roberts gazes at her subject with a characteristic blend of toughness and innocence in *Closer* (2004).

George Hurrell, one of Hollywood's most acclaimed photographers, captures Clark Gable's elegant insouciance perfectly in this 1933 studio shot.

In *Carry on Cleo* Kenneth Williams gave us a memorable example of death by *double entendre*.

Endings

1937   A DAY AT THE RACES 1937

Dr Hackenbush takes his patient's pulse.

DR HACKENBUSH

Either he's dead or my watch has stopped.

Dir: Sam Wood • Scr: Robert Pirosh, George Seaton, George Oppenheimer • Cast: Groucho Marx (Dr Hugo Z. Hackenbush)

1938   THE LADY VANISHES 1938

A young woman returns from a tour of Europe on the eve of her wedding.

IRIS

I've no regrets. I've been everywhere and done everything. I've eaten caviar at Cannes, sausage rolls at the dogs. I've played baccarat at Biarritz and darts with the rural dean. What is there left for me but marriage?

Dir: Alfred Hitchcock • Scr: Sidney Gilliat, Frank Launder • Based on a story by Ethel Lina White • Cast: Margaret Lockwood (Iris Henderson)

1940   THE GRAPES OF WRATH 1940

The mother of a migrant family during the Great Depression remains convinced of the strength of the oppressed.

MA JOAD

That's what makes us tough. Rich fellas come up an' they die an' their kids ain't no good, an' they die out. But we keep a-comin'. We're the people that live. They can't wipe us out. They can't lick us. And we'll go on forever, Pa, 'cause...we're the people.

Dir: John Ford • Scr: Nunnally Johnson • Based on a novel by John Steinbeck • Cast: Jane Darwell (Ma Joad)

1948   THE NAKED CITY 1948

A murder mystery unfolds against the backdrop of New York with its myriad inhabitants.

NARRATOR

There are eight million stories in the naked city. This has been one of them.

Dir: Jules Dassin • Scr: Albert Maltz, Malvin Wald • Cast: Mark Hellinger (Narrator)

Most unusually for the time, director Jules Dassin filmed a good deal of the picture on location, often using hidden cameras to let actors perform amid crowds without the need for unconvincing background players. If he needed to control passers-by, he would stage diversions, on one occasion hiring a juggler and on another sending a crew member up a lamp post to wave a large American flag.

1949   THE THIRD MAN   1949

Black marketeer Harry Lime tries to justify his criminal activities to his friend Holly.

> HARRY
>
> Don't be so gloomy. After all, it's not that awful. Like the fellow says, in Italy for thirty years under the Borgias they had warfare, terror, murder and bloodshed but they produced Michelangelo, Leonardo da Vinci and the Renaissance. In Switzerland they had brotherly love: they had five hundred years of democracy and peace, and what did that produce? The cuckoo clock. So long, Holly.

Dir: Carol Reed • Scr: Graham Greene • Cast: Orson Welles (Harry Lime)

'A DELICATE MATTER'

With its ambiguous encounters in echoing alleyways, *The Third Man* perfectly captures the atmosphere of a divided Vienna in the aftermath of war. Robert Krasker's chiaroscuro cinematography won an Oscar and his tilted camera angles were hugely influential on thrillers thereafter, but they were not to everyone's taste; director William Wyler sent Carol Reed a spirit level with a note saying, 'Carol, next time you make a picture, just put it on top of the camera, will you?'

Although Reed had proven his talent with two earlier productions (*Odd Man Out* (1947) and *The Fallen Idol* (1948), the latter also based on a story by Graham Greene), *The Third Man* was dogged by rumours that Orson Welles was its true director. Welles' performance as Harry Lime is a tour de force and he seemed to enjoy the idea that he might also have been secretly in charge. In later years he did little to settle the controversy, giving one interview in which he hinted that it was 'a delicate matter', but subsequently that it was indeed 'Carol's picture'. The latter is undoubtedly the case since Welles spent much of the time when he was supposed to be on set travelling around Europe and many of his non-speaking scenes had to be filmed with body doubles.

Reed's role can hardly be doubted: he insisted on running three production units simultaneously to get all the location footage they needed within the six weeks scheduled for Vienna. One crew covered the daytime shots, another the night and a third was responsible for the sewer scenes. By the end Reed was reportedly working twenty hours a day and was relying on Dexedrine (speed) to keep his energy levels up.

Other ambiguities linger: the famous speech at the top of the Ferris wheel does not appear in Greene's original treatment and was reputedly improvised by Welles, although he claimed it was inspired by an unnamed Hungarian play. Whoever did write it should have checked their facts: the Swiss have never been famous for making cuckoo clocks (their true home is Germany) and Switzerland itself was not neutral but a proud and feared military power during the Renaissance.

1951 THE THING FROM ANOTHER WORLD   1951

After narrowly defeating an alien invader who adopts human form, Scotty warns humanity never to drop its guard.

SCOTTY

I bring you a warning. Every one of you listening to my voice, tell the world, tell this to everybody wherever they are. Watch the skies. Everywhere. Keep looking. Keep watching the skies...

Dir: Christian Nyby • Scr: Charles Lederer • Based on a story by John W. Campbell Jr • Cast: Douglas Spencer (Ned 'Scotty' Scott)

The producers asked the US Air Force for assistance with aircraft and locations but were refused because the government's official stance is that UFOs do not exist.

1956   THE TEAHOUSE OF THE AUGUST MOON   1956

A wise Japanese translator defuses tensions between American occupiers and the inhabitants of Okinawa.

SAKINI

Little story now concluded. But history of world unfinished. Lovely ladies, kind gentlemen, go home to ponder. What was true at beginning remains true. Pain make man think, thought make man wise, and wisdom make life endurable. So, may August moon bring gentle sleep. Sayonara.

Dir: Daniel Mann • Scr: John Patrick • Based on a novel by Vern J. Sneider • Cast: Marlon Brando (Sakini)

Brando's performance as the Japanese Sakini was so convincing that many viewers demanded their money back, believing that the actor had not appeared in the film at all.

1957   THE SEVENTH SEAL (*DET SJUNDE INSEGLET*)   1957

Antonius, a wandering knight, challenges Death to a game of chess in a bid to escape his fate.

DEATH

Are you ready?

ANTONIUS

My body is ready, but I am not.

Dir: Ingmar Bergman • Scr: Ingmar Bergman, based on his play • Cast: Bengt Ekerot (Death), Max von Sydow (Antonius Block)

1957   THE INCREDIBLE SHRINKING MAN   1957

After being exposed to a radioactive cloud, a man condemned to grow ever smaller makes peace with his destiny.

SCOTT

And I felt my body dwindling, melting, becoming nothing. My fears locked away and in their place came acceptance. All this vast majesty of creation, it had to mean something. And

then I meant something, too. Yes, smaller than the smallest,
I meant something, too. To God there is no zero. I still exist!

Dir: Jack Arnold • Scr: Richard Matheson, based on his novel • Cast: Grant
Williams (Scott Carey)

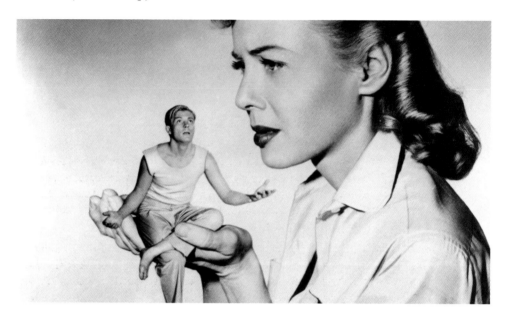

1958   **TOUCH OF EVIL**   1958

*Corrupt police captain Quinlan realizes it cannot be long before
justice catches up with him.*

QUINLAN

Come on, read my future for me.

TANYA

You haven't got any.

QUINLAN

Hmm? What do you mean?

TANYA

Your future's all used up.

Dir: Orson Welles • Scr: Orson Welles • Based on a novel by Whit
Masterson • Cast: Orson Welles (Captain Hank Quinlan), Marlene Dietrich
(Tanya)

In a world dying from radiation poisoning after a nuclear war,
a survivor opts to take a lethal sedative.

MARY

God, God forgive us, Peter. I think I'll have that cup of tea now.

Dir: Stanley Kramer • Scr: John Paxton • Based on a novel by Nevil
Shute • Cast: Donna Anderson (Mary Holmes)

'THE REST IS SILENCE'

If Shakespeare had handed in a draft of *Hamlet* to one of the
Hollywood studios, he would have found himself swiftly summoned
for a creative meeting. Executives might murmur that the Danish
prince's speeches are meandering and his character arc lacks
clarity. Worst of all, his final zinger — 'the rest is silence' —
doesn't come as the credits roll.

Even if Sam Goldwyn or Louis B. Mayer hadn't demanded a rewrite,
any decent star playing the prince would surely have asked the bard
to lose the closing speeches by Horatio and Fortinbras in case they
overshadowed his magnificent death scene.

Here are some examples of how a film should really end:

Oh, Auntie Em, there's no place like home!
The Wizard of Oz (1939)

Louis, I think this is the beginning of a beautiful friendship.
Casablanca (1942)

Remember, honey, on your wedding day it's all right to say yes.
Gentlemen Prefer Blondes (1953)

Well, nobody's perfect.
Some Like It Hot (1959)

Forget it, Jake. It's Chinatown.
Chinatown (1974)

The horror... the horror...
Apocalypse Now (1979)

Not everybody gets corrupted. You have to have a little faith
in people.
Manhattan (1979)

I'm the boss, I'm the boss, I'm the boss, I'm the boss.
Raging Bull (1980)

I'll be right here.
E.T. the Extra Terrestrial (1982)

Let's just wait here awhile, see what happens.
The Thing (1982)

Well, ma'am, if I see him, I'll sure give him the message.
Blood Simple (1984)

Roads? Where we're going, we don't need roads.
Back to the Future (1985)

I'm too old for this.
Lethal Weapon (1987)

Asshole!
A Fish Called Wanda (1988)

VINCENT: I think we should be leaving now.

JULES: Yeah, that's probably a good idea.
Pulp Fiction (1994)

I find I am so excited I can barely sit still or hold a thought in my head. I think it's the excitement only a free man can feel, a free man at the start of a long journey whose conclusion is uncertain. I hope I can make it across the border. I hope to see my friend and shake his hand. I hope the Pacific is as blue as it has been in my dreams. I hope.
The Shawshank Redemption (1994)

You met me at a very strange time of my life.
Fight Club (1999)

I'm going to show them a world without you. A world without rules and controls, without borders or boundaries. A world where anything is possible. Where we go from there is a choice I leave to you.
The Matrix (1999)

Now, where was I?
Memento (2000)

*Handsome but self-centred ladies' man Alfie begins to wonder what
his string of conquests really adds up to.*

ALFIE

You know what? When I look back on my little life and the
birds I've known, and think of all the things they've done for
me and the little I've done for them, you'd think I've had the
best of it along the line. But what have I got out of it? I've
got a bob or two, some decent clothes, a car, I've got me health
back and I ain't attached. But I ain't got me peace of mind
- and if you ain't got that, you ain't got nothing. I dunno.
It seems to me if they ain't got you one way, they've got you
another. So what's the answer? That's what I keep asking
myself - what's it all about? Know what I mean?

Dir: Lewis Gilbert • Scr: Bill Naughton, based on his novel and stage
play • Cast: Michael Caine (Alfie Elkins)

*Dragline tells his fellow convicts how Cool Hand Luke kept his
dignity even as he was shot down by prison guards.*

DRAGLINE

He was smiling... That's right. You know... that Luke smile of his.
He had it on his face right to the very end. Hell, if they didn't

know it 'fore, they could tell right then that they weren't gonna
beat him. That old Luke smile. Oh, Luke. He was some boy. Cool Hand
Luke. Hell, he's a natural-born world-shaker.

Dir: Stuart Rosenberg • Scr: Frank Pierson, Donn Pearce • Based on a novel
by Donn Pearce • Cast: George Kennedy (Dragline)

A complete prison set near Stockton, California, was constructed for the shoot, including
barracks, mess hall and warden's quarters. Truckloads of Spanish moss were shipped from
Louisiana and the cast actually tarred a mile-long stretch of highway while filming. A passing
building inspector thought the buildings had been put up by migrant workers and posted
'condemned' notices on them for shoddy construction.

1970   CATCH-22   1970

*The eccentric Yossarian tells his lover about a fellow soldier he
saw buried that day.*

YOSSARIAN

He was very old.

LUCIANA

But he was a boy.

YOSSARIAN

Well, he died. You don't get any older than that.

Dir: Mike Nichols • Scr: Buck Henry • Based on a novel by Joseph
Heller • Cast: Alan Arkin (Captain John Yossarian), Olimpia Carlisi
(Luciana)

1972   CABARET   1972

MASTER OF CEREMONIES

Meine Damen und Herren, Madames et Messieurs, Ladies and
Gentlemen. Where are your troubles now? Forgotten? I told
you so. We have no troubles here! Here, life is beautiful.
The girls are beautiful. Even the orchestra is beautiful.
Auf Wiedersehen! A bientôt.

Dir: Bob Fosse • Scr: Jay Presson Allen • Based on a play by John Van
Druten and stories by Christopher Isherwood • Cast: Joel Grey (Master of
Ceremonies)

Liza Minnelli worked with her own father, acclaimed musical director Vincente Minnelli, to design
her hair and make-up. She said she could tell she was the star of the nightclub because she was
the only performer with shaved armpits.

THE SHOOTIST

An ageing gunfighter contemplates his mortality.

BOOKS

You told me I was strong as an ox.

DR HOSTETLER

Well, even an ox dies.

Dir: Don Siegel • Scr: Miles Hood Swarthout, Scott Hale • Based on a novel by Glendon Swarthout • Cast: John Wayne (J. B. Books), James Stewart (Dr E. W. Hostetler)

THE DEER HUNTER

A Vietnam veteran searches for an old friend in Saigon but is shocked to discover he has become a heroin addict.

MICHAEL

I came twelve thousand miles back here to get you. What's the matter with you? Don't you recognize me? Nicky, I love you, you're my friend. What are you doing? We don't have much time, Nick.

Nick holds a revolver to his own head. He pulls the trigger but it clicks on an empty chamber.

Is this what you want? Is this what you want? I love you, Nick.

Michael pulls the trigger again. Another empty chamber.

Come on, Nicky, come home. Just come home. Home. Talk to me.

He sees Nick's needle marks.

What did you do to your arms?

He reminds Nick of their hunting days.

Do you remember the trees? Do you remember all the different ways of the trees? Do you remember that? Do you remember? Huh? The mountains? Do you remember all that?

NICK

One shot.

He smiles and laughs, remembering their old catchphrase.

                        MICHAEL

    One shot, one shot.

Without warning, Nick pulls the trigger and shoots himself.

    Nicky, Nicky, don't, Nick, no!

Dir: Michael Cimino • Scr: Deric Washburn • Cast: Robert De Niro (Michael
'Mike' Vronsky), Christopher Walken (Nikanor 'Nick' Chevotarevich)

De Niro suggested the gun used for this scene should contain real bullets to heighten the
tension. Only on the takes where the trigger was pulled did the actors check there was no live
round in the chamber.

1982   BLADE RUNNER   1982

*An android fascinated by the possibility of his own humanity
faces death.*

                        ROY

    Quite an experience to live in fear, isn't it? That's what it
    is to be a slave. I've seen things you people wouldn't believe.
    Attack ships on fire off the shoulder of Orion. I've watched
    C-beams glitter in the dark near the Tannhäuser Gate. All those
    moments will be lost in time, like tears in rain... Time to die.

Dir: Ridley Scott • Scr: Hampton Fancher, David Webb Peoples • Based on a
novel by Philip K. Dick • Cast: Rutger Hauer (Roy Batty)

Ridley Scott had been impressed by Rutger Hauer's performance in several films and cast him
without ever having met him. In this project, Hauer was to play an icily murderous android
(Batty), so for a joke he turned up on the first day wearing green sunglasses, pink satin trousers
and a cuddly white sweater with animals on it. One production executive recalls that when Scott
first saw him he 'literally turned white'.

'TEARS IN RAIN'

Blade Runner, Philip K. Dick and Ridley's Scott's provocative
dystopian vision, polarized reactions on its first release and
even if it is now widely agreed to be a masterpiece its ambiguities
continue to intrigue. Rick Deckard (Harrison Ford) is a cop whose
task it is to seek out and destroy escaped replicants — robot
workers ostensibly indistinguishable from humans. The story, set in
2019, invites us to explore notions of consciousness and emotion.
Director Ridley Scott believed Deckard himself was a replicant,
producer Michael Deeley and Harrison Ford felt he must be human,
while writer Hampton Fancher wanted the audience to decide for
themselves.

The uncertainty worked in reverse, too. Rutger Hauer, playing replicant Roy Batty, was determined to make his character as human as possible and felt the scene of his death was a perfect opportunity to challenge Deckard's — and our — preconceptions about artificial intelligence. The lines he speaks in the film's various released versions differ from all the earlier scripts and Hampton Fancher's draft of 24 July 1980 contains no final speech at all apart from Batty taunting Deckard with the words:

Time to die.

Fancher's script with David Webb Peoples from December 1980 has:

I've known adventures, seen places you people will never see, I've been Offworld and back...frontiers! I've stood on the back deck of a blinker bound for the Plutition Camps with sweat in my eyes watching the stars fight on the shoulder of Orion ... I've felt wind in my hair, riding test boats off the black galaxies and seen an attack fleet burn like a match and disappear. I've seen it, felt it!

Fancher and Peoples' draft dated 23 February 1981 reads:

I've seen things... seen things you little people wouldn't believe... Attack ships on fire off the shoulder of Orion bright as magnesium... I rode on the back decks of a blinker and watched C-beams glitter in the dark near the Tannhäuser Gate. All those moments... They'll be gone.

Hauer described the speech in the shooting script he was given as 'opera talk' and set about revising it the night before the cameras rolled; his amalgamation of scripted ideas and improvisation is frequently cited as the greatest dying speech on film.

1983   MONTY PYTHON'S THE MEANING OF LIFE   1983

A group of friends at dinner receive an unexpected visitor.

> GRIM REAPER

Silence! I have come for you – to take you away. That is my purpose. I am Death.

> HOST

Well, that's cast rather a gloom over the evening, hasn't it?

Dir: Terry Jones, Terry Gilliam • Scr: Graham Chapman, John Cleese, Terry Gilliam, Eric Idle, Terry Jones, Michael Palin • Cast: John Cleese (Grim Reaper), Graham Chapman (Host)

1985   BRAZIL   1985

Sam, a government employee in an Orwellian world, asks his boss Kurtzmann what has happened to a citizen named Buttle.

> KURTZMANN

You see? The population census has got him down as 'dormanted'. The Central Collective Storehouse computer has got him down as 'deleted'.

> SAM

Hang on.

Sam checks another computer terminal.

> KURTZMANN

Information Retrieval has got him down as 'inoperative'. And there's another one – security has got him down as 'excised'. Administration has got him down as 'completed'.

SAM

He's dead.

Dir: Terry Gilliam • Scr: Terry Gilliam, Tom Stoppard, Charles
McKeown • Cast: Ian Holm (Mr Kurtzmann), Jonathan Pryce (Sam Lowry)

1986 ALIENS   **1986**

*Ripley reassures Newt, the child she has rescued, that the alien
threat is over as they prepare to return to Earth from deep space.*

NEWT

Are we gonna sleep all the way home?

RIPLEY

All the way home.

NEWT

Can I dream?

RIPLEY

Yes, honey. I think we both can.

She tucks Newt in.

RIPLEY

Sleep tight.

NEWT

Affirmative.

Dir: James Cameron • Scr: James Cameron • Cast: Carrie Henn (Rebecca
'Newt' Jorden), Sigourney Weaver (Ellen Ripley)

Despite the apparently lavish budget, the film-makers had to cut corners wherever they could.
The room with the hypersleep capsules was made to look larger with the use of mirrors; only six
alien suits were used, constructed from a handful of latex appliances stuck on black leotards.
The assault vehicle was a modified airport towing vehicle and Ripley's cabin bathroom is actually
a British Airways toilet.

1986 **STAND BY ME** **1986**

The narrator recalls an unforgettable summer from his childhood.

NARRATOR

I never had any friends later on like the ones I had when I was twelve. Jesus, does anyone?

Dir: Rob Reiner • Scr: Raynold Gideon, Bruce A. Evans • Based on a novel by Stephen King • Cast: Richard Dreyfuss (Gordie Lachance/Narrator)

1991 **CITY SLICKERS** **1991**

Mitch attends Career Day at his son's school.

MITCH

Value this time in your life, kids, because this is the time in your life when you still have your choices, and it goes by so fast. When you're a teenager, you think you can do anything, and you do. Your twenties are a blur. Thirties - you raise your family, you make a little money and you think to yourself: 'What happened to my twenties?' Forties - you grow a little potbelly, you grow another chin. The music starts to get too loud and one of your old girlfriends from high school becomes a grandmother. Fifties - you have a minor surgery. You'll call it a 'procedure', but it's a surgery. Sixties - you'll have a major surgery, the music is still loud but it doesn't matter because you can't hear it anyway. Seventies - you and the wife retire to Fort Lauderdale. You start eating dinner at two o'clock in the afternoon, you have lunch around ten, breakfast the night before. You spend most of your time wandering around malls looking for the ultimate soft yogurt and muttering: 'How come the kids don't call?' 'How come the kids don't call?' The eighties, you'll have a major stroke. You end up babbling to some Jamaican nurse who your wife can't stand but who you call mama. Any questions?

Dir: Ron Underwood • Scr: Lowell Ganz, Babaloo Mandel • Cast: Billy Crystal (Mitch Robbins)

1991 **THELMA & LOUISE** **1991**

Two women on the run are surrounded by police but decide they would rather die free than return to their former lives.

THELMA

OK, then listen - let's not get caught.

LOUISE

What're you talking about?

THELMA

Let's keep going!

LOUISE

What d'you mean?

Thelma nods at the sheer drop ahead of them.

THELMA

Go.

LOUISE

You sure?

THELMA

Yeah.

The car begins to gather speed...

Dir: Ridley Scott • Scr: Callie Khouri • Cast: Geena Davis (Thelma Dickinson), Susan Sarandon (Louise Sawyer)

1991   THE SILENCE OF THE LAMBS   1991

A killer known for his cannibalistic tastes has escaped from prison.

LECTER

I do wish we could chat longer, but I'm having an old friend for dinner.

Dir: Jonathan Demme • Scr: Ted Tally • Based on a novel by Thomas Harris • Cast: Anthony Hopkins (Dr Hannibal Lecter)

1992   UNFORGIVEN   1992

Reformed gunfighter Will consoles a young colleague who has shot an adversary.

WILL

It's a hell of a thing, killin' a man. You take away all he's got and all he's ever gonna have.

SCHOFIELD KID

Yeah, well, I guess they had it comin'.

WILL

We all have it comin', kid.

Dir: Clint Eastwood • Scr: David Webb Peoples • Cast: Clint Eastwood (Will Munny), Jaimz Woolvett (The Schofield Kid)

The long-suffering David Webb Peoples wrote the script in 1976, sixteen years before it was filmed. Eastwood resisted reading it for a long time because his assistant didn't think it was any good; when he finally did, he loved it but felt his character should be older – and delayed production for a further ten years.

1992 THE PLAYER 1992

A jaded Hollywood executive has rejected another unpromising screenplay.

GRIFFIN

It lacked certain elements that we need to market a film successfully.

JUNE

What elements?

GRIFFIN

Suspense, laughter, violence. Hope, heart, nudity, sex. Happy endings. Mainly happy endings.

Dir: Robert Altman • Scr: Michael Tolkin, based on his novel • Cast: Tim Robbins (Griffin Mill), Greta Scacchi (June Gudmundsdottir)

To add realism, Altman called on many of his showbiz friends and acquaintances to play themselves in the film. The roll call included Bruce Willis, Anjelica Huston, Jack Lemmon, Susan Sarandon, Julia Roberts, John Cusack, Cher, James Coburn, Elliott Gould and Burt Reynolds. A trade paper estimated that if they had all charged their normal salaries the budget would have risen by $100 million [$165 million].

TINSELTOWN

No business in history can have been so widely associated with a landmark which cost a mere $21,000 [$280,000]. The sign, originally reading 'Hollywoodland', was put up in 1923 by property developers encouraging Los Angelenos to colonize the hills. In the 1940s it was damaged when its caretaker drove his Model A Ford into the letter 'H', and in 1949 the local Chamber of Commerce entered a contract to restore the sign on condition it was amended to say 'Hollywood'. By then the district was already a household name.

In its earliest years, American motion picture production was based on the East Coast where manufacturers of cameras and film stock were involved in bitter rivalry to establish supremacy through patents and rights agreements. When Thomas Edison began sending agents to impound unlicensed equipment, many film-makers headed west and in 1910 D. W. Griffith was the first director to complete a film (*In Old California*) shot entirely on location in the village of Hollywood, Los Angeles.

Since the slow photographic negatives of the time required a huge amount of illumination in order to yield a good image, and the crude artificial lighting then used was cumbersome and expensive, the wide open spaces and reliable sunshine of California proved a huge advantage. By 1915, Hollywood was established as the industry's movie capital.

'Industry' is often seen as a pejorative description by the writers, directors and actors who work within the system but its founders, such as the Warner brothers, Louis B. Mayer at MGM and Adolph Zukor at Paramount, were under no illusion that what they wanted to create were empires — personal fiefdoms, where the talent they hired was kept on a tight leash to ensure affordable, efficient delivery of product for their audiences. Despite this, the studios liked to imagine their productions carried the gloss of respectable creative endeavour and MGM's official slogan remains 'ars gratia artis' — art for art's sake.

Thus was born a long-running rivalry between employers and employed. The talent, bound by lucrative contracts, found solace in snide remarks, while the paymasters took consolation from their profits and smiled tightly. The *amour-propre* of the industry is such that even when hit movies such as *Sunset Boulevard*, *The Player* and *L.A. Confidential* portray Hollywood as corrupt, venal and philistine, their producers are all too happy to stand on the red carpet and share the glory.

This is merely a smattering of the insults that have been hurled at the industry over the years:

> Those who do not study history are forced to get it from Hollywood.
> Allen Barra

> Half the people in Hollywood are dying to be discovered and the other half are afraid they will be.
> Lionel Barrymore

There are only three ages for women in Hollywood - Babe,
District Attorney, and Driving Miss Daisy.
Goldie Hawn

I'm a Hollywood writer, so I put on my sports jacket and take
off my brain.
Ben Hecht

Every country gets the circus it deserves. Spain gets bullfights.
Italy gets the Catholic Church. America gets Hollywood.
Erica Jong

Hollywood amuses me. Holier-than-thou for the public, and
unholier-than-the-devil in reality.
Grace Kelly

I always thought the real violence in Hollywood isn't what's
on the screen. It's what you have to do to raise the money.
David Mamet

Hollywood is a sewer with service from the Ritz Carlton.
Wilson Mizner

Hollywood is a place where they'll pay you a thousand
dollars for a kiss and fifty cents for your soul.
Marilyn Monroe

The only -ism Hollywood believes in is plagiarism.
Dorothy Parker

Hollywood is a place that attracts people with massive holes
in their souls.
Julia Phillips

In Europe an actor is an artist. In Hollywood, if he isn't
working, he's a bum.
Anthony Quinn

In Hollywood the woods are full of people that learned to
write but evidently can't read. If they could read their stuff,
they'd stop writing.
Will Rogers

Agents are like tires on a car; in order to get anywhere
at all, you need at least four of them, and they need to be
rotated every 5,000 miles.
Billy Wilder

In Hollywood a marriage is a success if it outlasts milk.
Rita Rudner

Hollywood is loneliness beside the swimming pool.
Liv Ullmann

1994   FOUR WEDDINGS AND A FUNERAL   1994

*Two old friends caught outside in a rain storm finally find
the courage to confess their feelings.*

> CHARLES

The truth of it is, I've loved you from the first second I met
you.

Carrie tries to digest his words.

> CHARLES

You're not suddenly going to go away again, are you?

> CARRIE

No. I might drown. But otherwise, no.

> CHARLES

OK, OK. We'll go in.

They head inside but Charles turns to her again:

> CHARLES

But first, let me ask you one thing. Do you think - after
we've dried off, after we've spent lots more time together -
you might agree not to marry me? And do you think not being
married to me might maybe be something you could consider
doing for the rest of your life?

He waits for her answer.

> CHARLES

Do you?

> CARRIE

I do...

Dir: Mike Newell • Scr: Richard Curtis • Cast: Hugh Grant (Charles),
Andie MacDowell (Carrie)

1995   SE7EN   1995

*An ageing detective is left shocked by the brutality of the serial
killer he has apprehended.*

SOMERSET

Ernest Hemingway once wrote: 'The world is a fine place and
worth fighting for.' I agree with the second part.

Dir: David Fincher • Scr: Andrew Kevin Walker • Cast: Morgan Freeman
(Detective Lieutenant William Somerset)

1999   AMERICAN BEAUTY   1999

*A man fighting for joy and dignity narrates the story of his life
– after he has died.*

LESTER

I had always heard your entire life flashes in front of your
eyes the second before you die. First of all, that one second
isn't a second at all, it stretches on forever, like an ocean
of time... For me, it was lying on my back at Boy Scout camp,
watching falling stars... And yellow leaves, from the maple
trees, that lined our street... Or my grandmother's hands, and
the way her skin seemed like paper... And the first time I saw
my cousin Tony's brand new Firebird... And Janie... And Janie
... And... Carolyn. I guess I could be pretty pissed off about

what happened to me... but it's hard to stay mad, when there's so much beauty in the world. Sometimes I feel like I'm seeing it all at once, and it's too much, my heart fills up like a balloon that's about to burst... And then I remember to relax, and stop trying to hold on to it, and then it flows through me like rain and I can't feel anything but gratitude for every single moment of my stupid little life... You have no idea what I'm talking about, I'm sure. But don't worry... you will someday.

Dir: Sam Mendes • Scr: Alan Ball • Cast: Kevin Spacey (Lester Burnham)

Writer Alan Ball claimed the film – originally intended as a play – was inspired by his memory of watching a paper bag swirling in the wind at the World Trade Center plaza.

1999 EYES WIDE SHUT   1999

Victor reassures a friend that the death of girl they knew was just an unfortunate accident.

VICTOR

Life goes on. It always does: until it doesn't.

Dir: Stanley Kubrick • Scr: Stanley Kubrick, Frederic Raphael • Based on a novella by Arthur Schnitzler • Cast: Sydney Pollack (Victor Ziegler)

Director Kubrick hated travelling so the New York exteriors had to be built in London. The film holds the record for the longest ever continuous shooting schedule; on one occasion, Kubrick repeated a shot of Tom Cruise walking through a door ninety times until he felt it was right. Kubrick died four days after completing his edit, for which he had the contractual right of final cut, so Warner Brothers were bound to release the film exactly as it stood.

Among the various props in the movie can be seen a VHS copy of *Rain Man*, a hit for Tom Cruise in 1988, and DVDs of several Kubrick films including his previous production *Full Metal Jacket* (1987).

1999 FIGHT CLUB   1999

The leader of an anarchic self-help group warns his audience to seize the day.

NARRATOR

This is your life and it's ending one minute at a time.

Dir: David Fincher • Scr: Jim Uhls • Based on a novel by Chuck Palahniuk • Cast: Edward Norton (Narrator)

Selma finds the fantasy world of cinema a comfort amid life's challenges.

                          SELMA

You like the movies, don't you?

                          BILL

I love the movies. I just love the musicals.

                          SELMA

But isn't it annoying when they do the last song in the films?

                          BILL

Why?

                          SELMA

Because you just know when it goes really big...and the camera goes like out of the roof...and you just know it's going to end. I hate that. I would leave just after the next to last song...and the film would just go on forever.

Dir: Lars von Trier • Scr: Lars von Trier • Cast: Björk (Selma Ježková), David Morse (Bill Houston)

END

Titles

Cast

Dreyfuss, Richard 412
Driver, Minnie 179
Dullea, Keir 219
Dunaway, Faye 169
Dussollier, André 365
Duvall, Robert 281, 285
Duvall, Shelley 226
Dzundza, George 149

Eastwood, Clint 17, 41, 306, 307, 414
Ekerot, Bengt 401
Ermey, R. Lee 286
Esposito, Giancarlo 33
Esposito, Jennifer 99
Ewell, Tom 141

Falk, Peter 360
Farrell, Colin 100, 183
Ferrell, Will 129
Fields, W.C. 358
Fiennes, Ralph 123, 229
Finch, Peter 310
Finney, Albert 80
Fiorentino, Linda 205
Firth, Colin 101
Foch, Nina 194
Fonda, Bridget 348
Fonda, Henry 32, 246, 302, 334
Fonda, Jane 13
Fonda, Peter 12
Ford, Glenn 141, 245
Ford, Harrison 31, 311
Ford, Paul 245
Foree, Ken 223
Fowler, Harry 305
Francis, Kay 68
Freeman, Morgan 16, 418
Fugit, Patrick 37

Gabin, Jean 328
Gable, Clark 46, 138
Garland, Judy 106
Garner, James 38
Garr, Teri 33
Garrett, Eddie 200
Gere, Richard 147
Giamatti, Paul 351
Giordano, Domiziana 202
Gish, Lillian 386
Gleeson, Brendan 100
Goldblum, Jeff 227
Goldstein, Steven 314
Gordon, Ruth 31
Grant, Cary 68, 70, 191, 192, 330, 380
Grant, Hugh 128
Grant, Richard E. 343
Graves, Peter 74, 90
Green, Nigel 279
Greenlees, William 118
Greenwood, Joan 329
Grey, Joel 406

Griffith, Melanie 204
Guest, Christopher 341
Guilfoyle, Paul 50
Guinness, Alec 278
Gyllenhaal, Jake 390

Hackman, Gene 60, 170, 176, 180
Hagen, Jean 53
Haley, Jack 106
Hall, Hanna R. 388
Hall, Philip Baker 265
Hall, Porter 328
Hamilton, Margaret 214
Hanks, Tom 34, 290
Hannah, John 417
Hansson, Maud 215
Harlow, Jean 188
Harrelson, Woody 319
Harris, Richard 38, 281, 291
Harvey, Laurence 80
Hauer, Rutger 408
Hawke, Ethan 98
Hayakawa, Sessue 278
Hayden, Sterling 29
Haydn, Richard 333
Hayworth, Rita 141
Hedebrant, Kåre 372
Heflin, Marta 340
Hellinger, Mark 399
Helpmann, Robert 221
Henn, Carrie 411
Hepburn, Audrey 8, 80
Hepburn, Katharine 28, 32, 50, 73, 250
Heston, Charlton 12, 246
Hill, Jonah 353
Hinds, Ciarán 183
Hitchcock, Patricia 245
Hoffman, Dustin 33, 198, 339
Holcomb, Sarah 339
Holden, William 51, 74
Holliday, Judy 50
Holloway, Stanley 248, 381
Holm, Ian 14, 225, 411
Holmes, Taylor 7
Homolka, Oskar 141
Hopkins, Anthony 228, 386, 413
Howard, Leslie 106
Hudson, Kate 37
Hudson, Rock 74
Hull, Josephine 7
Hunter, Kim 112
Hurt, John 360
Hurt, William 201
Huston, John 253
Huston, Walter 72
Hyde-White, Wilfrid 248

Jackson, Samuel L. 93, 348
Jaeckel, Richard 83
James, Clifton 250

James, Sid 81
Janssen, Famke 94
Johansson, Scarlett 388
Johnson, Celia 380
Johnson, Reggie 286
Jones, Gene 236
Jones, Terry 255
Jones, Tommy Lee 292

Karloff, Boris 28
Keaton, Diane 13, 116, 167, 200
Kelly, Gene 53, 194
Kennedy, George 406
Kidder, Margot 117, 312
King, Chris Thomas 350
Kinski, Klaus 118, 253
Klanfer, François 388
Kline, Kevin 94
Koch, Marianne 306
Koonce, Kelly 391
Korman, Harvey 169
Kotto, Yaphet 225
Kristofferson, Kris 360

Lancaster, Burt 75, 360
Laughton, Charles 213
Lawhon, Margaret 261
Leandersson, Lina 372
Ledger, Heath 62, 390
Lee, Spike 33
Leigh, Janet 215
Leigh, Vivien 2, 46, 138
Leitch, Donovan 15
Lemmon, Jack 76, 333, 382
Liotta, Ray 178
Ljunggren, Sten 37
Lockwood, Margaret 398
Lone, John 258
Lorre, Peter 359
Loy, Myrna 300
Lugosi, Bela 212, 213
Luna, Diego 206
Lynch, John Carroll 41

McCambridge, Mercedes 223
McCormack, Catherine 206
McCrea, Joel 328
McDormand, Frances 318
MacDowell, Andie 363
McDowell, Malcolm 116, 221, 250
McGann, Paul 343
McGinley, John C. 60
McGregor, Ewan 20
McKellen, Ian 266
McKern, Leo 248
McKinney, Bill 222
McLaglen, Victor 53
MacLaine, Shirley 382
McNamara, William 344
McQueen, Steve 279
Maffia, Roma 260

Maley, Peggy 164
Mara, Rooney 63
Marais, Jean 214
Martin, Steve 83
Marvin, Lee 58, 285
Marx, Groucho 46, 190, 398
Matthau, Walter 329
Maxwell, Edwin 274
Mayo, Virginia 193
Melville, Jean-Pierre 10
Ménochet, Denis 295
Miles, Sarah 343
Milland, Ray 7
Miller, Jason 223
Mirren, Helen 132
Mitchum, Robert 115, 218
Monroe, Marilyn 7, 194
Morán, Patricia 218
Moreau, Marguerite 207
Morley, Robert 244
Morse, David 420
Mortensen, Viggo 23
Moseley, Bill 233
Mosley, Bryan 166
Moss, Carrie-Anne 20, 365
Mostel, Zero 335
Mullins, Bartlett 142
Murray, Bill 339, 363, 388
Myers, Mike 149, 232, 364

Napier, Charles 260
Neal, Patricia 329
Neeson, Liam 323
Nelson, Tim Blake 267, 350, 371
Newman, Paul 12, 30, 143, 250
Nicholson, Jack 23, 82, 143, 169, 226, 362
Nielsen, Leslie 150
Niemczyk, Leon 247
Niven, David 112
Norton, Edward 62, 94, 419
Novak, Kim 75

Oates, Warren 168
O'Byrne, Brian F. 388
O'Connor, Carroll 165
O'Donnell, Rosie 123
Oldman, Gary 180
Olsen, Moroni 2
Olson, Nancy 51
O'Neal, Ryan 59
O'Neal, Tatum 59
O'Shea, Milo 221
Osment, Haley Joel 22
O'Toole, Peter 258, 305, 306
Owen, Clive 131

Pacino, Al 93, 123, 143, 149, 167, 171, 231, 254
Page, Ellen 373
Palance, Jack 168
Palin, Michael 255, 257

Crew

Hitchcock, Alfred 70, 75, 192, 215, 245, 330, 379, 398
Hodge, John 20
Hodges, Mike 166
Hoeber, Erich 132
Hoeber, Jon 132
Hoffenstein, Samuel 49
Hooper, Tom 101
Hopper, Dennis 151
Howard, Gregory Allen 97
Howard, Ron 125
Howard, Sidney 2, 46, 85, 138
Howlett, John 116, 250
Hsiao, Rita 36
Hudson, Hugh 14
Hughes, Howard 188
Hughes, John 15, 342
Hughes, Ken 221, 281
Hurd, Earl 2
Hurd, Gale Anne 87
Hurlbut, William 28
Huston, John 3, 72, 73, 85, 163, 359

Idle, Eric 255, 257, 313, 410
Iliff, W. Peter 60

Jackson, Peter 38, 88, 266
Jacobs, Alexander 165
James, Rian 2
Jankiewicz, Tom 179
Jay, Jay Presson Allen 12
Jeunet, Jean-Pierre 365
Jewison, Norman 121
Johannson, Dave 41
Johnson, Diane 226
Johnson, Kristine 37
Johnson, Nunnally 302, 398
Jones, Grover 68
Jones, Kirk 36
Jones, Terry 143, 255, 257, 313, 410

Kalmar, Bert 46, 190
Kalogridis, Laeta 237
Kamen, Robert Mark 323
Kanin, Garson 50
Karaszewski, Larry 319
Kasdan, Jake 353
Kasdan, Lawrence 31, 90, 201
Kaufman, Charlie 100
Kaufman, Millard 54
Kaufman, Philip 31, 313
Kazan, Elia 329, 382
Keighley, William 48, 244
Kelland, Clarence Budington 300
Kelly, Gene 53
Kennaway, James 280
Kenney, Douglas 339
Kenton, Erle C. 213

Kenyon, Charles 106
Khouri, Callie 38, 413
Kinberg, Simon 100
King, Michael Patrick 23
King, Rick 60
King, Stephen 86
Kloves, Steve 38
Koch, Howard 48, 85, 108
Koppelman, Brian 94
Koster, Henry 7
Kramer, Stanley 247, 403
Krizan, Kim 98
Kubrick, Stanley 29, 86, 219, 221, 226, 279, 286, 419

LaGravenese, Richard 17
Landis, John 84
Langley, Noel 85, 106, 214
Lasseter, John 36, 88
Laughton, Charles 115
Launder, Frank 398
Laurant, Guillaume 365
Laurents, Arthur 54
Lawton, J.F. 122, 147
Lean, David 278, 305, 380
Lederer, Charles 7, 68, 194
Lee, Ang 26, 94, 390
Lee, Spike 33, 62
Lehman, Ernest 8, 54, 75, 113, 246, 330, 333
Leigh, Mike 95, 317, 387
Leland, David 143
Lemkin, Jonathan 123, 231
Lennart, Isobel 85, 384
Leone, Sergio 306, 334
Lerner, Alan Jay 194, 248
Levien, David 94
Levinson, Barry 260
Liman, Doug 100, 262, 370
Lindqvist, John Ajvide 372
Linklater, Richard 98, 350
LoCash, Robert 150
Lochhead, Seth 133
Logan, John 22, 291, 320
Lonergan, Kenneth 152
Lubitsch, Ernst 47, 49, 68, 138, 275
Lucas, George 31, 86, 311
Lumet, Sidney 246, 310
Lurie, Rod 180
Lynch, David 147, 205, 386

McCarey, Leo 46, 190
McCullers, Michael 232
McDonagh, Martin 100, 183
MacDougall, Ranald 140
McGuire, Don 33, 54, 339
McKay, Adam 129
McKean, Michael 341
Mackendrick, Alexander 75, 246
McKenna, Aline Brosh 234
McKeown, Charles 411
McMurtry, Larry 390

McQuarrie, Christopher 229
McTiernan, John 315
Maddow, Ben 163
Madsen, David 344
Maibaum, Richard 85, 177, 195, 221
Mainwaring, Daniel 158, 381
Makavejev, Dušan 253
Malick, Terrence 337, 391
Maltz, Albert 399
Mamet, David 176, 180, 259, 314
Mandel, Babaloo 412
Mankiewicz, Herman J. 242, 358
Mankiewicz, Joseph L. 29, 50, 74, 193
Mann, Abby 247
Mann, Daniel 245, 401
Mann, Michael 93
Marber, Patrick 131
March, James Moncure 188
Marks, Leo 142
Marshall, Garry 122, 147
Marshall, Rob 98
Marshman, D.M., Jr 51, 381
Martin, Steve 83
Martin, Troy Kennedy 337
Matheson, Richard 402
Mathison, Melissa 86
Mayer, Edwin Justus 49, 275
Mayo, Archie 106
Mazer, Dan 153
Medioli, Enrico 11
Mendes, Sam 101, 349, 419
Meyer, Russ 199
Michell, Roger 387
Milestone, Lewis 274
Milius, John 281
Miller, George 59, 361
Minghella, Anthony 20, 123
Minnelli, Vincente 194
Mitchum, Robert 115
Moffat, Ivan 74
Monahan, William 23
Monroe, Thomas 138
Moodysson, Lukas 37
Moore, Robert 360
Morel, Pierre 323
Moresco, Robert 99, 267
Mottola, Greg 353
Myers, Mike 149, 232, 364

Naughton, Bill 115, 405
Neame, Ronald 12
Neilan, Marshall 188
Nelson, Jessie 37
Neville, John T. 358
Newell, Mike 417
Newhouse, David 165
Newhouse, Rafe 165
Newman, David 117, 312
Newman, Leslie 117, 312
Newman, Walter 164, 329

Nichols, Mike 131, 198, 204, 406
Nicholson, Jack 362
Nicholson, William 291, 320, 363
Night Shyamalan, M. 22
Nolan, Christopher 62, 237, 365, 373
Nolan, Jonathan 62, 237
Nolan, Ken 292
North, Edmund H. 113, 245, 281
Nugent, Frank S. 8, 53
Nyswaner, Ron 260

O'Bannon, Dan 225
Odets, Clifford 75, 246, 380
Oppenheimer, George 398
Ormonde, Czenzi 245
Ossana, Diana 390

Pakula, Alan J. 256
Palin, Michael 227, 255, 257, 313, 410
Parker, Alan 60, 176
Parks, Gordon 171
Parsonnet, Marion 141
Pascal, Gabriel 244
Patrick, John 245, 401
Paxton, John 164, 277, 403
Payne, Alexander 152, 351
Pearce, Donn 85, 250, 406
Peckinpah, Sam 83, 168
Penhall, Joe 23
Penn, Arthur 170
Peoples, David Webb 408, 414
Peploe, Mark 258
Perrin, Nat 46
Perry, Eleanor 360
Perry, Frank 360
Petersen, Wolfgang 292
Pierce, Charles B. 87
Pierson, Frank 85, 250, 406
Pileggi, Nicholas 178, 344
Pink, Steve 152, 179
Pirosh, Robert 398
Pogue, Charles Edward 227
Polanski, Roman 91, 169, 247, 253
Pollack, Sydney 33, 339
Pontecorvo, Gillo 280
Potter, Dennis 202
Powell, Michael 112, 142
Prebble, John 279
Preminger, Otto 49
Pressburger, Emeric 112
Price, Jeffrey 202
Proft, Pat 150
Proyas, Alex 23
Pryor, Richard 169
Puzo, Mario 86, 117, 167, 254, 312

Radford, Michael 343

Ramis, Harold 152, 339, 363
Ranft, Joe 88
Raphael, Frederic 80, 197, 419
Raphaelson, Samson 47, 68
Raucher, Herman 285
Ravetch, Irving 143
Ray, Billy 260
Ray, Nicholas 113, 305
Reed, Carol 399
Reiner, Carl 83
Reiner, Rob 121, 146, 228, 288, 341, 412
Reinert, Al 87
Reinhardt, Elizabeth 49
Reisch, Walter 138
Remarque, Erich Maria 274
Renoir, Jean 328
Richlin, Maurice 141
Rickard, Dick 2
Riesner, Don 307
Riskin, Robert 300
Ritt, Martin 143, 334
Roach, Jay 232, 364
Robbins, Jerome 54
Robbins, Tim 261
Roberts, Ben 50, 158, 193
Roberts, Marguerite 165
Roberts, William 279
Robinson, Bruce 343
Robinson, Phil Alden 15, 87
Rodat, Robert 290
Rogen, Seth 353
Romanek, Mark 365
Romero, George A. 223
Rose, Reginald 246
Rose, Ruth 213
Rosenberg, Scott 123, 152
Rosenberg, Stuart 250, 406
Rosner, Mark 319
Ross, Herbert 385, 387
Roth, Eric 34, 87
Rothwell, Talbot 55, 81
Rubin, Danny 363
Ruby, Harry 46, 190
Ruggles, Wesley 191
Rush, Richard 260
Rydell, Mark 32
Ryerson, Florence 85, 106, 214
Ryskind, Morrie 85

Salt, Waldo 86
Samuels, Lesser 164, 329
Sargent, Alvin 59
Sarne, Michael 199
Sather, Drake 350
Schaffner, Franklin J. 12, 281
Schamus, James 94, 265
Schenk, Nick 41
Schiffer, Michael 151

Schisgal, Murray 33, 339
Schlesinger, John 197
Schoedsack, Ernest B. 213
Schrader, Paul 86, 171, 385
Schroeder, Barbet 174
Schulberg, Budd 329, 382
Schulman, Tom 14
Schwentke, Robert 132
Scorsese, Martin 23, 171, 178, 237, 340, 344, 385
Scott, Ridley 225, 291, 292, 320, 408, 413
Seaman, Peter S. 202
Sears, Ted 2
Seaton, George 398
Segal, Erich 86
Segal, Peter 150, 371
Seidler, David 101
Serling, Rod 12
Seymour, James 2
Shaffer, Peter 341
Shanley, John Patrick 121
Shapiro, Stanley 141
Sharp, Alan 170
Shaw, George Bernard 244
Shearer, Harry 341
Sheekman, Arthur 46
Shelton, Ron 204
Sherman, Vincent 358
Sherwin, David 116, 250
Showalter, Michael 207
Shusett, Ronald 225
Siegel, Don 307, 311, 407
Simon, Neil 360
Sinclair, Stephen 88
Singer, Bryan 229
Siodmak, Curt 378
Skolimowski, Jerzy 247
Smith, Earl E. 87
Smith, Webb 2
Soderbergh, Steven 261, 266, 320
Sokolow, Alec 88
Solinas, Franco 280
Solt, Andrew 113
Sorkin, Aaron 63, 288
Sorrentino, Paolo 389
Southern, Terry 221, 279
Spaak, Charles 328
Spheeris, Penelope 149
Spielberg, Steven 31, 86, 170, 229, 290, 307, 371
Stallone, Sylvester 311
Stanton, Andrew 36, 88
Stefano, Joseph 215
Steinberg, Norman 169
Stevens, George 74
Stevenson, Robert 80
Stewart, Donald Ogden 28
Stiller, Ben 350
Stinson, Joseph 87

Stone, Oliver 87, 143, 171, 259, 286
Stoppard, Tom 411
Stuart, Jeb 315
Stupnitsky, Gene 353
Sturges, John 54, 279
Sturges, Preston 68, 158, 277, 328
Swarthout, Miles Hood 311, 407
Swerling, Jo 379

Tally, Ted 228, 413
Tarantino, Quentin 93, 178, 288, 295, 348
Tarkovsky, Andrei 202
Taylor, Jim 152, 351
Taylor, Samuel A. 8, 75, 113
Tewkesbury, Joan 255
Thomas, Gerald 55, 81
Thompson, Ernest 32
Thompson, J. Lee 218
Thompson, Jim 29
Thurber, Rawson Marshall 352
Tidyman, Ernest 171
Tolan, Peter 152
Tolkin, Michael 414
Tourneur, Jacques 158, 378, 381
Towne, Robert 82, 169, 253, 362
Towne, Robert (as P.H. Vazak) 14
Trosper, Guy 334
Truffaut, François 10
Turner, Bonnie 149
Turner, Guinevere 233
Turner, Terry 149

Uger, Alan 169
Uhls, Jim 180, 419
Ulmer, Edgar G. 69
Underwood, Ron 412
Unkrich, Lee 36

Vadim, Roger 221
Van Druten, John 358
Van Dyke, W.S. 300
Van Sant, Gus 348
Varda, Agnès 81
Verhoeven, Paul 149
Victor, Mark 86
Vidor, Charles 141
Viertel, Peter 73
Vintar, Jeff 23
Visconti, Luchino 11
von Trier, Lars 420

Wachowski, Andy 20
Wachowski, Lana 20

Wade, Kevin 204
Wain, David 207
Waititi, Taika 352
Wald, Malvin 399
Waldman, Frank 338
Walker, Andrew Kevin 229, 418
Walsh, Bill 80
Walsh, Fran 38, 88, 266
Walsh, Raoul 50, 158, 193
Washburn, Deric 408
Webb, Chris 36
Webb, James 292
Webb, James R. 218
Weir, Peter 14
Weisberg, David 319
Weiser, Stanley 259
Welles, Orson 49, 242, 246, 328, 358, 402
West, Claudine 275
West, Mae 191
Wexley, John 214
Whale, James 28
Whedon, Joss 88
Wilder, Billy 7, 8, 51, 69, 74, 76, 113, 138, 141, 164, 329, 333, 381, 382
Willingham, Calder 198
Wilson, Gerald 168
Wilson, Michael 12, 278, 305
Wilson, Michael G. 177
Wimperis, Arthur 275
Wing, George 371
Winner, Michael 168
Winterbottom, Michael 323
Wise, Robert 54, 245, 333
Wisher, William, Jr. 87
Wood, Edward D., Jr 9
Wood, Sam 398
Woolf, Edgar Allan 106, 214
Wray, Ardel 378
Wright, Joe 133
Wurlitzer, Rudy 83
Wyler, William 275, 384
Wylie, Philip 213

Yakin, Boaz 97
Yordan, Philip 305
Young, Waldemar 213
Younger, Ben 266

Zaillian, Steven 229
Zapponi, Bernardino 116
Zemeckis, Robert 34, 202
Zimmerman, Paul D. 340
Zinnemann, Fred 248, 305
Zombie, Rob 233
Zucker, David 86, 90, 150
Zucker, Jerry 86, 90
Zwick, Edward 22

PICTURE CAPTIONS AND CREDITS

All the images in this book are from the archives of The Kobal Collection which owes its existence to the vision, talent and energy of the men and women who created the movie industry and whose legacies live on through the films they made, the studios they built, and the publicity photographs they took. Kobal collects, preserves, organizes and makes these images available to enhance our understanding of this cinematic art.

The publisher wishes to thank all of the photographers (known and unknown) and the film production and distribution companies whose publicity images appear in this book. We apologize in advance for any omissions, or neglect, and will be pleased to make any corrections in future editions.

TEXT CREDITS

Excerpts from *Apocalypse Now* granted courtesy of Faber & Faber Ltd.

Excerpts from *Inglourious Basterds* granted courtesy of Faber & Faber Ltd.

Excerpts from *Cool Hand Luke* granted courtesy of David Higham Ltd.

Excerpts from *Without Feathers* and *Getting Even* from *Woody Allen: Complete Prose* (Picador, 1998).

Excerpt from David Benioff, *The 25th Hour* (Hodder & Stoughton, 2002), copyright © 2000 by David Benioff, reproduced by permission of Hodder & Stoughton Limited.

Excerpt from William Goldman, *Adventures in the Screen Trade: A Personal View of Hollywood* (Abacus, 2003), copyright © William Goldman 1983, granted courtesy of Little, Brown Book Group.

Excerpts from *Casablanca* granted courtesy of Warner Bros. Entertainment Inc.

Excerpts from *Mrs Miniver* granted courtesy of Warner Bros. Entertainment Inc.

Excerpts from Syd Field's *Paradigm*, en.wikipedia.org/wiki/Screenwriting.

The editor and publisher apologize if any material has been included without the appropriate acknowledgement, and would be pleased to rectify any omissions brought to their attention at the earliest opportunity.